AQUILES DELLE VIGNE

THE INNERMOST
JOURNEY OF A PIANIST

Original title: voyages dans l'intimité d'un pianiste

Editor: first english edition Associação António Fragoso, 2016
Translation from the French edition: Ms. Sheila Cardno
Technical Revision: Prof. Manuel Araújo, assistant of the author

ii

AQUILES DELLE VIGNE

THE INNERMOST JOURNEY OF A PIANIST

Preface of this Edition MANUEL ARAÚJO

Foreword by NANCY BRICARD

To Chantal, my wife,
and to Laurence, Gabrielle and Guillaume, our children,
for their constant support to my utopia.

To the memory of Claudio Arrau, Eduardo del Pueyo and
Georges Cziffra, the three Masters who taught me
always to never condescend.

To the memory of Saint Augustine, Leonardo and Franz Liszt,
who have been a constant inspiration in my life.

To my assistants and to my pupils who, through their devotion,
have taught me so much!

A.D.V.

Table of content

BOOK I

Part one
The ontological relationship between the work and the artist's thoughts, or the fifth element of Nature

Part two
The struggle

Part three
The art of teaching and the art of learning

BOOK II

Part one
Meditation on our work or « Meditation on the Passion » by Carpaccio

Part two
The protagonists, the actors, the figurants, the mimes, the doubles, the angel, the devil, and the « Tuttologists»!

BOOK III

Part one
The years of apprenticeship or Salvador Dali's "Christ of Saint John of the Cross"

Part two
The Old and the New Testament: Bach's Preludes and Fugues and Chopin's Etudes

Part three
The Etudes of Chopin ... or the « 24 » works of Hercules ... and the wonders of the world

BOOK IV

Part one
The great "enemies" of our work: Tendinitis, Memory, Stage fright

Part two
International Competitions: the neutrality or the stalemate or « The last Judgement » by Luca Signorelli… or rather « The card players», by Paul Cézanne.

BOOK V

Part one
Liszt's Sonata in B minor
Years of career

Part two
The Career, the random, the ephemeral... and the market

BOOK VI

Part one

Sonata Op. 111 by Beethoven or the return to Silence, « Moses » by Michael Angelo, « Le Prieur » by Brancusi

Part two

BOOK VI

PREFACE
By Manuel Araújo, pianist

We live an ambiguous epoch. Never classical music produced so many and such competent pianists.

New huge auditoriums, acoustically studied to detail, multiply within large cities and invade each and every small town. The mechanics of the latest instruments almost approaches perfection. Such reliability, sensitivity and keyboard balance enabling a dizzying clarity in the most virtuous of the works of the repertoire, as well as the production of the most beautiful sounds by the expert hands of any of the millions of professional and competent pianists which exist today. And the recordings? Supreme art, apogee of technology. Carnegie Hall especially transported to a small studio in London, to crown the new perfect interpretation, like a revelation, of a great competent pianist. Perfection note by note,

a recording worth filling with shame Cortot, Richter, Schnabel or Fisher. Starting with photo on the cover.

However we live in constant dissatisfaction. We praise the great pianists of the beginning of the century that has passed. Although they performed on dubious pianos and were clearly negligent in relation to wrong notes ... And were fat! We dream of that personal encounter (enough a breakfast! ...) with an incontestable idol of the eighteenth or nineteenth century (or XVII), whom we know only through his abundant private correspondence that he has forgotten to destroy. Perhaps because he expected to survive the fourth decade of his life, but God has granted exclusive anticipation of every moment with such genius and striking personality.

We further regret that the first prize of Brussels' major international competition plays approximately the same way as the first prize of Tokyo, who was similar to the pianist who won in Texas resembling the winner of Sydney which was a copy of his classmate who triumphed in South Africa.

Why do we live then with such mixed feelings? Maybe because we have forgotten for almost an entire century, intoxicated by a dizzying rise of new technologies, and a remarkable improvement of social conditions, something fundamental: a universal high qualilty art education is innocuous if forgeting the uniqueness of the individual. The privileges of the twentieth century should have served to form, in quantity, unique and enriching personalities. However, we formed a Kafkaesque musical cloud. Large, but poor in results for eternity. Or at least well below those obtained in the fifteenth century.

Assumes at this point historic significance the figure of Maestro Aquiles Delle Vigne. His light radiates the four corners of the world, an inexorable torch he carries in his eternal, restless pilgrimage on Earth. As the Lighthouse, his light, supported by huge pillars of limestone and marble, is ubiquitous, mutiplied by mirrors facing the flame. Pupil of Claudio Arrau, he is a legitimate follower of the school of F. Liszt (through Martin Krause). True Monk of music, he is a missing link between two epochs that we worship. The one that vanished in the early twentieth century and one that is yet to come. Times when the artistic personality breaks through the cloud of conformed and competent bodies, sometimes through high gloss other times through humble discretion, to inspire the World for eternity. Where music, literature, philosophy, painting, sculpture and other arts merge to understand and enhance the human condition. Times where the inspiration of the moment does not give way to the formalities and conventions that separate us from composers we admire. Where, in the name of rigor and scientific analysis of the score, we do not lose the historical culture that allows us to reincarnate every epoch with the specificity of Thought that corresponds to it. "*A metronomical performance is certainly tiresome and nonsensical; time and rhythm must be adapted to and identified with melody, the harmony, the accent and the poetry... But how indicate all this? I shudder at the thought of it*". Through these words of F. Liszt, we understand the limitations of a composer of the nineteenth century. However, it is not unusual to hear a musicologist arguing that the fermata over a pause at the end of a meditative sentence of the Hungarian composer must have the duration of the pause plus half its value. No more, no less! ... We must therefore urgently realize how lucky we are to be able to hear the words of a Professor that carries the weight of the direct oral tradition of Liszt.

Pianist with unique inspiration, Maestro Delle Vigne cultivates his own sonority (identifiable among hundreds of recordings), being able to withstand the longest and most complex of works from first to last note without any fracture in the structure. Especially sensitive to the expressive value of harmonic modulations, he is incapable of playing a single note without an ulterior motive and the finest of sounds. The Hippocrene may have provided him the inexhaustible inspiration and Work his solid technical resources. Being one of the most sought after teachers in the world, he is the perfect balance between demand, beauty, tradition, kindness, erudition and truth. Added to a sincere respect for the own personality of each pupil. We would hardly be able to find, among the thousands of young pianists that he has inspired, from many different countries, two that perform the same work equally. Unable to compromise, especially to smaller arguments, his ideals despise easy success. Respect for timeless transmission of the human genius imposes on him a relentless dedication to work, year after year; as if every day he lost an opportunity to learn or share some of his unique knowledge.

For all this, and more, "The innermost journey of a pianist" is an alternative bible for the pianist. A sincere view of the current sociological context of the false profession that Liszt accidentally created; a reflection on the ideals of our art; a technique study guide; a moving technical, historical and philosophical interpretation of Liszt´s Sonata and Beethoven's Last Sonata. A book where you can see a little, which is a lot, of the endless knowledge of the great professor and to which I will always come back as memory betrays me. Fate allowed me to share many years of interaction with such a figure in modern music history. May this same fate allow me to say, within 82 years, that I personally met Master Aquiles Delle Vigne, one of the drivers of the new cultural renaissance, world scale, which will manifest by the middle of the twenty-first century. Until then, we will be Hans Castorp. Artists of fragile personality, happyly facing the disease, without perception of time and away from the real world.

This publication of António Fragoso Association is commendable and very opportune. António Fragoso also lived for the ideal, being unable to identify himself with the system of his epoch. His letters were visionary; He would surely be a big influence on the Portuguese music scene and beyond. Pneumonic Flu took his live at 21, in the preparations to leave to Paris. Interestingly the same misfortune that stole Krause from Arrau. God writes straight with crooked lines: the legacy of both would not die in 1918.

FOREWORD

This marvelous book is a moving documentary of the inner journey of Delle Vigne through a lifetime of love and dedication to music, as well as his artistry as a pianist. In my many years of teaching and performing, I have seldom read such a lively, comprehensive and detailed chronicle with such important messages and lessons for musicians at all levels of professional experience. Marguerite Long once said: "Music does not have a permanent existence and only an interpretation can give it life". That ability to "give life" to a musical score is dependent on a myriad of factors that are lucidly addressed by the author. The result is a book that it will impact all who read it, be they performers of merely lovers of music.

I first met Aquiles Delle Vigne in Australia, where we both were adjudicating the 8thSydney International Piano Competition. I was immediately impressed by his musical sensitivity and pedagogical acumen, as well as his knowledge of the vast repertoire that was being performed at the competition. His intellectual depth was coupled with an irresistible charm and joie de vivre, as well as an innate kindness and empathy toward contestants, judges and observers. These qualities have made him not only a treasured friend, but a very valued colleague. George Bernard Shaw once proclaimed: "He who can, does. He who cannot, teaches". Shaw was of course wrong! This is amply illustrated by Delle Vigne who has a world-wide recognition as a performing and recording artist, coupled with well merited respect as a Professor and Master Class teacher throughout the world. His book does not merely chronicle or proclaim, but sensitively instructs.

For example, I believe that it was Olivier Messiaen who once noted that silences are the most expressive moments in music! This is also true, of course, in everyday life… as demonstrated by how many people become uncomfortable with any stop in the conversation. There is pressure to rush in and fill the silence, so as to replace the emotion that mounts   to fill the void. Delle Vigne speaks at length about the importance of silence in creating mood, musicality and expressiveness.

His approach is poetic, philosophical and religious; but it is never pedantic. He supplies an abundance of practical information on aids to students, teachers and performing musicians. These aids include suggestions on practicing methodology and technical study, the importance of an educated ear, differing ways of producing sound, the use of pedal and he even addresses the issue of choice of teachers. There are wonderful and pertinent quotes from famous interpreters, painters and writers which illustrate his insights and knowledge about the material being presented. Physical problems (e.g. tendonitis), memory problems (usually due to loss of concentration), and performance anxiety are all discussed at length and with possible solutions. Career building is one of the most stressful and difficult parts of achieving recognition as a performer and musician. It is rare to find this topic comprehensively addressed in the literature, and it is desperately needed by young and aspiring musicians. Personality, social relations, money and managers are among the topics discussed. The pro's and con's of international competitions are explored from the point of view of both the contestants and the jurors.

Four monumental works in the piano repertoire have been chosen for a detailed description and analysis. They include the 48 Preludes and Fugues of Johann Sebastian Bach, the 24 Etudes of Chopin, the Sonata of Franz Liszt and the Sonata Op. 111 of Ludwig van Beethoven. *His insights and comments about these works are truly phenomenal.*

All journeys must ultimately come to an end, and so it is for the pianist. This Götterdämmerung, or twilight of the pianist, is usually signaled by signs of fatigue, and a decline in technique, concentration, strength and endurance. In reading this, one cannot help but experience the profound sadness and emptiness of this demise.

Delle Vigne's commitment to music expresses his belief that it is a privilege, a responsibility and an enormous reward to be a pianist. His deep love of music is evident on every page! In writing my performance editions of works by Fauré, Ravel and Moussorgsky, I emphasized how the cultural and historical events of the times affected the composition and ultimately the performance of this music. Delle Vigne's "Voyage" is living testimony to how the shaping of the "interior" ultimately determines artistry. To read his manuscript has been a tremendously moving experience for me, both intellectually and spiritually. This book is destined to be a timeless source of knowledge and inspiration for this generation and those yet to come.

Nancy Bricard
Emeritus Professor of Keyboard Studies
Flora Thornton / University of Southern California School of Music Los Angeles, California, USA

PREALUDIUM

The major concern in these reflections on Music is to refocus on ethical and aesthetic problems in looking at the work of art and the composer, such values being supreme in any artistic feat

The principle of their *existential independence* must be re-established vis-à-vis *the self*, the pianist, and consequently vis-à-vis my ego, just like my *causal dependence* vis-à-vis them, the true origins of my current artistic presence.

It is clear that *the self*, that is, my own presence, in the social phenomenon known as the concert, becomes *a focal point*. It is therefore a displaced experience in this new hierarchy of values, because the concert in our day and age has become a world event that is superficial and, as a result, dependent on powers other than those of Music.

That can only be explained by the upheaval in the order of concerns involved in the artistic act, and this gives rise to a new phenomenon: this presence, mine, *is the prime object of admiration*, and so comes before the work and the composer.

In other words, we are now part of the *star system*, abandoning the intrinsic essence that was once the phenomenon of the concert.

This book is an appeal for a return to a purer form of art that is, at the same time, healthier, closer to the truth and more dignified, while less infected by the musical business and the servitude of *the star* to the system.

Hegel taught is in his Aesthetics *"We are not dealing with something merely agreeable or useful, but rather with the deployment of Truth"*. This problem is always pertinent and makes itself felt constantly.

Seeking the true aesthetic and moral position must be done, without a doubt, in the true spirit of Gottfried W. Leibniz, that is, not only based on the fact that we are capable of reasoning, a faculty that we may or may not exercise correctly, but above all, on the important fact of being able to bind together scrupulous assumptions of basic truths, *"because one truth can only produce another truth that will not contradict the first one"*.

When I talk about *moral problems*, in speaking about ethics and aesthetics, I do this in the sense of Plato and Aristotle: I am suggesting the incorporation of a moral code in Art alongside the totally different sentiment of frenzy and fits of passion. This comes through the elevation of all hedonistic sentiment and by *allowing the interdependence of values other than sublime to flow without interruption*, through the fervor and balance of the artistic feat; or through the mysticism, for example, of St Teresa of Avila, or any other religious being, so that beauty, religion and art are brother movements and currents, given that God cannot dictate to His artist any *magnificent inspiration that is neither true nor just*.

This moral code also involves the moral subjectivism of Kant where everything is affected by the ethical imperative. In other words, by *"this world that is an incarnation of music as well as an incarnation of Will "*, so dear to Schopenhauer. Through these expressions on the work of art that bring with them a sediment of significance and that represent several of its existences, such as the physical, phenomenal, symbolic and transcendental; invisible but *indivisible*. In short, through the solidarity of all its composing elements. Clearly, through the alchemy that represents an artistic work, not only as a blend of more or less personal ideas on beauty, but above all through a work of art seen *as an independent being and the complete and consubstantial expression of the human soul*.

The five major individual elements that concern us - *music, composer, work, piano and concert* -

seek, as in the work of Luigi Pirandello, *the sixth personage*, that is *the self*, the pianist, to broach a troublesome situation that is not being resolved and to which I do not think I can give a final answer. These reflections evoke this history of internal struggle and enigma, because *"science itself teaches us to doubt"*, in the words of Unamuno. They examine *questions without answers*, recalling Charles Ives and Leonard Bernstein. There are disappointments and successes, bitterness and joy. They sometimes become tragedies, when the outcome remains confused, and at other times great good fortune when light floods the path and makes it intelligible.

A glimmer of hope is then shown to the spirit. From this time on it is filled with superior powers that change it into a messenger such as the Archangel Gabriel, in Leonardo's Annunciation. It is almost like accomplishing the impossible mission of reconciliation already attempted by Erasmus. But because *"the middle road it is the only one that does not lead to Rome"*, as Arnold Schöenberg used to teach his pupils, one must try to draw near to that which has all the characteristics of the irreconcilable. Like this, the spirit of the artist draws close to God, and gradually the obscurity dissipates. But nothing can be definitive because, again, it will be a question of *becoming constantly obsessed by an inaccessible end.*

These reflections aim at no more than that: they are an approach to the desperate struggle *to assert the uniqueness of each artist*, his inalienable right to difference, his ontological specificity to mark his distance from the laws of subordination - whether these are commercial, racial, hierarchical, political or aesthetic. The artist has the right not to be compared as well as the right to make a mistake and to correct it.

In short, he has the right to what is advocated by Saint Augustine in his Confessions -*"Go forth on your path, as it exists only through your walking"*- and, as a result, the artist has the right to follow his path alone. That is, alone, he has the right to involve his soul in minds superior to his own, similar to his own, but above all *never inferior to his own.*

These reflections strive to assert the elevation of each artist, a supreme contribution to the unwavering approach of Art itself that cannot stop to consent to certain pettiness on the part of those who serve it. They are also a self-defense against servitude: one cannot serve two gods at the same time. We must choose: either Art or… whatever else remains.

But to be able to do this we need, above all, the strength to say *"no"*, because saying *no* is the most implacable proof of the human personality and will prevent this personality becoming complicit with the wheels of power that, themselves, make finding an individual aesthetic identity impossible.

This has been true of all systems, whether communist, capitalist or a mix of both.

Today, with globalization at all levels, and becoming practically the taskmaster of our daily life, *we have an even greater need of personality*. Because the artist, as well, has become standard, ordinary, impersonal and trivial, and no more than an every day product. The artist has become like the moving picture in the *gouache* by Carle Vernet and his *seasonal* violinist.

To make culture commonplace, commercialize it or make it cripplingly vulgar, because it would be an illusion to believe that *everyone* is capable of grasping and embracing the ultimate message of Beethoven's *Hammerklavier*, follows the common route of *sacrificing the personality*. Almost destroying the personality by developing *a so called public awareness* that in reality does no more than diminish the last vestiges of the uniqueness of the artist, either with the Music, first of all, or latterly, with the very artist.

This leads me to say that I am skeptical about the current idea that claims *the piano is being played better than ever before.*

I agree the major arguments in this concept. But... let us look closer... Now, the general level is *tremendously higher* considering the number of young pianists who practise the profession successfully.

They are so fantastic from the instrumental point of view that personality and genius have been forgotten, relegating these quaint elements to the romantic relics of another age, *but always invoking the exteriority of these values*.

So there is something that hinders the mechanism, which we will try to analyze.

What is missing, in particular, is what Ravel wrote about Mozart: *"His great lesson today, is that he helps us free ourselves of the Music, to listen only to ourselves and the eternal background, and to forget that which precedes us immediately"*.

Subsequently, the *Master thinker* is lacking.

It is clear, therefore, that we lack guides because of the democratization of the media, through easy, false, uncommitted, elementary and populist access made available to those handling art, meaning that any one can discuss, exchange ideas and even become controversial on television with Luciano Berio, for example.

Perhaps Schiller's idea will reveal all its merit in the near future, and *"we will call upon the genius to save us when danger becomes imminent, but* - perhaps also - *when this genius appears we will be afraid of him"*.

But the motives are very clear: today is not about creating an art that is pure or of continuing it, but about the sale, in industrial quantities, of the products designed by our mediocrity under the pretext of their universality.

The range of action of this so-called *culture* then becomes a doubtful sensitivity because the final aim is *to reach the greatest number of people without bothering about the quality of the message*.

I must take this opportunity to quote a passage from the Philosophy of the New Music by Théodore W. Adorno, which should be a Bible for all budding musicians: *"In fact, an adequate recital of the works of Beethoven, the themes of which one whistles in the subway, demands a far greater effort than that of the most sophisticated music; it must be cleared of the veneer of a false interpretation and sclerotic ways of reacting. But since the cultural industry has set up its victims to avoid every effort during the leisure time allowed to them for the consumption of spiritual goods, people cling with ever greater stubbornness to the appearance that separates them from the essence"*.

So how can we fail to understand the distance between current composers and the public? The abyss that separates them deepens mercilessly, because their interests have ceased to be the same.

Why be surprised at this historical, aesthetic and ethical descent - collapse would be a better word - that comes from *The Passion* according to Saint Matthew by Johann Sebastian Bach, from *The Ninth Symphony* by Ludwig van Beethoven, to *"Souvenirs de Voyage"* to *"Idylles des fleurs"*, or to *"Feuilles d'Album"*, to *"Espaces"* or to *"Sans forme"* of certain composers, whom I refuse to name but who will be known to any serious musician, prototypes of the decadence of the nineteenth and twentieth centuries?

The effects of this *twilight of the gods* are evident, heartrending and irrefutable.

For example, comparing the *off-the-shelf* melodies played in a salon of bad taste with a diminished seventh chord - decadent, one says - forming an organic whole in Liszt's Sonata or in the Introduction to Beethoven's Sonata Opus 111, is a sign of intellectual bad faith, of incompetence or quite simply a lack of vision.

It is the same chord but *conceived and integrated* by two different minds: one commonplace, that of the salon, and the other of a genius, that of Beethoven or Liszt.

There is, therefore, a distance of dissociation between a severe concept of things and the extravagant illusions of pseudo, pre-packed music, labeled and ready for use.

"The past does not fascinate us when it resembles our own day and age; certainly we are more fascinated by the forms that man has adopted on earth and through which we try to understand him", the verdict of André Malraux, when he had, and he had increasingly, a burning desire to remove from Art and its expression, that is, from an artistic career and from the audience attending the concert, *all the suffering inherent in this process.*

You might say *we no longer want to suffer to create*, as if that were possible!

You might believe then, or better *swallow*, that Frederic Chopin would have composed his Preludes Opus 28 after the lovely blue eyes of his Countess of the moment, because his inspiration was only triggered on hearing his *note bleue*, according to sources… authorized by George Sand.

So we should take the author of Lelia as an historical reference!

The endless novels, interviews, paparazzi, the life of artists of every type, whether artistic, biographical or political, often do no more than increase market literature, an indecent business of an industry *also* musical that develops human gullibility and imbecility to their utmost. All of that used to take place in the Coliseum. Currently, the final aim of all of this is to strengthen power groups and to use the *stupefied muscles* - or brains, should they exist, of the masses and their incapacity to reflect, *"Art has to reveal to us ideas, formless spiritual essences. The supreme question about a work of art is out of how deep a life does it spring".* These magnificent words from James Joyce in his Ulysses illustrate far better than any other discourse. And so we move from the Golden Age of Art to the Age of Argent, to the Age of Lead and to the Ages of the Absurd and Ineptitude.

However, we cannot speak about awkwardness or poverty of mind because our day and age is a marvel of intelligence, talent and progress. We should speak rather of intellectual diversion to the service of a variety of gods.

This lack of propriety in social and aesthetical behavior, this artistic irresponsibility and acceptance of mediocrity, is nothing more than the result of leveling everything off to the lowest common denominator, piloted with aplomb by forces foreign to Art itself.

Politics is one of the major causes of this: the mediocrity of world leaders, their lack of vision on the true importance of culture and their own lack of culture have led to so many projects never getting off the ground.

We should not forget that the queue forms, each time with greater enthusiasm, from first thing in the morning, to enter the Prado Museum, the Louvre, the National Gallery or the Uffizi Gallery, in order to nourish the soul on eternal works.

If you were to ask who the Prime Minister was of a certain country fifty years ago no one would be able to reply as ministers are easily forgotten.

Look to the immortality of the creative, never granted to those who *decide on the budget.*

On reading the lectures of Thomas Mann, when he established the connection of historical, aesthetic and philosophical continuity between Schopenauer, Wagner and Nietzsche, you find surprising words concerning the *nationalistic* issue to things.

The great German thinker writes, among other things, asking a question far deeper, and ambiguous, than its aesthetic scope: *"Can one be a musician and a philosopher if one is not German?"*

Undeniably one cannot reply easily to such a great mind, although he was completely wrong: History has already given this response, and far better than anyone or anything else…

It is also clear that the problem must be returned to its true context and that Thomas Mann was perfectly familiar with *the lights from elsewhere* travelling under other passports. It would be sad to put together such inconceivable words to ask the question in reverse, by replacing *musicians or philosophers* by less spiritual words.

We would be accused of being *barbaric* writing like this, but we might deduce that the achievements of some nations are incontestable, but not at all enviable.

Such suggestions do not move things forward but tend to create a lot of confusion and ill feeling.

This does not prevent us from recognizing the remarkable influence of German thought in the world over the past three centuries. And the same goes for French, Italian, British, Spanish, Greek, Russian, Chinese and Japanese thought.

Plato, Aristotle, Plutarch, Cervantes, Molière, Racine, Dante, Tolstoy, Dostoyevsky, Shakespeare, Marlowe, Byron, Bacon, Darwin, Newton, Calderon de la Barca, Confucius, Lope de Vega, Mishima, Visconti, Sartre, Bernard-Henri Levi, Borges, Marx, Mao and also Che Guevara, have not only influenced, but also marked, History.

As much as Mann, Heidegger, Hegel, Brecht, Hölderlin, Hoffmann and Goethe.

But above all, Kant, who understood better than anyone the fundamental questions of existence by placing the reason for the human being at the centre of such a moral problem: *"What can I do?"*, *"What can I know?"*, *"What is my moral relationship vis-à-vis other beings in Nature and society?"*, because for him all morality includes the values of each individual.

Who would not recognize the artist's duty in this sentence?

But it is for Signor Settembrini himself to put an end to this misunderstanding, when he replies to Hans Carstop in The Magic Mountain: *"The malady is no more than a question of deregulation"*.

It goes without saying that Art has no nationality, other than minor manifestations.

But when an art, even folkloric, achieves universality, as with Chopin's Mazurka, a Rhapsody by Liszt or Gershwin's Rhapsody in Blue, we are in the presence of *a superior art* that only *began in a minor element.*

Similar intentions are intrinsic to artists: it is not a country that produces artists of genius, but rather the genius that brings glory to his or her country, which does not always deserve it.

There was a time, however, when the fact of belonging to a particular nation was enough to determine the quality of the artist: the Russian artist, for example.

Personally, I love many of them, but not all.

A similar concept only goes to enhance the false stereotypes of a society that does nothing more than seek its identity beyond and that includes itself among the famous errors of History. Or, better said, famous political errors. But just as History has proved, *there are no superior races on earth*, only *superior beings* from the point of view of mind and intelligence.

And, of course, Thomas Mann is one of them.

I have tried in this book to analyze the pinnacle of music for the piano. This Music that accompanies a pianist throughout a lifetime and that remains the clarification of the human spirit: Bach's Preludes and Fugues, Chopin's Etudes, Liszt's Sonata in B minor and Beethoven's Sonata Opus 111. I associate them with specific periods in the life of an artist. They take part in the early years of training, also on the social and ethical confrontations of his career, whether with glory or failure, and they follow the artist in his decline.

I have written with little talent because I am a musician and not a writer. Do not expect in what follows *a style of writing*, but quite simply reflection into the problems we face *all the time and every day*. Far more modestly, this has almost been written in the style of the Diary of Vaslav Nijinsky, where many things jostle without order, but also without compromise. Or perhaps, better expressed, in the ironic style of Jean-Jacques Rousseau when he used to say, *"you have to make grammatical mistakes to be crystal clear and have the right to belong to the art of writing"*.

I can only say I have followed this closely with grammatical mistakes and the logic of the writing!

Other works could have been chosen by some other author, maybe. Not by me.

But I would like to assume all my errors and in particular recall the Cardinal in the film by Federico Fellini, *8½*, when his feet are being washed, and who said, with great sadness, to the character of the artist, the director in mid-creative crisis: *"Who told you that we were put on earth to be happy"?*

BOOK I

Part one

The ontological relationship between the work and the artist's thoughts, or the fifth element of Nature

1 - Silence and the artwork, or Botticelli's "The Birth of Venus"
All music is born of silence, and to silence it returns. This is the case with Liszt's Sonata, Beethoven's Arietta, op.111 or Ravel's *Gaspard de la Nuit*.
It is a circular path to Silence, and it is the path of Life in that we leave from God and return to Him. The space between is no more than a simple adventure, "*a moment between two eternities*", in the words of the poet. Brilliant for some, less brilliant for others, at times dark, at times full of light, but always different and always with the same outcome: the relentless return to this lethargy and this Silence, which is common to them.
It determines the sole, unique principle of human equality, that which makes all of us the children of someone: God. It is this sole principle that decides that we come into the world naked and that we leave it in the same way.
Life then becomes the flight of time in its spatial perception.
It is perhaps what Bach felt in his time: do the Goldberg Variations not begin with the Aria to make an extraordinary, visionary journey in time and space, before returning once again to where they began, in the Aria that gave rise to them? Does Beethoven in his Variations, op. 109 not do the same thing?
The Silence that follows is almost more important than the vibrations heard.
Endless variations because they return always to the beginning: the Silence. With God. And then they begin the cycle once again. So the music becomes the language of the eternal circle; it is the perpetual return to Silence and confrontation with the inner self. One must become impregnated with this noble, solitary Silence. One must listen to it, feel it; and understand, in the words of Flaubert "*the abyss that separates it from me*", because it is solely in the Silence that the Essential can be heard.

One must also *think* this Silence. Because *thought* for the artist is the *fifth element* of Nature. One must also understand the vacuum created by it just before the music is performed. This allows the forces to descend, the muscles to relax in order to receive the vital energy of *the earth*, the reference element that consolidates and strengthens before it rises into space, to the cosmos and the spirit. The vibration is explored, an attempt made to discover what Chopin, Liszt and Brahms felt before us, and to isolate it, in isolating ourselves with it.
The thoughts of the artist must move in this way to an encounter with the musical work. And it is the meeting of these two powers and the communication between these two thoughts

that will make the voyage successful where even the Roman army failed: challenging time and crossing the centuries, *"because Art"* in Rodin's words *"is the most sublime mission of mankind because it is the exercise of thought that tries to understand the world and to make it understood"*.

We need, then, to love this magic Silence. Cultivating and preparing it in secret. For it is with it, and *beginning with it,* that we shall *reach others*.

2 - The home of the artwork

Silence is the source of creation. Of all creation *including our own*. For it allows us to put our inner confusion in order in a fertile way. And it is *from here* that the Sound is born.

The catharsis must be produced *within us*, but *"given the very abstract, formal nature of the musical element of the sound and the interiority that affects the content, it can only be dealt with using technical determinations referring to the mass relationships between them"* as Hegel informs us in his Aesthetics.

To this end, we must study the relationships between the Silence, the Sound and the self.

It is also within this Silence that the work lives. Being entirely musical it adores the Silence. It lives in obscurity and obsesses us. It does not belong to us. It belongs now, and always, to God. It is also *to home* that its loves to return after its zenith and glory in concert. According to Rainer Maria Rilke, it adores its *"infinite solitude"* .... and *"there is nothing worse than criticism to upset it. Only love can grasp it, hold it and be fair to it"*. In this way, the musical work loves its refuge. It leaves it reluctantly. All attempts at seduction, all the courtesy that we show it seems to leave it indifferent. It only reveals itself on occasion and makes us pay dearly for its consent *to come to us,* very rarely. And when it does, we think that we possess it. But this is false. We avidly enjoy a moment of ephemeral relationship because immediately the work is off on its capricious flight. And, immediately after its final vibration, its final fall begins, and we look on sadly as it disappears.

But everything will begin again.

But it is also this rarity, the certainty of this disappearance, that makes the work remain so beautiful at all times, because, as so magnificently put by Jorge Luis Borges, *"the face is beautiful at all ages but you must wait until Death to discover it in its infinite beauty"*.

3 - Coming in contact with the work

Oh, what joy when we come in contact with the work of art for the first time! What a miracle it is to discover its sonority and purity! So many ideas come to mind for its interpretation… So many hopes for how it will be performed… How many promises!

However, very quickly, once we have fallen into the arms of the work, it imposes on us its laws and makes its demands. It becomes uncertain and illusive and reminds us constantly that we have sworn to serve it steadfastly. The problems begin to disappear gradually when we try for the first time at home, well before the concert. We hear its voice without any references, but rather projected into the future, no doubt awkwardly, timidly and not yet polished. But what joy, and what a sense of power! Perhaps, faced by our novice emotions, it pardons our errors and accepts our faltering progress in exchange for our vague promise of trying to serve it better the next time.

And what a sensation when we interpret the music for the first time in concert! Not having mastered still the reflexes required to perform it in public. Being still unaware of our emotional limits and still with no idea of the extent of the real assimilation on our part. These are rare moments for an artist. Each one of these steps is a marvel. They lead to unexpected and unimagined regions, and sometimes to fundamental corrections, to changes that are often quite radical, to quite revealing adaptations and revisions, because *"prior to the musical work lies obscurity and after closer study comes the light, and following the execution comes the return to the shadows"*, according to Diderot. These steps lead us to the fundamental truth: *there is more work to be done*, because the level required to produce this music with dignity has not yet been achieved.

At times the work proves demanding, even distant. It makes us feel that we are living on different planets but sometimes gives us the vague hope that we can love one another. The concert teaches us that. At that moment - alone with the piano and the music – we learn the greatest lesson in life, in technical, artistic, philosophical and, above all, psychological terms. And so, we discover that the true strength of our chain is in its weakest link.

We want to discover the sometimes incredible paths that this music assumes to throw us off track. We want also to penetrate its treasures as well as its traps. Although, in the words of Vladimir Jankélévitch, *"one can penetrate a secret, but one cannot pierce a mystery"*. At the most one can conjecture and interpret, but not explain or rationalize.

Drawing close to the music is to blur the frail boundary between artistic inspiration and madness. Philippe Brenot, in analyzing Beethoven's character, through Panizza and Schindler, underscored this. The whole paragraph is quoted below:

"Anyone who has read Schindler's description in the biography of Beethoven and who could see hallucination in the initial stage of his illness, could have no doubt that it was a question of two closely linked situations belonging to the same family". And it goes on: *"The brilliance of musical inspiration may indeed resemble acts of hallucination, if we consider comments made by composers who claim they perceive the melody and that they do no more than transcribe it. This is not a false perception, nor an illusion, nor indeed is it an interpretation of reality, but very probably it is a true delirious intuition, self-generated, that allows us to think that the creator manages, in an advanced perceptive search, to unleash automatic thought and, as a result, an automatic perception, an undeniable sign of a moment of dissociation from the self"*.

Similar to the travels of Ulysses, the voyage towards the musical work goes through much suffering. Step by step and stone by stone, it has to be built to get release from the bonds that prevent our Ondine from reappearing.

The technical obstacles obstructing this route must be confronted, and the lack of constancy, indiscipline and the absence of professionalism in the work must be overcome. Many other difficulties that upset and impede concentration on the Music must also be dealt with, the many psychological obstacles that prevent the transfer and the symbiosis of personalities between the composer, the work and the self, a true artistic and spiritual communion that allows souls, of apparently different natures to meet and complete one another. And above all, it must also be borne in mind that, even after the suffering and the work, all of this will result in only the ephemeral joy of a moment. Despite all our efforts, Ondine will evaporate and disappear, as in the verses of *Gaspard de la Nuit* by Aloysius Bertrand. But Charles Baudelaire as well, from the depth of his melancholy, wrote: "*we must work if not out of pleasure then out of despair*".

Nevertheless, our passionate dream, our desire to have contact with the musical work, is no flighty, fickle summer love, but rather a commitment that will last throughout our short lifetime.

4 - The work lives in us, or the confessions of St. Augustine

The work lives in us. It is in the depth of our being and in our spirit and we must find it, even when there is no guarantee that we will find it each time nor that we will be able always to reach the end of the journey. An artist must search his soul with humility. Even Leonardo saw his paintings as unfinished.

This understanding implies the cultural and spiritual development of the pianist. We must, then, speak of *a whole*. Technical perfection as advanced as is possible will be required, as this will produce a better translation of the Music initially, although this must not hide from view the *final conception of the work*. And even if all additional control gives access to relatively higher worlds, technique alone is not enough. It must be accompanied by musical and general culture, by an insatiable curiosity, a musical instinct, artistic intuition and an acute sensibility. Spiritual elevation is inevitable for an artist worthy of the title. This is what will open the gates of Heaven. A mature approach to the work is necessary, as well as tenacity, concentration and interest, and an obvious willingness clearly attached to the fervent desire to make progress. Any distraction must be avoided and, above all, in the words of Claudio Arrau, "*studying very slowly because I am in a great hurry*".

Opinions on this type of work are contradictory. However, three stages can be distinguished: *feeling*, as the initial element; *reasoning,* as the element of planning and *spirituality*, as the final element.

As we know, *feeling* is common to all species. For example, just think of the affection your dog or horse has for you. Every living being is capable of feeling. Emotion is always the *moving force of creation*, the driving force behind inspiration in a work of art. *Reasoning* comes at a higher level because it belongs in the human mind.

Analysis and synthesis, or method, dear to Descartes – order, in other words, must be part of musical practice. Of course, it is not by reasoning that *one is* or that *one becomes* an artist, but surely one cannot be an artist without it. Order in the mind and the secret underlie our artistic construction.

Lastly, the third stage, recommends achieving a *certain spirituality* that is, finding the mysticism and moral aspect of the work. Examples are the spirituality of the Trio of Chopin's Funeral March or that of Franck's Coral. Works like these achieve a level of perception, vibration and transcendence that goes beyond the scope of mere mortals. This stage, however, does not go *beyond* human scope because works, although divine, remain the fruit of human labour.

Two contrasting opinions are quoted in full to illustrate the problem from a different perspective.

One from Arnold Schoenberg: *"The more an interpretation follows the instructions, that is the more it is able to bring out the true intention of the composer, the more sublime it is, because the interpreter is not the tutor of an orphan work, nor its spiritual mentor, but its most faithful servant; even before they take shape, the interpreter seeks out the least of its desires, the least of its thoughts to avoid letting them escape. But there are two things that frustrate this project: the imperfection of the notation and that of the servant. The latter is generally a person who wants to express his own personality rather than penetrate that of the composer. He becomes, therefore, a parasite who remains on the surface of the work although he could nourish it from within"*.

At the other extreme, Franz Liszt wrote: *"The musical work is no more than the tragic, moving stage production for the virtuoso, because he is trying to reach his own sentiments"*. The pianist, the interpreter of these divine works, *has the moral obligation* to set out in search of his own limits. Hence *the obligation to aspire to transcendence*.

5 - Aspiring to transcendence

Aspiring to transcendence implies being prepared not just to *execute a work*, but to participate in a more *divine* activity. Nietzsche used to speak of the desire to become a *demi-god*. There is a need to feel – here is the feeling, once again – that this creation is not only produced *under* our fingers but *above* our heads.

We could speak, then, of two emotions: one a *driving emotion because it drives our fingers*; the other a *unifying* emotion that leads us to being *in unison* with something higher than ourselves but which, at the same time, *passes through us*.

We could also speak of two feelings: one closer to *desire* and *appetite* and the other closer to a *beatific and celestial* sensation where, in some way, a revelation is found, a need for peace and non-movement, or better, *"a still movement"*, according to Hermann Hesse.

This *still movement* is probably the most difficult thing to achieve and even a lifetime is not sufficient in which to do so. The pianist must aspire to this rather than thinking he can achieve it completely. Partly aspiring and achieving while accepting his limitations, partially accomplishing our dream of Icarus, in a way, knowing that at any moment we can be mercilessly returned to earth in punishment for our insolence at attempting this *prohibited flight*. This limit and this hope of achievement are the elements that help us mature. They are the most complete vitamins for the human soul. Lastly, it is wiser to accept this imperfection, confront it daily, treat it with familiarity and try to overcome it.

In Kempff's words, *"being an artist is the capacity to begin over again"*.

This perseverance is our indispensable weapon. Without it, we would not only be lost but also disarmed, impoverished in the extreme, and, above all, deprived of our winning trump card. Without it, all is lost before it begins. This perseverance allows us, because in its very blood passion and courage circulate in perfect harmony, to win all the battles with great dignity, if not with success.

In view of the fact that our technique is fallible like everything else, we must be armed - *and develop this sentiment to the full* - against the depletion and constant decline in our capacities. This reinforcement will be the only guarantee against the continuous decline in all aspects of our work. There is, therefore, a constant trade-off between qualities and non-qualities.

6 - The creation or « The Lute Player » by Caravaggio

But how can we aspire to such dreams, and throw ourselves   into such projects, without an intelligence of the highest level, accompanying and guiding everything, arranging the elements, prodding each thing into its place?

We are teaching nothing new to any one by saying that you   need to know Hoffman and his Tales to understand Schumann's Kreisleriana, or Dante Alighieri's Divine Comedy to express more correctly the Fantasy quasi Sonata of Liszt. What can we say of pianists who have never read the Poems of Bertrand and who play *Gaspard de la Nuit* only to show off *sonorities* or *repeated notes*, although the verses are published together with the music?

The cultural development of an artist must be on-going and constant, at the risk of rendering him limited and *primary*. *Culture is that artist's daily bread*, and his true freedom. Cultivating the self is to nourish the self.

I remember well the magic formula from the Middle Ages, the three eights: eight hours for work, eight hours for rest and eight hours for leisure. The first two concepts are very clear. The third, the idea of *leisure*, is less clear. *Leisure*, to me, means *having time available to learn more*. What could be more agreeable than spending a few hours wandering in the Orsay Museum in Paris or the Uffizi in Florence? What could be more delightful than visiting the Sainte Sophie in Istanbul, the skyscrapers of Kuala Lumpur and New York or the canals of Venice? What could be more impressive than observing how the engine of a Ferrari or the reactor of an Airbus functions? And what about the hours spent exploring literature, theatre, philosophy, theology, the exact sciences, pedagogy or aesthetics? The *Trivium* and the *Quadrivium*, so dear to Liszt, can only but influence artistic growth at the highest level and create a man that is in harmony and free.

The wonders of nature and the products of human genius contribute to improving our intellectual, spiritual and scientific *state*. They help the artist to develop, make him reflect, learn, stir his curiosity, making him avid for explanations and enigmas to resolve, avid to feel that the absolute escapes him. All this makes him aware that he *knows* very little and that the way ahead is far longer than that already travelled. It means that all this must make the artist fervently desire that his mind should think of things other than playing octaves on the piano faster than anyone else.

The active or passive cultural store helps the artist in his work. The old principle "*mens sana in corpore sano*" still holds and will continue to do so as long as man is on earth. This learning must take place in harmony and be as thorough as possible. Nothing is to be gained from developing one part of the body without the other parts following. This would only create parts that were *monstrous*, abnormal, disproportionate and ridiculous.

Cultivating recalls the idea of sowing and reaping as well as the idea of *transmission*. I am thinking, for example, of Michael Angelo's work in the Sistine Chapel – those two fingers that reach out to touch one another, in The Creation. The Finger of God almost touches that of Adam.

This painting shows us divine transmission.

7 - The unfathomable threads

Ralph W. Emerson said: "*Metaphorically, there is only one body, in which all parts make the whole: the head, heart, muscles, organs, skin, bones, and nothing can be missing, or it risks destroying the rest*».

Similarly, the Arts, Knowledge, Culture, the Sciences and even Nature taken together are all parts of one thing. Each element   is itself, but it represents *others as well*. Of course, they are all interdependent. Music is also closely linked to the other arts. The different artistic spheres have an influence on one another and nourish one another mutually.

Goethe and Liszt; Hölderlin, Jean-Paul Richter and Schumann; Victor Hugo and Berlioz; Victor Hugo and Liszt; Mallarmé and Ravel; Lamartine and Liszt; Mickiewicz and Chopin; Heine and Schumann; and Schubert, and Debussy, and Moussorgski, and Prokofiev, and…? Goethe and Beethoven; Goethe and…, Schiller and…, the list is endless. As many names as artists, and these examples could fill a vast, endless book.

Music is also closely linked to Nature. An observation of Nature served to inspire Liszt's "Years of Pilgrimage"

How can we fail to associate the Pacific Ocean viewed in its infinity from Australia, from Chile or the western seaboard of the United States with the work of Bach, with the Partitas, the 48 Preludes and Fugues, with the Passions, the Masses, the great organ Corals, they themselves *infinite*? Is the immensity of Bach not comparable to an ocean?

How can we fail to associate the wonder of the working of the human heart with the vital mechanism of a Fugue? It is the very principle of Life, the generator of both. Albert Einstein, on Bach's Fugue in F minor said: "*I carried this Fugue into one of my finest equations and the result was perfect. Then, immediately, I carried my finest equation into musical phrases and the result was certainly not a Bach Fugue!*"

Spiritual associations that are created and established are in this way infinite, just like the circuits of our brain.

When you look at the Sistine Chapel – its tragedy, its power and its pain – that tells the whole history of human essence and its suffering in its relation to God, that touches even the Creation, that in its power reduces all reaction on our part, how can we fail to associate the genius of Michael Angelo with the Quartets, the great Sonatas and Beethoven's Symphonies, even if the latter never saw the work of the painter?

There is a whole aesthetic theory that associates the works of Raphael and of Mozart.

My extraordinary professor of musical aesthetics and musicology, but more importantly the composer Juan Francisco Giacobbe, himself a pupil of Ravel, used to say, "*The mysteries turn certain Inca scales into certain Chinese scales although these peoples never met nor crossed one another's paths.*

8 - « The paths of the Lord are impenetrable ... »

Religion inspires men and, therefore, artists. The cathedrals and temples that pay homage to God in all towns and cities throughout the world, from Rome, Lima, London, New Delhi, Paris, Brussels, Tokyo, Vienna, Kyoto, Chartres, Florence, Mexico, Seoul, Pretoria, Casablanca, Istanbul, are innumerable. Every human community, no matter how small, every village, however poor, has its church. For Music they have Bach, Palestrina, Handel, Mendelssohn, Fauré, Mozart, Haydn, Liszt, Rimski Korsakoff, Verdi, and so on. For Painting and Sculpture, they have Rubens, Dürer, Raphael, Leonardo, Giotto, Jeronimo Bosch, Murillo, Andrea Mantegna, Rodin, Primaticcio, Dali, David, as well as Praxitèle and so many others. For Literature I write nothing because the list would be endless.

For every human manifestation, whatever it is, religion is a source of phenomenal inspiration that goes on through Time.

9 - The Message or Leonardo's « Annunciation »

The artistic message, as a moral and aesthetic value, must involve an *understanding of Time.* No perfection, no skill, no technical or expressive capacity, no acoustics of a fairly fine hall in fairly good order, no interpretation no matter how magnificent it is, cannot replace this *"something extra"* that certain artists have: *this understanding of Time.* It is a determining factor in transmitting the artistic message from one mind to another.

And, certainly, it does not depend on the reputation of the artist, nor the age of the artist, nor on the instrument, nor on the concert hall where the performance is given.

Why is it that certain orchestras sound different under a different conductor?

Why is it that the same piano, in the same concert hall, will sound according to the nervous or emotional discharge of each pianist? Why is it that these same mechanics are sublime or not?

This understanding of time depends on the capacity to give each thought, each note, each phrase, each sequence its own breath required to guarantee an existence independent of the metronomic speed inherent in each work.

We need a new artist who does not change the notes but who, in the words of Schnabel in referring to himself, *"plays the notes like almost everyone else with just a few added faults. The difference between me and other pianists lies "before" and "after" my notes, not 'during' them."* It is the space *between* the notes that should be different, and seeing what lies *behind the notes, between them and in front of them* is what is important.

The *Tempo* of a musical work - and not its speed - depends on this. This Time is found not just in the keyboard (because only the keyboard *permits it*) and, in particular, determines the distances between the notes. It gives them their capacity to breathe. It is this Time that gives them life.

There is no purpose in producing stillborn notes.

The search for this *Tempo* (the Lost Time of Proust, or rather Time Recovered) should be done without the keyboard, in solitude and only in harmony with the *other* Time. It is this that determines its own life with that of the musical work. It is arranging a *tempo* instructed by the composer (and not by the metronome) with *our vital vibration* that connects us to it. That is my definition of *tempo*.

The dexterity of the spirit should, in this way, join the vibration of eternity. *"Where is the Time? What is the purpose of this mobile image of an immobile eternity?"*, were the questions raised by Rousseau.

The magic thread that weaves through any major work of art, through all its genius and love of being, comes down through the centuries without the slightest crease. *It defies Time*. Its more secret rules escape us and probably will never be completely transmissible.

Just look carefully at the paintings of the well-known disciples of the major Italian or Flemish painters to see that they too, the greatest Masters, were unable to communicate or transmit the deepest secrets of this magic thread.

This sign of powerlessness, this incapacity to truly pass on the legacy of something impossible, this utopia, this illusion, this dream of becoming a *Maestro* by decree, should underlie all teaching: the idea of encouraging the search for the unique being,

for the unrivalled artist, for the non-comparison, denying the *truths* of competitions or, at least, *the relativity of opinions*. In the end, the idea of ensuring the identity of each artist with himself. This is our only hope of finding, perhaps, a person still capable of producing this vibration. This training and his intellectual development are felt, very strongly, in a supreme interpretation: just think, for example, of Chopin's Third Sonata played by Dinu Lipatti, this unrivalled Virtuoso who would say to his pupils at the Geneva Conservatory: *"Not only Urtext is required, but above all Urspirit'*.

10 - The work or « Venus at the Mirror » by Rubens

All these players, the pianist, the composer or any artist, the instrument itself, are going to disappear. Only the music remains. And it will last and become eternal.

It is proof of the immortality of the human soul. It is the music that provides the human representation of the artist, the image that sustains our imagination.

It is the tree that links Heaven and Earth. Its roots cover our heart and mind. It is the music that allows us to irradiate out towards others.

This Whole is found in us because God chose us as His own dwelling place.

It is God that decided this.

The musical work follows Him: it is in us. It lives in us.

It is for the artists to get to this Whole to flow to others, without troubling them, but convincing them.

However, before radiating the music out to others, even before building it, there has to *be a prior conception*.

Before learning Brahms's Third Sonata, you have to know what you want to do with it, to have an idea of how to interpret it. We should feel the *ideal* vibration played by an *ideal* pianist who does not have our problems, feel a Sonata that does not depend on our playing, a trembling that is not conditioned by our personal participation: compare how this Sonata *sounds* in the Infinite, in Eternity, regardless of *our* limits. We should come to know it beforehand in the purity of its conception.

This appeals not only to our honesty, but also to our culture, our knowledge, and our intellectual development, all elements that are indispensable for artists who aspire to being something more than just *sound smiths.*

If we do not understand Beethoven beforehand how can we study Brahms's Sonata, which follows his model and quotes him continually in his Tempest, in Scherzo for the Fifth Symphony, in his Four Notes of Destiny and in his Hammerklavier?

How do we solve the problem of the challenge to the world launched by Brahms when he himself is tributary to the Maestro of Bonn?

How can you be the *brilliant pupil of the brilliant Maestro*, but through him become one of the great musical geniuses?

For example, how can you place this great Sonata beside Liszt's Sonata, composed in the same era?

One refers to the past, that of Brahms, the other to the future, that of Liszt. "How many *aesthetic years* have elapsed between these two musical works, from the strictly historical point of view *(because in reality the two works date from the same year!)* Without a doubt this raises an ethical problem.

And we should be ready with the answer if we want to interpret the two works, and certainly *before we play them.*

11 - The relationship with the 'self'

Too often the pianist is tempted to reduce the music to his own scope, to his technical, intellectual and moral limits that will all determine his *conception of the work.* This is an unpardonable mistake on the part of the artist: *it does no more than make him seem insignificant.*

I do not think you can study a work mechanically and to see where you arrive by means of this work to then decide on the interpretation: fatally our personal limits impose a *primary* conception, because *we can only go there and no further.*

Like this we are limited by a lack of ambition, culture, love, art, power and sacrifice. We are fools. We do not have access to the world of Brahms. At the most we can *reproduce* in certain aspects that are no more than the tip of the iceberg.

On the other hand, if we know beforehand what we must do, and what we want to do, it is easier not to impose limits, but rather to spiritualize routine work and to charge it with a sublime outcome: that of bringing it closer to the *concept* of Brahms's Sonata.

Such an attitude will help us improve, because in this way *we are obliged* to excel, to develop, to learn and to make ourselves *aware* of the problems. In the first case, unfortunately, we will do no more than sidle past the work of Brahms.

12 - Giving to receive

What can we say about what we take away from a great concert, about what the great artist gives us?

Will the Music, the sound, die completely, or will it continue to live and be present in the soul of whoever receives it?

Perhaps we, the musicians, think that because the music lives in us, we are in some way bound to it by an umbilical cord. Every great interpretation means, as a result, *resurrecting something that is dead*. The code of a score, under the fingers of the pianist, becomes something living. *The work of the artist is therefore to give life.*

And because you must give it this life, the work almost becomes your child, to whom you can only tell the truth. You cannot lie to it. You must give it the best of yourself because, in the words of Rabindranath Tagore, "*we must draw it out of the limits of our sensibility and our mental vision to achieve a greater freedom, such as that of immortality*".

The exaggeration then, the artificial echoes, the search   for voices more interesting than the principal ones, the effects on the audience, sudden dynamic changes, the untimely *ritardando* and *accelerando*, all super-charge of sonority in volume or the fleeting *morendo*, cannot, fortunately, correct the situation should there be a lack of musical conception.

The poor musician is one who does not understand what he is playing.

The average musician is responsible, and he realizes, despite all, what he is doing, but without inspiration and *without knowing what to do* with the sound.

The great musician *is the one who conceptualises the sound before producing it and above all he hears the silence afterwards*, because the work for him is a prior concept, an idea, sonority, an image, a living being and not just a printed page.

Certainly, one can play the piano with extreme sensitivity, with great beauty and with no thought at all, interpreting sonorities and their magic effects on the brains of others. This is the same as the picture of a beautiful woman, of no special interest other than her beauty. A hollow beauty, that holds neither mystery nor secret and that one quickly tires of.

Similarly, *the beautiful sonority is but a part of a great interpretation but in itself it is not a complete interpretation*. We can imagine the *Arioso dolente* of Beethoven's Sonata, op. 110, played *with sensitivity* although in no way transcendent. The contrary would be impossible in the hands of artists such as Arrau or Gilels. A great musical thought certainly manifests itself with a sensitive sonority, but this is no more than one of its elements. *The sound is not an end in itself, but a means.*

It is important in this case to dissociate these two elements: *sensitivity and thought.*

The first element does not depend on the second, but the second, *the thought, uses the first as a vehicle*. By deduction, Sensitivity is part of the Thought and not the other way around. It is the Thought that fills the artist, this conception of the work of Art, and not the opposite. We must constantly seek it in ourselves. We must seek out in the convolutions of our brain and in the disorder of our affections the channels that communicate mysteriously like true communicating vessels.

I really do not believe in a great interpretation that does not belong to the Elevation. Beethoven thought that Music should be the maximum expression of all Philosophy. *The Thought is, therefore, the ultimate state of Art*, because it is the only fundamental aspect through which we feel God in our work.

Beauty, in the Emotion, should inspire any work of art, and Truth transforms it into a message

that can be received by others, according to the eternal principles of Plato and Aristotle.
Teresa gave Beethoven her portrait with the following dedication: *"To the great pianist, to the great composer, to the noble man"*.
And there we have a scale of values.

13 - Vulgarity as a concept

To empty music of its major content is not a crime, of course. An artist unable to overcome the usual problems is not to be *condemned*. He too has the right to exist. It is not his fault if he has no charisma, no gift of being able to make others vibrate in a dimension other than that of fine sonorities and adequate formal relationships: he has the notes as a belief, the technical problems and the bravado as an end. And so, his destiny is sealed. Access to the upper realms of Art is reserved for a category of artists who think differently to *most people practising the profession*.

Fabricating idols without talent is, on the hand, a major fault because it implies a lie. It is not a sin if you do not own a luxury apartment in Monte Carlo, but to try and sell something that is deteriorating, dirty and horrible for the same price as the luxury apartment in Monte Carlo would be immoral.

However, this is common currency in current musical life. One could talk about trafficking in artists, pupils, juries and organisations. The market is, so to speak, *open* and there are all sorts of authorised dealings going on. Of course, those conducting this type of business are sufficiently smart not to be taken in and, deep down, they know the *quality* of what they are selling. But why worry if the public *buys anything*?

What moral, artistic or human responsibility must then adopt a jury, a critic, a teacher, the director of a Conservatory, a journalist! It is sad to note that this educational mission, this religion, this behaviour and this moral sense are all too often completely stifled by the desire for *power*.

Human relations in this context become meaningless because words are used wildly, because *"the word is given to man to disguise his thought"*, according to Edward Young.

Suffice to call something genius when it is banal, for the two words to lose their intrinsic meaning.

14 - Arabesques

We should rather feel the smallness of our dimension compared with the infinite scale of Art and Life. To understand that the only thing that is *not indispensable* is us, the pianist and the instrument, because we are interchangeable and replaceable. *The musical work is the true protagonist*. Without it, we do not exist.

Of course, one might reply *without us, the music cannot exist either*. Without *the pianist* that is indeed true. But without *us*, in personal terms, it can indeed exist *someone else* will replace us. We learn the greatest lesson in humility the day we understand that *no one is indispensable, and particularly us*.

This idea should be to instil in the artist a steadfast modesty and not the idiotic airs of a *prima donna* that will do no more than besmirch his soul. Humility, an inestimable treasure for the artist, is the art of self-questioning every day and at all times.

Surprise, joy, fear and the unforeseen in concert, should motivate us and help us mature. We should not take our daily task as some routine activity of little worth: the concert must always be an event. Experience influences nothing, because experienced or not, we find ourselves alone, before the public and before the mystery above all. Nothing is certain at these times. *The only thing that is certain is the unknown.*

There are numerous artists, even the great ones, who love to believe that they are superhuman, as if touched by God. They feel themselves to be conquerors like Alexander the Great, nothing scares them, they say. I have seen some of them before they go on stage. The reality has nothing to do with what goes down in their *Memoirs*, in these wonderful fairy tales that are worth no more than their anecdotal or financial value.

The force of wanting to show off our nervous superiority only makes us more vulnerable.

15 - The inner journey or « The importance of The Wonders of Nature » by Magritte

We have already said several times that Music must pre-exist in us, before all else. So, it is a journey into our inner self, in some way to meet up with an old companion.

This process is full of obstacles, traps, false prophecies, demagogues, corrupters and the corrupt. The journey is full of discouragement and exaltation. It keeps every possible and imaginable surprise for us. Earlier, it was said that it resembles an Odyssey.

To undertake it we look for advice and the opinions of great teachers. We look at others and not at ourselves. We are afraid   of taking the wrong road. Nothing can replace our most trusty weapon, which is *patience*. We would only be cowardly and mediocre if we did not dare, either through fear or idleness, to realise our potential capabilities.

Putting *fine sounds* together, as was said earlier, is not sufficient. It would be a gross error to imagine that by assembling *fine words* we could produce works worthy of Rimbaud.

Nothing can be achieved if there is a gap between the Idea, Technique, Beauty, Analysis and Transmission. Without these, the interpretation of the work would only be partial. It would only throw light on one aspect of things, only one angle of the picture would be recognized, or it would be restricted by its own framework.

A great interpretation *must be visionary. It is not à la mode and it crosses time.* It is the Liszt by Busoni, the Chopin of Rubenstein and Lipatti, the Beethoven of Backhaus, the Schubert of Schnabel and Kempff, the Brahms of Arrau, the Scriabin of Horowitz.

Not only do the ears transmit such music. It is transmitted by sound waves that have an effect on the brain cells and it floods our whole being. These waves of sounds make the body vibrate until its trembles.

We breathe the desire for a brilliant interpretation, and we feel unrest when we do not find it. Often, we feel powerless when we feel we have failed to concentrate properly at the start of a concert. Sometimes, on the contrary, we are happy at having discovered what escaped us in a previous presentation. This discovery encourages us *and is not content just to cohabite* in us. It *guides* us, conditions our decisions, forces us to become better, teaches us and makes us suffer for *the good cause*. After all, it determines the major choices in our existence.

It is useless to want to describe it by a single sentiment, no matter how sacred it is. That would be too naive. One cannot imagine that such sentiments can be learnt like a geography lesson: if Music does not live in us, it is inconceivable that anyone else can put it into us. We may be extremely receptive but that will not help at all, quite the contrary, particularly when considering transcendence. *One cannot duplicate an artist.*

To fulfil life, we have Love and Friendship, but for us artists and musicians, when the music is not right then nothing is right. Taking the words of Nerval in speaking of poetry, we could say "*in my latest folly, I thought always of myself as an artist*".

We are influenced, affected, conditioned in this way. Music produces in us a veritable existential *inundation* and a total dependence on it.

16 - The return of the prodigal son

A one-thousand-kilometre journey always begins with the first step. Therefore we must return to the source, have the courage to question ourselves every day, be reinvigorated, return our score to zero at any moment, rediscover the marvels of the work as for the first time: never constantly repeat the same *effects* as if our palette of resources were so limited.

Recreate is a key word for the artist.

We need to get over our useless histrionic practices, rekindle our sensitivity relentlessly, *revitalise* and feel at all times the blood flowing through our veins.

Repetition kills Art. It is not the model that is to blame, *but the lack of creation*, the sale of the same product without variation or progress. It is the habit of minor sentiments, petty, false sensitivity and vanity, as well as being imbued with oneself. It is losing one's bearings and having no other reference stars but ourselves, forgetting the true stars at the party.

We need constantly to seek a fresh approach to our interpretations, nourishing oneself on music every day and all the time, such is the law. And we should never play pieces for the n'th time *without the ecstasy of the first time.*

This dimension of ecstasy, so dear to Chopin, Liszt, Debussy, Scriabin and Ravel, is almost absent from the concerns of whoever thinks only of *playing*. The idea of the pianist who restricts himself to playing should be banished from the education system.

Young artists today are drawn into a *vicious circle created by* the "musical market" that pushes them into "the maximum number of concerts". They are forced not to think or to wander away from the artistic approach by the need to play better than others to be able to survive. They become commonplace products, *to be used and then thrown away*. That costs less than repairing them. It is almost an ultimatum to their progress.

To be or to become an artist means experiencing deep down inside the pressing need to communicate, to give, to commune, to recreate, to love something madly in order to breathe life into it. It means giving to others that which is the finest, even when the representation of Good and Evil, as in certain paintings by Jeronimo Bosch, show *other facets that also exist* within the human being and that being's soul.

Although, according to Pierre Debray-Ritzen, in his attempt to contradict the principles of Plato, (the Great, the Good, the True and the Idea .... we will always return to this...), Art cannot *always* be great, true and just ...

Despite such harsh ideas, *we must always give without considering the cost.* This often means the cost is the self, as Saint Ignacio Loyola used to say: "*only the rich can give.... not only those who have material riches, but 'others' "*.

We should understand that Music bubbles in our heads, it warms the heart and makes the fingers itch, and none of this can be calmed until enjoyment, conclusion or at least the attempt at an interpretation are achieved. Like all human passion, that of music seeks to be realised and fulfilled. Without this desire, it is impossible to *become* an artist.

17 - The "other" trinity

And here we have our three great workers: the brain, the heart and the hands.

We could find the right formula by saying: "*a technique - which in Greek means Art-at the service of spirited reflection*".

Of course, there is the anguish felt in encountering the perfection of the work. It is a terrible struggle between *the self and what lies outside myself*: my egocentrism in encountering the work and all that its musical translation demands of me.

The moral brought by development is therefore evidence of my perpetual imperfection. A great artist can only see that which is still, and always, to be perfected, particularly without feeling this bourgeois conformity of an artistic position obtained.

This imperfection will be the most powerful driving force in helping the artist mature. This anguish can be only creative, because it justifies, stimulates and provokes. *It is suffering that will give life and not death.*

It is in these great moments of crisis that the true artist is formed and becomes stronger. It is a question of survival and not of death. Because all Art must, necessarily, resemble Life.

The connection between these three elements - the brain, heart and muscles - will be the aim of a great Master. And this connection will help the young pianist to become an artist. But the Master teacher will face many problems if just one of these elements is missing!

The artist without a brain will make no sense. Without a heart he will be no more than a machine. And without fingers he will be no more than an amateur.

If I recall correctly it was Vladimir Horowitz who spoke of a 33% balance in everything.

His labour will be *to carry his cross*. Firstly, the artist must feel the work as a musical creation, and then as the work of God, discerning the ascension to the pure spirit.

This crusade is always re-beginning, like an anathema: growing through pain, suffering to grow. This is the final lesson from any great Music, whether a Mozart Sonata or a Bartok Concert.

It presses on the chest, shapes our respiration, and blinds us like the vision of a great Gothic cathedral, the Niagara Falls or the Grand Canyon. It brings us down, almost, because it shows us the Infinite. We are humbled before such power. We respect it in silence; and in ecstasy as well.

18 - The 'quasi' Quartet

Of course, there is every type of artist in a great variety of qualities, but we may generally differentiate four main types:

1 - There are those artists who feel and know Music, breathe it, penetrate it,

conceive it and speak it as if it were their *mothertongue.*

2 - There are other artists who understand Music and feel it as if it were a *language learnt perfectly* and spoken without any foreign accent.

3 - There are others in whom the *foreign accent* is very audible. You can tell that they are foreign.

4 - And lastly, there are *the others,* those who *learn phonetically.* With each word they pronounce you can feel that they are not expressing the music and that they do not understand it. To refer to them as artists would be to exaggerate. They would be better called *parrots.*

Those artists who would breathe music, who speak it is as if it were their *mother tongue* have a natural, easy, fine and flowing style, that has no makeup, artificial colouring or lifting. Everything in them seems to have the strength of the four elements: they have the lightness and purity of Air, the firmness of the Earth, the transparency of Water and the vigour of Fire. They treat the Music with familiarity. They give concerts, which more than just leading us to wonder, lead us to think. They can move us, and in fact they do very often, but above all prove to be masters *of thought.* These are the *greats.* Everything is evident at their concerts. Only the musical message fills the mind and when it comes to the last note, you do not even feel like applauding. As Monsieur Croche said in talking to Debussy, "*do you feel like applauding when you see the sun set?*"

The artists belonging to the second category are very good. They have learnt music so well, with such dedication, that you cannot hear an accent when they talk.
It is all very perfect and thought-out. There is no sign of any excessive make-up. It is all excellent quality and the result is splendid.
However, they address the music with more formality. After the concert, we are more than ready to raise a glass to toast this admirable work, this good taste and *intuitive skill.*

The third category includes those who *have learnt music* but whose accent in this language is intolerable. They give more and more concerts. They are integrated in musical life, take out subscriptions for recitals, network constantly and survive in a profession that is not theirs.

And lastly, the fourth type, those who learn phonetically and repeat like *parrots.*
There is no evidence of talent, unless that of the ridiculous imitation of others. After the concert you go home. You turn on the television to try to forget this unfortunate incident.
Why are they there? This is probably the most irritating point. Who has taken them this far? Where was the teacher who was responsible, who did not tell them that music was not for them, at least as a profession?

I must say that I think most of the problems we are facing currently come, as in any other sector of social fabric, from a poor education. Money, corruption, misunderstood dealings and unhealthy ambition replace that which common sense and responsibility did not do correctly at the right time.
Every artist has the right to exist. There is absolutely no doubt about that. It is an inalienable

right; and far be it for me *to prevent* anyone from making music. I am talking here purely professionally. Above all, the artist should exist and be independent of all social career. Artists are like drops of water falling on marble: there are few who perforate it but all flow and end up by finding their way, despite the hardness of the material.

We have to agree that not everyone is cut out to be a star. What is given to each of us in exchange *is the strength required to solve our own problems.* And this is our *prime duty* as human beings.

BOOK I

Part two

The struggle

1 - The pianist and the piano or « Dante and Virgil in hell » by Delacroix

Machiavelli claimed that there were three types of brain. The first is the one that understands alone. A problem is raised, and it is able to solve it. The second is the one that learns only when it is taught. And the third type neither understands nor learns.

And he adds: "*the first is magnificent, the second is fine and the third is useless*".

And in this definition who does not recognize the different types of pupil we teach, current pianists and quite simply the people around us?

The pianist and the piano. An often-imbalanced pair.

In the words of the great Ferruccio Busoni, they can be unequal and more like a "*pair of enemies*". One is full of sensitivity, "*a whole nervous system*", according to Friedricht Nietzsche, and is sensitive, fragile and surprising.

The other is indifferent, almost like a music box, a very black and white tool, like our clothing, but ready to transform itself at times into song and vibration.

Once again, the price to be paid for this transubstantiation will be very high. By what mystery does this vibration want to be transmitted to others, to our public? It is not surprising to find that there is no "law of listening" that determines this mystery.

In fact, very often, at a great performance that might be defined as irreproachable, the interpreter or the public may not be satisfied because the delirium, being transported to another world, contact with the beyond, in a word, *the Vibration*, is not there.

So what are the rules that allow this *vibration* to be present? What is the mystery that allows the interpreter to achieve this role of medium, when, in Leonardo's words "*the greater the sensitivity, the greater the martyrdom*"? How can this symbiosis that brings together the vital *quartet* of composer – work - interpreter - instrument, and the public, be achieved in the concert, where thousands of people experience at the same time, in *Time stood still,* where the only reality is this Music in the pure state, in its principal vibration and in its superior emotion?

It is indeed a question of sustaining this whole musical crusade with a sincere, serene sensibility, which at the same time is keen and ready for anything, particularly the greater sacrifices. This sensibility must be intense and striking. It is the driving force behind the adventure. It is thanks to it that life is filled. It is through it that the whole is measured. It is the extraordinary motive that makes sure that our flame is always vivid red. It is this sensibility that tells us the story, the drama, the joys of the work, because it is the first to burn and catch alight. In the words of Novalis "*the chaos must shine through the veil of order*".

All of this must be transmitted as the Message to the public.

And teachers must help young artists to shape on the outside what is already beautiful within, but in a state of disorder, clearly *this chaos* referred to by Novalis.

At the age of 13 for example, the lack of training and culture in a young artist may be forgiven, if it is accompanied by natural talent and an innate charm. At the age of 20 this becomes inappropriate and unpleasant because the more one knows, the more one understands and the more one loves. All true love rests in fact on deep understanding and acceptance.

2 - The concert or « The Disquieting Muses » by Chirico

According to Luigi Pirandello, the process, the relationship and the rapport between his "*Six personalities seeking their author*" are endless. It is the same for the pianist for his, not six, but *ten personalities: his own fingers.*

However, our *personalities* are more or less ready to begin a mysterious ballet that should lead us, *by listening* to the strange movements of the fingers, to *Wonderland*.

Our fingers begin to move. Our ears to listen.

Our head to think and control. Our sensibility is on red alert.

Our whole being trembles with desire and fear before Venus, the goddess of Beauty. She does not smile at us. Her face seems so distant. And we tremble at *not being up to* the situation.

The *boards for the actors and the keys for the pianist* are so narrow! At any moment you can slip and fall. You are at the edge of the abyss. This journey into the infinite, which is unachievable because it has no limits, is terrifying.

However, this concert must begin because the audience is waiting. And with the first notes it is as if our whole musical life parades before our spirit in a single instant.

We realise then that we have not worked enough, we have not given everything, and we have not gone into sufficient detail. This single instant makes us feel guilty even if the act, the concert that we are going to begin, falls within Plato's outline: The Fine, the Just and the Good.

The head of Beethoven, in all his bad humour, comes to us also. His look is terrible! It is he who wanted to bring together all the Greek elements to respond to Beauty, to enter into dialogue with the authentic and truth, to go in search of a superior Ethics and a faultless Morality, that is just and not misleading, without wanting to transmit messages that only involve our personal success, but quite the contrary, to transmit messages that belong to the *great*, to

the visionaries and the thinkers.

Saint Augustine also appears. He wants to take part in this scene between Beethoven and Plato, his equals. He is there to re-affirm that all *truth* lives in us and that there is no better teacher than to persist in this search into the depth of ourselves. *It is there*, said the Saint, that *we find certain answers to certain secrets*.

An interpretation is indeed an act of love: it appeals to the best in us. It exposes us. We have nothing more to hide. Every secret is revealed. All fear is manifest. All anguish is raw and settles in us. It refuses to leave we are alone before Chopin, Liszt and Mozart. There is no doubt that the battle is unequal: we can but lose. But to an extent we feel that they also, the greats, do need us a little. And they also face the fear that we experience.

This recognition gives us strength and courage and so we dare leaping into the vacuum. And it is at this precise moment, as Victor Hugo said, that we experience *"the melancholy and the happiness of being sad"*.

3 - The first meeting or the Love at first sight

How can we get to know the work?

We love it, we have loved it and we want always to love it. Firstly, we want to observe it and analyse its place in time and its aesthetic characteristics, in other words *its own life*. We want also to know about the composer, its creator, and his artistic trends, his moral, psychological, spiritual and existential crises. We want to do a formal, comparative harmonic analysis with other *similar* works. We want to investigate the motives of his composition, that is, the *raison d'être of his creation*. We want to study the emotional effect it has on us, the way it affects our brain, our heart, our ears and skin, in fact the whole hedonistic effect, the religious desire, the moral pleasure of serving it and giving it to others, the selfish satisfaction that it gives to our hands in making them shine because of the magnificence of the virtuosity, the austere position it demands of us, the suffering it forces on us or the aesthetic pleasure it finds for us in filling our soul with joy and happiness or, at times, with profound sadness.

It is getting to know how a great Master has seen it *before* us and, above all, *better* than us.

In short, we must do everything to form *our* concept, *our* idea and *our* definition of that work. What will we do with it? Has it already been done before?

If we love it as much as we say, we must do these analyses and ask these questions.

4 - The first steps and the ascension

It is only now that we should begin to study the music.

Our work at the piano is going to achieve the elevation and the spirituality because this work on the instrument is now on the way towards the model, towards the *ideal*. We are not in the process of repeating *more forte and faster, and later we shall see the consequence*. What can we see later if we do not know beforehand what we want?

This model forces us to use our imagination. It inspires us to playing the music ideally for a *sublime god*, without obstacles and with miracles, regardless of our means. In this way we can get a bit closer to it.

According to Giovanni Papini *"without intelligence, imbecility itself would have no meaning"*.

Our act of love for this music, this movement towards it, this   true ascension, assumes the ardent desire to know the music and not just the desire to play it. You can tire of anything *"except for understanding"*, according to Virgil.

It is like wanting to channel the cosmos and the universe, after correct and gentle screening, contained in us in a macro cell, and presenting it to the public for them to love it equally.

We aspire to discovering it note by note, to understand what it holds between its notes, as well as before and behind them. All our emotions are therefore en route and *"a long staff in hand, I wandered through the greenest pasture and soon my vessel will be full of starlight, under which I want to sing aloud*", as in the verses of Hus Chi Mo.

In this way a great movement of love and elevation is created. It is the ascension towards God.

5 - The medium

How can we deny, then, the religious and mystic role of the artist? And as a result, how can we assess the role of the interpreter? Why press the keys to produce a beautiful sound, with style and "savoir-faire"?

Why have in your home as decoration "The Trinity" by Masaccio or "The Adoration of the Magi" by Leonardo da Vinci?

If the artist does not feel responsible for this great mission then we understand, from the strictly human point of view, the reason for his egoistic fear at concerts: this fear is proof that his artistic act only *exists in relation to himself.*

One cannot *fill* an artist. The vital elements that will be the backbone of his interpretive act must be *extracted* from deep within him.

BOOK I

Part three

The art of teaching and the art of learning

1 - Teaching is learning from the pupil or « Saint Francis preaching to the birds"
   by Giotto

Someone said once that you learn what you already know.

Since the work *already* lives in us, even if in an embryonic state, in finding it we are not really producing a *creation*, but rather making a *discovery*, because *"to teach is to learn twice",* according to Joubert.

Is this discovery part of us, and the best part of us? Does it not rather belong to the cosmos? Are we not, as a result, only the partial owners? Is that our direct relationship with God?

There are so many questions that suggest that the work is built *from within* to then be pushed outwards. The role of love is therefore fundamental, as it is for a mother who gives life to her child. Remember the words of Ernest Hemingway: *"eternity or the lack of daily eternity"* because the idea of 'mother-child-eternity' could be compared with the trio "work-composer-pianist".

The role of the teacher is vital here. He is the guide, the one who helps *to discover* and not the one *who discovers*. For heaven's sake let us leave this role to the pupil. Through our teaching we must make this possible. We learn ourselves because *"I know no better teachers than my own pupils"*, claimed Arnold Schöenberg. We should learn *to be and to become,* and not just *to do*. It is a major lesson in humility for the maestro who carries and receives the secrets of the oracle, because, once again … *each time we teach do we not also learn*?

2 - "Il duetto" of teaching or Ravel's Sonata for violin and cello

In each act of teaching there are *two pupils* and, above all, *two teachers*.

The only true teachers are those who teach to think. To want any pupil to be dependent on us, the teachers, is a sign of egoism, what I call "reasoned stupidity". The relational and psychological aspect then becomes catastrophic. The more the pupil is dependent the more the teacher feels himself to be a demigod. His judgement takes on immense importance. How many false prophets are created like this!

The duty of the teacher is rather to help find the unique being, the being that we should help to find its freedom.

At the time of *separation*, when the pupil will exist alone, the teacher and the pupil become friends. The finest rapport and the warmest relationship begin then, between two developed beings. They are equal in their ideals, *but different in their personalities*. But there can be much sadness when there is a breakdown at the time when pupil and teacher separate, where there has been failure, or triumph. These are no more than displaced ambitions on the side of both!

3 - Difficult relations

A music lesson can take place in a modest studio or in a vast hall with an audience. It may be seen or not as a good *show*, a performance with an exchange of fingerings, dynamics and *tempi*. It may be seasoned with tasty gossip and some good jokes, but all this is scene setting.

True lessons, on the other hand, are those in which anaesthetics, morals, art and life are questioned. A look is sufficient to tell the pupil whether his aesthetic choice has won approval in the eyes of the teacher.
The price may vary from three hundred dollars an hour or the gratitude of a lifetime. This does not depend only on the skills of the pupil or of the teacher, but on their moral qualities. I can still remember today some great teaching moments, and fantastic lessons I received from my Masters. They illuminate my whole life. They are my chosen and preferred companions. Nothing can erase such feelings or memories. Such lessons are priceless. Money is good for paying the heating bills, tuning pianos, the telephone bills and the rent. It cannot commonly purchase deep knowledge and understanding, *that which is learnt for a whole lifetime*.
This is the duty and obligation that Liszt teaches us. It is the sacred duty that God did not give to "traders" in Music. One does not give pearls to swine. He did give it to some who should, if not change the face of the world, have the dignity to take up the fight. The teacher and his pupils should form a spiritual community where the prime rule is not to accept *the axis of Evil*, in the words of George Bush, because genius being inspired by God can only lead to the Truth.

4 - « To be an artist by the grace of God»

The teacher should persuade his pupils, and this is his principal role, *to exceed his performance*, to establish a chain leading to progress and purification. The teacher should not be seen as God, nor should he wish to be seen as such by his pupils. He should not decide on their lives for them. As Niels Bohr said to Einstein: "*Who are you, my dear Albert, to tell God what he should do*?
Do you not believe, then, that the Conservatories and the great Schools of Music urgently need a new morality? When will we teachers know everything? Where do these pretensions come from, if not from our weaknesses?
When are we going to reveal the mystery of Bach's Fugues, the smile in Mozart's Sonatas, the melancholy and sadness of Schubert, and declare at the same time that we hold the Truth? Many teachers have no scruples in declaring such things, and I am angered by such statements.
A good teacher must help his pupil to delve into his very depth, without creating in him any inopportune, displaced expectation. He should not encourage the incubation *of the superfluous but rather develop talent*.
Many dramas among young pianists come from the fact that they are not warned of the

dangers *at the time of their training*. There is no need to send anyone to the slaughter of competition knowing in advance that, winning the first prize or not, he is incapable of performing a work with dignity and off competing honourably. Creating ambiguous situations and giving false hopes assumes that the pupil, as a musician and as a human being, counts for nothing in the eyes of the teacher.

Because "*science without consciousness only ruins the soul*", expresses the clear sentence passed by Pantagruel in the work of Rabelais.

daily on these words.

5 - The gift of filling oneself with wonder

I remember when a very important American surgeon, Professor Denton Cooley, visited Buenos Aires, at the time when medicine was attempting the first heart transplants. He said something at the time that I have never forgotten. Watching a human heart beating in open-heart surgery shown on television, he said the following, while watching the heart movement in wonder:

"*This beating heart is Life. We know that when this heart stops, it will be Death, which clinically we can define as a stop to all functions. But we cannot know why this heart beats. We do not know the cause of its movement. All we know is that when it stops it brings Death without our being able to do anything. We cannot know 'why' there is Life*".

We are powerless before this mystery, as with any mystery, and exactly as we are before God. If His Existence and His Presence could be proved and defined as we explain how a car engine functions, the beauty of Faith would not be necessary.

As explained by Jean d'Ormesson, *it is we who have created God*. Throughout time, man has felt the need to create a superior being to explain his own existence.

Is it plausible then to hope to know the secret of the *creation,* artistic or otherwise, and the ontological relationship between the *work and us*?

Is it the work that creates us, or do we create the work? Does Music give us life, or do we give it life? Do we need music to exist? Do we create it because we exist?

Necessity certainly has a creative role. We are certainly in a position to build instruments and to use their soul, but perhaps it is only to launch an ascending scale towards the heavens, as with the Greeks, to aspire to immortality, carried by a desire to feel God close to us.

BOOK II

Part one

Meditation on our work or
« Meditation on the Passion » by Carpaccio

1 - Trade and business in Music or « Brussels trades" in Petit-Sablon Square

A musical occupation - the *job of musician*, its apostolate, its mission - is not a common route towards money or a senseless "flight forward". Take the example of Liszt: he left his great career as a soloist to become one of the greatest musicians of all time leaving the financial benefits of Music to others. We will always have a halo over our heads if, firstly, we have something to say and similar high ideals. Otherwise, this will just be one way, like any other, of doing a job; and in this case we would have to say as sadly as Thomas Mann that *"Art is not a power but a consolation"*.

What is the point, if we ourselves are not convinced or simply not sufficiently capable of being able to succeed to a great extent in convincing thousands of people who have come to listen to a concert, if in your own mind you do not know what to do? We are always peeping into our neighbour's garden without understanding that each career, like each life, *is different*. There is no sense in repeating what others do and often better than us. The austere and noble career of an ascetic, a missionary and amorous of his privilege in serving Music has as much value as a career based on false lights, trade and nothing else.

However, and thank God, the role of the artist is a *major* role.   It is the means by which the work is revived: *it is, therefore, the medium*, as already mentioned. But it is not an end in itself, far from that.

Emile Bernard, in his "Understanding Art" writes that *"the highest thought expressed in the most grandiose way should be the unflagging guide for the artist",* because it is the system that has made him a star in place of the musical work, and with no more than a commercial end.

This "ambiguity" will bring serious consequences in the long- term: among others, it will lead to fear, because this system teaches me *that I am the centre of everything.*

Very egoistically the whole changes into an education in which "I am" the centre of the problem. To get rid of this is an almost impossible task, because this fear grows as the career develops, with the coming responsibility and prestige.

The older one gets, even at an advanced age, the more one has to defend, said Arthur Rubinstein, who, jokingly, recommended to a young pianist not to be too concerned about not feeling fear too soon. *"Everything comes to you in life, my dear, sooner or later"*, said the great pianist.

2 - Sharing responsibilities

When I talk of the *major role* of the artist, I mean by that from an early age the pupil must be made responsible for the exact meaning *of his work*. He should not be deviated on to paths that *do not lead to Rome*. What a great teacher will do is to help the pupil realise that the composer is not *the pupil himself* but *another being*. The one who first felt the vibrations of the work *"it is he and not you"*. I would like to transcribe here a sentence from Constantin Stanislavski who understood artists better than anyone: *"May old wisdom guide young courage and young strength; and may young courage and young strength sustain old wisdom. Only in these conditions can art flourish and have a future"*. The teacher   and pupil, that is *you* and *I*, belong only *in the second degree,* even if we force ourselves to feel *the same thing* as *the composer*. What we need is mutual support and a complete synergy.

Any interference or change introduced will deform the musical work and, as a result, change the message. My *feelings* count for little here: I must serve at the risk of becoming a peddler of junk, at the risk of selling illegal goods to the non-initiated, activities far from our task and duty.

Claudio Arrau, already at an advanced age, was asked one day why he repeated over and over a passage from a Beethoven Sonata that he had already played thousands of times. Very calmly the Maestro replied that he did this because, probably, on this particular evening *"some people would be listening to the work for the first time. So he had to give the best of himself"*. It was not simply the doubt that made him repeat, *but the desire to achieve perfection*. An incredible example, but true in an artist as great as Arrau, for whom Music, as for Beethoven, was the *supreme* expression of all philosophy.

What a responsibility, then, in *translating* the work *of another* while loving and rejecting! What proof of synergy must be manifest between the composer, the work, the interpreter, the piano and the audience! What balance! But, in the words of Buddha: *"The man is not forsaken who comes to the end of his journey, who has thrown off all care, who has freed himself from all association, who has rejected all his goods"*.

There are numerous religious men who in their efforts to build churches, kingdoms or armies have forgotten to teach the gift of self, and how to forget oneself to serve others better and to love them. Many are the men who in the drive to accumulate wealth and power, in the name of the Lord, came to replace Him and speak in His Name.

The austerity, humility, devotion and love with which to build and present a work of art should be at the core of all education, whether musical or not. This is not an accumulation of diplomas (necessary, but not central to humanist education), nor blind participation   in an endless number of idiotic international competitions (I am not speaking of the major competitions, but I will come back to this), where I was taught that *I am superior to my neighbour because I play faster and louder than he does.*

Each time that his hands play a Chopin Ballad, all the *other* hands that have played it before must be felt, as well as all *others* who have passed that way. Only the Ballad is eternal. 'I 'and my hands form part of the weak, the poor and those seeking consolation.

3 - Business as a musical law or the merchants in the temple of the Lord

We could mention and repeat the example of Liszt: *serving Music and not serving ourselves by it.*

This example is magnificent because it implies renunciation, recognition and consecration, as well as an awareness of the *true values* in accepting our *own errors*.

The Liszt-type personality, although full of contradictions, mood swings and human error, never sacrifices the essential, artistic and/or aesthetic values. Liszt was aware of his own faults. This personality strikes me as not being just exemplary but grandiose, because it brings into play, on the one hand, the star pianist and, on the other, the complete musician and the exceptional human being. Liszt is almost the *symbol* of our problems. But it is sad to note that we are far today from the values that he upheld.

Quite simply because the prime social end - although it does not always emanate from the artist - is to *produce* money, otherwise any career comes to a halt.

But *"provided that my conscience does not chide me, for whatsoever Fortune I am ready "*, as we read in Dante's Inferno. No other reason than that may justify performing more than 250 concerts a year.

The dictates of the market are difficult to subdue; it would be perilous and presumptuous to want to change them. It is the artist who must be different. It is the artist who must help to change the world through the strength of his personality, as Liszt did in his day and age.

Too often the world changes the artist.

All of this is, of course, disguised, covered up; claims are made, and justification given. It is possible to kill, to launder wars, to *understand* the hypocritical attitudes of governments and pressure groups, and to *collaborate*, to an extent, with these monstrous principles by closing one's eyes to everything. This is known as pure cynicism, present in all epochs, but very obvious in ours.

In such a context, we should not be surprised to see the artist become *a sales product similar to a common fizzy drink.* It is no longer a Bordeaux *vintage*, a fine Burgundy or a great Brunello de Montalcino. It is a common supermarket wine.

Geniality has become such a common concept that no one is surprised any longer to hear Chopin's Third Sonata played at the age of 14 or the Sonata of Dutilleux at the age of 15. Who has not heard a young male or female prodigy who at the age of 13 has already played Rachmaninov's Second Concerto or Tchaikovsky's B Flat, better than Sviatoslav Richter at 50? How many times has the *new Horowitz* not been announced?

The gift packaging is concocted by the managers, the uproar of advertising, the record companies, the journalists, the critics, radio, television, all the media; and the public approves. In short, it is the approach opened up by widespread corruption.

Pandora is right there.

4 - Verdi's « Chorus of the Hebrew Slaves » or anaesthetizing the intelligence

Young pianists of today, the ones who are our products, have only but little time to *think* and to *reflect*. The daily routine, training and labour consist, above all, in repeating *ad infinitum* the same difficult passage until they can play it *faster, louder or softer* than anyone else. More anything than anyone else, in any case. Comparison has become the key word.

They work so much that they have no real time to *understand* anything. They train their muscles and destroy their brain with the same exercises, in perfect synchrony. I remember Sacha Guitry, when he was making humorous comments on these serious problems: *"all gestures are good when they are natural. Those that we learn are always false."*
In the world of music, competitions, the schools of music and the conservatories are full of pupils of this kind. Their studies are based on this *parrot-style* repetition. Having no *inner life*, no principles and no solid musical ethics, they are ready to accept the laws of the market without a thought, mainly due to blind ambition.
Their work, at any time, at home or in concert, becomes a true massacre. There are even those, and I know of them, who hold the record for the highest number of competition appearances: they sometimes appear in the record books.

5 - The « dolce far niente»

We must be guided by conception and by the forces of the mind, because in the words of Kierkegard, *"they must pilot the experience of our human, aesthetic and social endeavour, our whole existence"*. Otherwise it is chaos.
It is sad and frustrating to find that that in this new approach to piano playing Music is deprived of all its true difficulty and its entire problem. *We empty it of its intrinsic, essential substance.*
Resolving the technical problems prevents young people, and less young people, to see the forest for the trees. Like this Music has no chance of survival: *it is we who are killing it.*
In all these sterile interpretations today, we note an incredible mental lethargy, a deplorable mechanical imagination and an artistic level bordering on indifference, not to say non-existent.
Our system consists of fabricating people *incapable* of understanding what Music is. Their intelligence seems to be impeded. They no longer think for themselves. All these pianists think about are fingerings, sonorities and movements, in their boring, stereotype performances.

How we admire those *artists* who change Sonatas as they change shirts!
They are so incredible that two days are sufficient for them to learn a Beethoven Concerto, and one day alone for a Mozart Concerto. The Hand of God brushing their forehead must be seen in this talent, a revelation more important than even the coming of Beethoven!
How can we dare think that our brain is faster than that of Mozart? How can we be content with a fast interpretation of a work, no matter how good it is? Is our intelligence limited or not sufficiently developed to make us act like this?
Clifford Curzon said so admirably to his pupils: *"If Beethoven reflected at length on each note, how do you think you can interpret him by giving so little"?*
Similarly, think about the pieces demanded in competitions that are learnt so quickly and forgotten the next day. These pieces are demanded by powerful composers, and by radio and television producers with few scruples.

This formidable capacity for learning does not mean everything can be learnt quickly and negligently. That would be like wanting to grow from the age of five to fifty without going through the years in between. That would be to deny the evolution on which every species depends.

6 - Shakespeare's « Merchant of Venice»

When the Music *is not there*, all the dynamics, techniques and physical gestures are useless. This is no more than an *attempt* to sell *non-existent* goods.

It all becomes a show: something like an *almost immoral (or amoral) performance*. All artistic ethics are relegated to oblivion. Why did Schumann, Brahms and Beethoven compose their works? Was it to entertain the public as you would   in a musical *crèche* for adults? Was it to show how pretty sounds can be combined without any thought? Was it all to serve as background music in elevators?

Muscular idiocy sometimes intoxicates, because speed is no longer a constraint. You feel *energised* because at least you have this. You can hold a record, for example, for the jumps in Schumann's Fantasy, for the octaves in Tchaikovsky's Concerto or for the contrary movements in the Don Giovanni of Mozart - Liszt.

Here we are entering a *pianistic bodybuilding*: toning muscles and showing them off by laying them on the piano. They are exhibited to the crowd with a smile from the one who thinks he *"has arrived"*.

However, *there is nothing to be gained from developing a muscle without a brain and a mind to accompany it.*

In a human being, it is balance that helps build a work and its interpretation with a minimum of faults. Certain forms of this *pianistic bodybuilding* die at the height of youth, in all their *beauty*. They have never achieved the true strength that would have brought balance.

Once I heard a frightful parody on Belgian radio, in which, in a programme of so-called classical music, some of the most distinguished pianists played the passages at high speed in the Finale of Chopin's Second Sonata pianists, reminiscent of an imitation of a Formula One Grand Prix.

It was in this style: *"Rachmaninov going at record speed and overtaking everyone! This is wicked! Wow! He is winning by two seconds over Horowitz and five over Benedetti Michelangelo!"* The programme was am attempt at irony, or at least I hope so. It must be recognized, however, that there is a ready public for this type of broadcast. I, among others, was dumbfounded.

7 - "Everything in the past was better", or the lyricism of Jorge Manrique

Harold Schoenberg, critic of the New York Times, a writer and a very good friend of mine, said to me one day on the Jury for the Masters in Monaco, that he thought that the technique used by pianists had been far better in the past than currently.

This is a fairly uncommon concept that risks upsetting a good number of our current virtuosos. However, I share it absolutely. Who, in fact, has exceeded the technique of Maurice

Rosenthal, Rachmaninov, Lhevinne, Busoni, Cziffra, Horowitz or Argerich? Is it our current *protégés*? Perhaps it is *the average* out of the current level? They play faster, you say? What does *great technique* really mean? What does it mean to be a great *virtuoso*? Who, in our day and age, which current virtuoso, apart from exceptional cases such as the young Kissin, is capable of *taking the risks* that were taken before?

I am thinking here along the lines of Kempff when he said: *"Busoni played La Campanella without a safety net and managed not to fall"*.

The true virtuoso is a juggler *familiar with danger* and not only *that surrounding him*. It is he who can play with fire without burning himself.

Currently, young pianists count how many wrong notes they have played and compare the result with that of their colleagues. Since we no longer have a message to transmit, all that remains is to press the notes. They cannot go wrong otherwise there will be nothing else to offer. The whole recital would backfire. The one thought is not to make too many mistakes. Just as in football, what is important is for the other side not to score goals. If we score, it will be because of the mistakes made by the opposing team, and not because of our qualities. The principle rests on negation. One could not be more anti-artist. The satires of Sacha Guitry are still pertinent.

In a live recording of a performance by the major pianists, for example, a few wrong notes are of little significance and scarcely affect the essential. Suffice to recall in Alfred Cortot's rendition of Chopin's Preludes the strength of his interpretation, which is so colossal that the poor little wrong notes are nothing compared to the expressive power of the Maestro. He himself considered his discs to be like "wax". They were *only a moment of execution and not the definitive execution*.

Obviously, David Oistrakh thought as Cortot did. He did not want to listen to his own recordings. He considered he was *not listening to himself* but to the sound engineers who, with the debris of his performance, had fabricated another Oistrakh, under the same name. Both Cortot and Oistrakh put the message first. This is no doubt why true artists like to return to live recordings, because what we fabricate using machines and computers has nothing to do with a normal recital.

Art is not the reproduction of a false technical perfection, but the reflection of a supreme truth, performed by man to draw closer to God, with all our faults, grievances and successes. The example of the great artists shows that we need to go in search of the unique being and not to ask the media to create idols, iconoclastic creators and candidates aspiring to star roles. Today, the mistakes of virtuosos without genius, the wrong notes, and the pedals placed badly, mean that the whole performance tumbles like a house of cards, and so there is no message and no notes in place.

We have almost become the interpreters of a dead Music - in the literal sense of the word, because as Borges said: *"you can be dead at the age of twenty and go on walking in the streets, and be more alive at eighty without ceasing your own inner journey"*. We are almost dead before we play, and while we are playing.

Nothing is alive *except the ego*.

8 - Communicating vessels

I believe that every great, and truly great, musician is at the same time a great virtuoso. The opposite is not necessarily true.

Every time I hear a *great* musician, I only think of the Music. His technique is magnificent because it allows him to "transcend" the problems, and I, the listener, concentrate only on the artistic message and not on whether he knows what he is doing.

An American critic said some time ago, when he was listening to the very young, almost infant, Joseph Hoffman, that his technique was so perfect that it couldn't be heard. When I listen to Arrau playing *The Emperor*, I am not thinking about the way he plays the arpeggios, scales, thirds and broken octaves. I see the head of Beethoven, his pride, his dignity and his morality through this brilliant interpretation. Such true technique allows the Music to flow and it does not hinder it.

The technique forms part of the Music. It is not separate from it. It does not live alone. The whole is sustained as in the human body. When I see a good-looking person, you see the whole image that he or she reflects. I see a whole. This being is not shown in its separate parts.

When a pianist exhibits his technique stupidly, I cannot help but think of the muscles, the volume of which is inversely proportional to the intelligence of their owner.

9 - Commutation of our baggage

Every great pianist has whole arsenal of means he uses to perform great interpretations objectively. Perhaps within he feels less secure (we are now comparing the idea with the great, in the plural) than the image portrayed, but I think that we only achieve the technique as we conceive it. If we do not have a vision that transcends the work, our technique remains primary. If our conception dictates to us an Olympian idea of the work to be interpreted, then our technique follows it to its last breath and as a result will develop.

This must be a fundamental principle in any teaching. The problem is the failure to make demands on ourselves.

If we restrict ourselves to developing our muscles to meet the speed demanded by Chopin in his Études, without any ulterior motive as Mozart used to say, our performance will probably be rapid, clean and polished. And that is it. We look no further, and the essence of Chopin's message is therefore not there. So, we stop the journey mid-way. Boredom sets in with the audience and the situation cannot be reversed.

If, on the other hand, we start from the opposite direction, from the point where we determine the essential as the fundamental point to be achieved, we develop not only our technique but also the outcome of our journey will be completely different, because our muscles will serve but will not control.

This idea at the start will provide the muscles with a warning, orders and information. This work accomplished, although important, will not impart the essential idea of the Études. Nothing vital comes *a posteriori*.

10 - The games or « A Game of Boules » by Matisse

The gossip that passes for wise and knowledgeable comments, the games, the competitions and the tombolas that accompany trade in Music and from which so many mediocre parasites live, currently dictate the laws of the world of music.

Unfortunately, this type of trade has all too often become indispensable in attracting to the concert hall a mass audience that is scarcely sensitive to music or even minimally cultured. Changing the programme or the name of the artist (due to illness or some other reason) would scarcely bother this audience: they are there simply for the show and the social events but not for the love of art.

A few tricks have been invented, such as free entry or a lucky draw to fill the halls, perhaps driven by fear of having more people on stage than in the audience if this type of enticement is not applied.

The laws of politics and those of the musical career seem to be identical. Success is measured in the voices of preference and the volume of applause.

But I do refuse to believe that the finest days of Music lie behind us. Particularly bearing in mind that we, the players in musical life, are the first to be found guilty of the massacre: we are the ones who have killed the goose that laid the golden egg.

I am alluding here to the major schools of music and the great conservatories. Submerged in management and administration, they launch themselves into the production of mediocre musical products that can only give rise to mediocre concerts, terrible recordings and, as a result, an insignificant audience before long. And this is even in the major cities that think they are carrying on a great tradition: just because your city was the birthplace of Mozart or Beethoven does not mean that genius is found in every cultural and social event organised there.

As Gustav Mahler pointed out "Tradition is sloppiness"

11 - The Mafias and discouragement due to ignorance

The decline of quality is no more, basically, than a lack of culture and good taste. It is thanks to, or because of it, that the mafias, circuits and groups profit for their own development. The artistic limitations of our products underlie their creation.

Is it reasonable to expect our artists to think and reflect when they are influenced by such groups? They are too busy struggling to survive and trying to avoid being devoured by these creatures that control us musically. Trained without a healthy basis for thought, without spiritual development, they do not have the weapons to face them. They have weak and malleable personalities.

They lack patience to hope. They do not know how to be happy in their work, in the accomplishment of their major task. They want only to play in concerts, live off their work and earn money because they have studied music. But since they have been neither trained nor informed, they find themselves miserably ill equipped in this relentless jungle. What indeed do they really know about Music, these *products of ours*? And what do they know about the works they *play*? Where did they get this egoism and vanity? Why not accept quite simply that if your career is not like that of Rubinstein this is principally because you are not playing as well as he did? Why is there this need to be at the centre of the universe? Why this obtuse, unhealthy and irrational ambition, without the necessary preparation? Why is there this lack of culture?

Most of them do not even know how to analyse what they are doing because their work is not underpinned by education but   by repetition. They play based on the primary instinct, without conception, or vision or revelation and, above all, without asking themselves why they are doing this. They are not true professionals, but they have been made to believe that in less trustworthy schools and in deplorable competitions. They have a miserable repertoire and do not even know the most basic works, but their ignorance feeds their pretension.

12 - Sad reflection!

So, we have a youth that is sometimes adrift, a sad reflection of   a society that has respect neither for its own existence nor for its moral integrity, and far less for the quality of its spiritual life. It is content to survive and takes to its heart the desperate struggle for subsistence, a sad fact that is more comprehensible than reprehensible.

So, why become a pianist at such a time?

The only good candidates, among so many called, are those who, despite all the discouragements that a life of music, or indeed life itself, throws at them, have the guts, the resilience and the dignity to continue as expressed in the words of Berlioz, *"even if I know in advance that the struggle is lost, I continue out of dignity."*

All of us in our youth have dreamt of changing the world.   All of us have thought at some time that we could play better than Backhaus, Solomon or Pollini. We have all believed we could win the greatest international competitions and, as a result, of taking our place on the most distinguished concert circuits. We have all dreamt that the greatest manager in the world, or the greatest recording company, would one day knock at our door and say that it was waiting for us as the new prophet of Music and the concert world.

But between dream and reality there is a gap to be crossed. This led Ruben Dario to say *"this is my weak point: dreaming. Poetry is the iron shirt with a thousand cruel prongs that I carry on my soul. The bloody thorns let the drops of my melancholy flow down."* Most of these would-be pianists are eliminated by pure natural selection: they have no spirit of sacrifice and far less the courage to get down to the basic work with the necessary abnegation. Nor do they have the talent. They are weak willed, and their capabilities are also weak. It is a relatively easy elimination.

Many others, among the survivors, are eliminated by the competitions or by the weakness of their professional performance, in all types of more advanced examinations, for example. This is something more complicated to accept and so we then hear speak of injustice.

Among those who persist, some are eliminated because of age, because of marriage and their obligations to family. In short, they have to earn a living to survive, and sometimes not by music. They feel they have been unfortunate. They think they are the victims of society. It is sad and also pathetic. It is even dramatic because, too often, their own resentment reflects negatively on the young people they train.

A few rare individuals manage to achieve something but eliminate themselves due to a lack of endurance, the weakness of their nervous system, real or imagined tendinitis, and they invent excuses or accidents. These are often the most distressing cases because for a brief moment they managed to get a taste of the life to which they aspired. The depression that follows can be extremely serious.

Most of those eliminated become bad critics, bad teachers, dubious organisers, etc.
Their common denominator is *their true lack of love and passion for the job*, replaced, over the years, by a bitter, harmful resentment. On the contrary, the only good musician is the one who is good from the very start, from the first the day he comes in contact with the instrument and with Music. This is the musician who treats every situation, good or bad, with the same enthusiasm and who remains a musician and artist until the day he dies.
A person cannot become a musician despite himself. It is not something that you choose. You are chosen.
I repeat again, and as always, the words of Liszt: *"To be an artist by the grace of God"*.

13 - « Eldorado » …again?

If we do not find new minds ready to unleash a new dynamic approach, the situation can only become worse. And perhaps it will become even harsher because of this ferocious struggle to survive.
We need a new type of artist, a new model that will adopt moral integrity and aesthetics as core principles as well as constantly seeking the highest ideals. We need an artist who understands Mozart's symbolic words *"silence is the finest moment of the Music."* Silence and the Waiting. In all areas, *particularly in hurried careers*.
The arrangement of these spaces, or mottos, must be seen as   a reflection of an organised brain. We must be able to accept, struggle and relentlessly approach this superior ideal.
Try to make only the musical law transmissible between the generations the guide. Then we will get movements in order, although often the wrong order, as created by our imagination, managed in disorder; and this in a universe far greater than our own personal range.
And then the mind will open up. Aspire to belonging to another race, to that of sincere artists, who carry the flame with justice and dignity.
Being a musician is above all the art of thinking about music without losing sight of it for an instant, just as being a medical doctor is the art of curing patients and not distancing himself from them. Both work to preserve Life and not to destroy it.
Basically, any performance, and quite simply a lifetime that does not respond to such criteria is condemned to a brief existence. It is almost *stillborn*.

BOOK II

Part two

The protagonists
The actors, the figurants, the mimes, the doubles, the angel, the devil, and the
« Tuttologists»!

1 – Sturm und Drang

According to Aldous Huxley we have in us both angel and demon. We are only here on earth to accomplish our two most important tasks: Creation or Destruction.

Any social behaviour implies this choice, whether it is conscious or not, of working in one of these two fields, which, like love and hate, complement one another. Their edges touch one another.

You can create or destroy by thinking. You can create or destroy by controlling. You can create or destroy by educating.

You can create or destroy by being a warrior or a musician, or by doing any other job.

Any activity assumes, then, adopting moral responsibility and at least minimum intelligence, whereas awareness, after a certain time, can lead to a dangerous automatism.

However, nothing can be truly imposed on man. He alone is the master of his decisions. He has what one calls free will.

Consequently, he can accept Good or Evil. Often, he accepts slavery through lack of courage, education or intelligence: this is the destiny of the masses.

Tyrannies can only develop where there is cultural and spiritual illiteracy. A great Argentinian teacher, Domingo F. Sarmiento, said *"it is impossible to kill ideas"*.

Therefore, you can buy muscles and bodies, such as gladiators or builders of pyramids, weapons and killers, such as mercenaries, but it is far more difficult to buy *minds*.

2 – Infallible recipes for killing Music: the "tuttology"

Robotization didn't wait for the creation of true robots to exist. Habit became then *"our second nature"*, as Saint Augustine said in his Confessions. This *second nature* is found in all professions. By cracking a whip, you can get an elephant to stand upright on a ball.

Using the same methods, perhaps without the whip, you can achieve muscular development in a person without, however, the mind developing at the same time. However, in the artistic field, you should not use the semiquavers of Beethoven or Mozart in order to attain that! Hanon's simple exercises are sufficient to prove and develop this type of "talent".

Did the famous piano teacher and pianist Friedrich Wilhelm Kalkbrenner, who tried to give lessons to Chopin (!), not advise his pupils to read a book while they were practising their scales or arpeggios? Concentration was not indispensable! To criticise such nonsense would be a waste of time. How not to feel indignant at such comments made by a teacher who rubbed shoulders with Chopin and Liszt!

However, there are people who do not have the assets of a Kalkbrenner, because this gentleman was despite all an accomplished pianist.

This is a category of person quite apart from the others: that which I call the *tuttology*.

Tutto: all, in Italian.
Logos: the science, the speech.
Tuttologist: human species who knows absolutely all.

This kind of person has always existed, but not in the almost industrial quantities that we find today. These know-alls know everything there is to know about all things and all people. They spread like weeds and have become the current *politicians* of Music.

One wonders why young pianists who are often brilliant study with such people.

The only explanation is the so-called support they can give them in competitions and in helping them get some concerts. Because of course, all these *know-alls* are on organising committees, in concert associations, in orchestra programming, in the mafias of international exchange, in the Ministries of Culture, and so on, where they deploy their talents with aplomb. They hold these *key* positions and spread an unhealthy "knowledge".

There is an ever-increasing number of these *theoreticians* and *charlatans* who tell pianists how to play without the slightest shame. It would be sad and cruel to ask them to show by example. However, they are so *intelligent* that they could reply saying that *they do not do this because for fear of imitation* (!)

I do not understand why and how we have dropped to such a level. The transcendental teaching of the piano should be reserved for pianists. It seems to me impossible to correct someone who is playing a Ravel Concerto better than I can and tell him what he should be doing. This would be the world in reverse. How can you give advice to a young pianist on something that you do not know how to do yourself: how to react when he plays with the orchestra, for example; how to behave on stage, how to approach the *cadenzas*, what is the technical rapport between the musicians and me, between the conductor and me, how and why is this fingering better than another, how to study Tchaikovsky's octaves, etc., if I have never played this work myself?

Would you let yourself be operated on your heart or brain by a *tuttologist* who has never performed surgery? Of course not. You might reply by saying this situation does not exist among surgeons. But it does exist *in politics and music*. Anyone can rise to being President or Minister, and similarly anyone can become a great teacher or a great musical critic without understanding his notes and scores

A good number of today's ministers lack competence and knowledge, and this can be seen in all present governments. Similarly, it is possible to become a great teacher in whatever great school anywhere in the world without playing the piano or any other instrument.

Someone once said somewhere, in a country of pianists: *"if you want to teach the piano close your own instrument"!*

No comment.

3 – The "tuttologists" and rotten fruit

Our world is shameless and as a result if full of false prophets. Just by organising a competition, for example, the person in question, the organiser, has the authority to become the President of the competition, as well as being on familiar terms with the pianists that make up the jury. Consequently, they are at a level with those who spend their whole life suffering before a piano, constantly confronting the public, aware each day that *everything must be improved, corrected or redone,* questioning themselves, studying even more to attain an illusory perfection, who have but one idea and who to seek to understand that *the more you know, the less you understand and the more there is still to be done.*

Sadly, we have to say that there is even a certain agreement among these *tuttologists* and the young pianists, who are blinded by the desire to shine and to build their career at all costs. Some young people *jack of all trades* even change teacher depending on the performances and competitions, for example. The *tuttologists* are aware of this and behave accordingly.

The repercussion is felt on the amounts paid, not to mention more intimate areas. Once it is known in advance that a particular *tuttologist* will be in the jury at a certain competition, some participants will come to ask for his advice because, according to the sacred formula, *for some time it has been their most fervent desire!*

Certainly, all this cynicism always existed, but in our day, it has reached its peak in all its splendour.

I do not think that one could speak on these terms to Liszt.

You might then ask where the purity of relationship between the young pianist and professor is at present. Many have forgotten the ethical dimension of Art.

The Greek concept of the word Art has been made ridiculous, sullied, neglected with abandon while the Machiavellian principle is now the order of the day: the end justifies the means. Reward is demanded immediately for what has been invested (time, money, life, sacrifice and much more): identification goes with the image of a career, but since this is completely distorted ....

No doubt to we can count our true artists on the fingers of one hand, as always. But the abundance of today's market is such that it is becoming not only worrying but also dangerous. At all times you realise that there are no ideals in the game. Now that musical practice responds to the laws of finance and trade, the objective is now a question of *earning a living,* because most of us *live* from Music. This means that it has become more of a job than an Art. All we can hope is that this decadence is only fleeting, and this way of acting temporary. People must be aware that   obviously you cannot go far with such ideas. However, whilst waiting, a lot of damage is being done.

4 - What remedies?

There has to be tremendous aesthetic and ethical control in playing the instrument, a faultless professionalism (rather than imagining yourself in the concert hall think rather of being in a laboratory where everything is being tested). Perseverance, constancy, sacrifice, enthusiasm, unwavering faith, endurance and, above all, the ability to remember at all times the essential condition: *the conception of the musical work to be interpreted.*

The fact of knowing, beforehand, the level to be achieved, indicates the mission of our muscles. They seek it out, *intelligently and guided* by the mind. They discover the finest approaches, the most attractive itinerary and the one most in agreement with this Thought. And this is the first rule established.

The second is to make music at all times avoiding empty exercises with no meaning.

It is often said that there are people, self-taught or craftsmen, who are guided naturally by intuition, by an innate sense of absorption in a particular problem, and by the capacity to find unexpected solutions.

Applied to music, this would suggest that intuition and instinct might lead to pure and spontaneous performances. Quite the contrary is true. Although indispensable, intuition and instinct are like a premonition, a confused perception prior to certain higher functions being set in motion. They are the closest neighbours to emotion. In the act of organised thought, they are a preview glimpse of a work.

An artist can and should put his trust in intuition and instinct at first. Similarly, they are precious to Politics and Science whether in the discovery of a new medication or in shaping the destiny of a people. However, they cannot alone replace pure thought, the mechanism of its action, its fabric and its final objective: The Concept.

Although *"man lives by bread alone"*, absolutely nothing can replace intelligence or at least an attempt at understanding, this embryo of capacity that helps penetrate areas to clarify, discover, explore and explain, and, as a result, to interpret.

It is in an intelligent work that these two elements, instinct and intuition, prove to be most sensitive and best perceived. And this because they cannot become the ultimate elements of reasoning, analysis, synthesis and information, no more than they can of culture or purged sensitivity, and far less of the cerebral mechanism in its vital functions. On the contrary, this implies higher spiritual levels, in the dignity of our work and in its morality.

Reasoning always remains the main driving force behind the work, even in the task of partially or totally *deciphering* a work of art, as in any other time of research or other spiritual operation. Because *"any technique that does not emerge from this reasoning is nothing, useless, sterile and without eloquence or meaning"*, as we have seen in Liszt. Above all empty of revelation, because it would lack *"wisdom"*, according to Raphael.

And this wisdom is demanded at the highest degree.

It would be difficult to believe that Beethoven composed Op. 127, or the Hammerklavier Fugue, by intuition and not knowing at any time what it was all about. Can we believe that the double columns of the Vatican (almost outlining St Peter's Square) were built by Bernini by instinct, without scientific calculations able to defy time and space? Could they have been built without mathematics or without architecture? The astounding sight we experience below the dome of Santa Maria della Fiori in Florence, by Brunelleschi, the ancient sacristy of San Lorenzo, or the Chapel of the Pazzi à Santa Croce, lead us to believe that the Master-builder knew far more about mathematics than our accountant. And this miracle that comes down through the centuries without the slightest blemish stands as proof that nothing is done by chance.

Perfection in simplicity and irreproachable constructions are proof of Picasso's idea that a straight line is without doubt the most difficult and most complicated to draw and that "*awareness is a creative act*", as defined by Carl Jung

The more one knows, the more one understands, the more one loves. Any true love rests on understanding, on a discovery and, as a result, on an acceptance.

But we know that our understanding is limited, sometimes non- existent because "*I know only that I know nothing*". Our task   to develop this intelligence is not just indispensable, but also imperative. It is a question of survival. Otherwise we become unconscious beings, as if we were under the effect of an intellectual anaesthesia. It would be regrettable to use the expression here of a generalised stupidification.

These bonds that unite us to the work through intelligence and sensitivity are the most lasting and most beautiful.
The limitations and the constraints are therefore easier to resolve because the "me" is forgotten more easily. They will more readily find, therefore, the approaches to finding the spirit and the vibration of the work, in an invitation to merge, in principle fully, with our feelings.
It is a bit like moving from a microcosm into a macrocosm, like reprogramming yourselves in the cosmos to be able to understand everything that escapes us and has escaped us.
It is like opening our window onto this universe, and just in opening this window the infinite dimension that we lack is transmitted to us.

5 - Methods? ...Ah, my dear René! Or « The adoration of the magi » by Dürer

To play better means representing the musical idea better, because the technique cannot develop without the mind and without the Music. I stress this point and I drive it as much as I can into the minds of my pupils: *technique on its own serves for nothing.*
It is not the scales or the arpeggios that help you play Sonata by Mozart, Haydn or Beethoven better; nor will they help with a work by Mendelssohn. It is the intelligent work of the music of Mozart, Haydn, Beethoven and Mendelssohn that helps improve the technical baggage to serve Art better: our scales and arpeggios have everything to gain from this.

Let us look at practical case: why do we want to improve our octaves, for example? Not just for an heroic specific passage, naturally, and nor is it for the octaves themselves, of course, but for us to use them in serving better the Music that demands octaves. Firstly, we must understand that all octaves are not the same. Those of Liszt and those of Chopin are different, for example. The octaves of Liszt are more virtuosistic, more decorative, more grandiose, more symphonic, and more amplified than those of Chopin. More specifically, just think of the octaves in the Sonata in B minor, those of the Eroica, those of the two Concerti, of La Campanella, the Spanish Rhapsody or the Sixth Hungarian Rhapsody (what else could be more difficult as octaves for both hands?)

Chopin's octaves are more polyphonic, with the exception perhaps of those of the Scherzi No. 3 and No. 4 or the Polonaise Op. 53, which join those of Liszt. Think, on the other hand, of those of the First Ballad, *legato cantabile*, or those of the Polonaise Op. 44, also *legato cantabile*. For heaven's sake let us speak only fleetingly of those of the Étude Op. 25 No. 10, a true work of voices, of *lines*, intertwining melodies, where *the whole* is *legato*. They are not at all as one hears them in competitions, *with no legato*! This insolent manner of doing it, only to play them *faster*, makes them grotesque to the extent that this sublime Étude might be called the *Étude of the grasshoppers*. We will come back to this in the Chapter on Études.

As a result, the work and practice of octaves, whether those of Liszt or Chopin, will not be the same, *because the aims of each are different*. Nevertheless, they will certainly assist one another. Firstly, we know that it is Chopin who created this type of *legato* octave. The only example I know of prior to him are the octaves of the First movement of Beethoven's Sonata Op. 7. They are rarely found in Mozart or Haydn. Those of Weber or Mendelssohn, the *Rondo Capriccioso* type, are, however, closer to Liszt.

Consequently, a separate study, that is without any specific application on the Music, without the final objective or without the sublimation of their destiny, in view of the musical material available, is neither necessary nor desirable. This would be really stupid, because this method causes us to waste time and would mark us out as the very dignified disciples of Professor Kalkbrenner.

For this exercise to become spiritual and lifted, what better than to study them, as already suggested, directly in the works mentioned above, in the Tannhäuser Overture of Wagner-Liszt, in the Scherzo of Chopin's Second Sonata, the passages of Tchaikovsky's Concerto, the Rhapsody on a theme by Paganini, by Rachmaninov, the American Prelude *for the octaves of Ginastera*, etc, in this way always bringing it into closer contact with *musical reality* and *musical material*? In other words, constantly playing and enjoying the Music. Because our beautiful octaves should serve for something far superior: to play these passages mentioned above even better, certainly, but also to rediscover the purity of the message of the composer and not to challenge the speeds of the metronome alone.

Let us speak of other methods as well, in order to be more thorough. What better, for example, to develop the *jeu perlé* than the Bach- Busoni Chorale in G major, Chopin's Prelude in B-flat minor for the right hand, the Prelude G major, this one for the left hand; Scherzo No. 4; the second Movement of the Concerto No. 2 by Prokofiev; the Finale of the *Appassionata* and other Beethoven Sonatas; Mozart's Sonata in A minor or that in D major K.576; Bach's Preludes and Fugues, for example the D major of the First and Second Volumes, the Fifth Partita; Mendelssohn's Études No. 2 and 3; The *Feux Follets* by Liszt, his Étude on Paganini in E; the *Huit doigts* of Debussy; the Fourth Étude by Stravinsky; Scarlatti's Sonatas, those of Soler, and Mateo Albéniz; Haydn's Concerto in D; those of Mendelssohn; Chopin's First Concerto and practically all that was written for the piano, in this way remaining in direct contact with Music?

When one is concerned with real material and not with accessory material, one develops the feeling of serving music *and not the feeling of getting married by correspondence*. The profound work of the *motor* Preludes and Fugues, as Neuhaus used to call them, develops and consolidates every type of articulation. The Preludes in C minor, D major, G major, F major, among others, will, according to him, and I am convinced too, spare us *a considerable number* of Études by Czerny, Clementi and company.

On the other hand, the Études of Mendelssohn, Chopin, Liszt, Debussy, Scriabin, Rachmaninov, Ligeti, Prokofiev, Bartok, Stravinsky, and sometimes, Cramer, Heller and Moszkowski, remain jewels to be visited every day.

The day when, for example, we can control *the mysterious thread* that holds the vibration in Ravel's Ondine, according to the definition of del Pueyo, we will be able to apply this thread, to tremendous advantage, in controlling the arabesques in Chopin's *Berceuse*, *Au Bord d'une Source* by Liszt, the *Feux Follets* and the Finale of Beethoven's Sonata op. 27 No. 2. We will have learnt much more about the extension of the wrist than many a hollow exercise can ever teach us.

The major principle is the interdependence of difficulties: nothing exists alone, and everything should be resolved by deduction. The advantages of one musical work over another are enormous, all the more when working with real musical material rather than artificial exercises, which helps add to the enthusiasm that moves mountains.

The same phenomenon occurs when a child is made to learn   the solfeggio apart from the Music and the instrument, without applying it to real music achievements using the instrument of his choice. If this child wants to learn to play the piano, while all we are doing is separating him from his desire, filling him with abstract ideas that do no more than discourage him, we are doing him no favours at all. We are distancing him from the Music, frustrating him in a way. The only thing that he wanted to do was to play some popular tunes on the piano. We will probably lose him as a musician, and possibly as an audience as well. Enthusiasm, desire, and readiness lead to incredible and marvellous results. The other method, only good for keeping obsolete teachers amused, people without ambitious goals, removes all desire to learn, all enthusiasm and all contact with a specific musical reality.

So, the ideal would be to have every musical problem analysed and explained in real terms and in a tangible application, if possible, all at the same time so as to establish technical, mental and aesthetic relations.

Bach already gave us the example: did he not compose during a lesson an Invention, a Symphony for three voices, or a Fugue, depending on the particular difficulty the pupil was facing at that moment? What advantage can there be in leaving a problem that should be solved quickly until later? This would only go to developing poor teaching.

6 – Great protagonists

To know or not to know; to discover, return, reject, reassess; to begin each time and each day as if it were the first. The work of interpretation is that of constant change and adaptation.
God seems to speak to us intermittently and to make us understand that our greatest understanding is that of Him who gave it to us and that it is Him who gives it at all times. This knowledge or understanding determines whether we gain access to the essence of the work or not, as well as penetrating its mystery, even if we cannot fully explain it, as said before. This understanding at least allows us to conjecture and imagine more closely.
A great interpretation assumes then harmony between Heaven and Earth. It flows of its own accord. It breathes the fire of creation. And so, it becomes a member of the family of the Elements.
The Earth will be the departure point for this great construction, its very foundations; the cathedral is indeed going to rise towards Heaven, towards God and Silence.
It is going to flow like *Water*, free of all constraints. Passion gives it life, making it full of *Fire*.
The Air draws it towards mankind, moves it on and gives it its own respiration.
All of this is governed by Equilibrium, by the Line and by Order. It is a movement that reincorporates itself into the Cosmos, almost without moving. Everything flows freely and calmly, in the sense that even the greatest dramas produced by the works of Chopin, Liszt or Wagner, are assimilated into an even higher, greater vision than that which conceived them. And so, the movement returns to the Divinity. The great musical work becomes part of this Universe that Emerson qualified as Eternal. Every great work of art belongs to only one Creator: God.
Bath would be his representative on Earth, like Peter, the one on which the Church would be built.
Mozart would be the Spirit, and Beethoven the Head. Chopin would be the Heart.
Schubert would be the Word, the expression of Pain and Song.
Liszt would be virtue, Abnegation, Pleasure, Generosity and Ecstasy.
Ravel would be Sensuality and the Perfection of Balance.
It is with this Equilibrium that Liszt conceived the art of interpretation: the composer can do no more than put down in code on paper a convention that must be animated by the mind, by intelligence and by sensitivity. It is therefore for the pianist to do the rest: that which the composer, himself, has not been able to do. To do this, he must put Life back into this code, not repeat the photograph of the paper, a symbol of the inherent and geographic existence of the work of art, but nothing to do with his own life. The fact of playing the piece well does not determine very much. Animating it, on the other hand, is something quite different: it is to give it transcendence. It is to raise it towards spiritual heights never imagined by average artists or by the public.

7 – Small protagonists … « Where do we come from? Who are we? Where are we going? » by Gauguin

There are so many concerts in which the instrument, the acoustics, the hall or the lighting are not in perfect condition. But is this enough for a concert to fail? Should other aspects to be taken into consideration? Where am I, the pianist, at this time? It would be naive to want to separate things, and wrong to view the problem just from the isolated factors involved.

Any musical act, given that it is a part of life, finds its origin in something that precedes it and goes on to produce different results. It is, therefore, useless to penalise someone for playing, or replaying, the wrong notes, or because the pedals are badly applied, or because the pianist's memory fails him during the concert. The analysis is unfortunately far more complex. The problem must be viewed as a whole.

The first thing to realise is that there is no such thing as the perfect concert, or perhaps only the concerts played by God in person. But even God would require some miracles.

Consequently, an educated public is looking for someone who *can come closest to the ideal of perfection*, and not someone aiming at *a non-existent perfection*.

Of course, we have in our ears recording techniques that have allowed us to make tremendous progress from the instrumental point of view, and I mean by this the global output. It would also be naive to look only at the coldness of CD recorded interpretations, because if a recording is particularly artificial, structured and assembled, it should at least aim at an ideal of the work in its independent existence.

The desire to achieve an ideal has, as a result, a certain influence on instrumental virtuosity, on social education and on the creation of a general musical reference to serve at least as a guide to those less initiated.

Recording has influenced the concept of "genius" and undermined the intrinsic value of the word, because in the editing it does produce technical perfection better than that of the concert; and that by the *same artist*.

A less gifted artist may then be seen as a dubious virtuoso.

This is not very positive but *render unto Caesar that which is his*. The main point is that this *non-existent perfection*, the recording, makes the artist extremely anxious so that for his recital he feels obliged to surpass himself and to work even harder and make progress beforehand. Such work was not done in a previous age when this method of control, or these parameters, did not exist.

This is an extremely positive fact.

On the other hand, recording has provided *ready-to-buy music* placed within reach of a lot of people. Everyone now has music available.

And that is another extremely positive fact.

But it is also because of this that there is no longer any need to go to a concert.

You can enjoy Brahms' Fourth Symphony at home, along with a good glass of Burgundy while talking business with a colleague.

Audiences are dwindling in the concert halls.

An extremely negative fact!

Indeed, so many people now have an excellent CD collection at home and never darken the door of a concert hall?

We are entering a terrain that is both ambiguous and complex. It's like a nod and a wink to Leonardo who used to say that Music was born to die right away!

However, we should accept this easy access, this massification of a world that seemed to belong only to the initiated.

In itself, it is an excellent thing.

But in this *socialisation* of Art we should avoid that excellence and the unique being become trivial, like my cousin or my neighbour in the railway carriage.

Human beings are equal before the law according to the French Revolution. Absolutely! But the minds and intellect of human beings are not all of the same quality. They have the same social rights but not the same spiritual and intellectual values. We have to admit, therefore, that in this socialisation or globalisation, we have far more geniuses than ever before.

This is a mathematical fact that is not just to do with demographic growth. Brilliance has become so common that it is open to many people of all kinds, and to artists of every level. It means that we can buy it "ready to use" at the corner supermarket.

Vélasquez, Musset, Victor Hugo, Debussy, Alban Berg, Delacroix, Cézanne, Paul Valéry, Murillo, Goya, Tolstoy, Sartre, Jaspers and Heidegger would be my all-time friends. Why should they be superior to us?!

For the same ridiculous reason that finishes so many artists so quickly.

If we counted the number of young artists in the world aspiring to become pianists, we could populate a large country. If we were to count the number of pianists over the age of 30, you could fill a small city. If you count the number of pianists working until over

the age of 40, you could perhaps fill a small town. If you were to count the great pianists working over the age of 60, you would have difficulty filling a house.

I say this, of course, taking account of the current world population.

This is not only the natural selection of all professions, but the *recklessness*, and I choose the word carefully, with which young musicians are guided.

In other words, the public should be educated in such a way that going to a concert seems quite natural. It will not be like attending a laborious task, but more like *attending the climax of human thought*.

It should be like attending a summit where you can no longer distinguish *who* speaks, whether the pianist or the composer, but only listen *what* is being said, because that conquest of freedom of spirit, of decision-making and courage would serve the Communion with Art. This would be approval for *non-vulgarity* and *non-mediocrity*.

Of course, a magnificent concert represents human genius in all its splendour. This would be, after all, agreeing that all the work of a human being at similar levels should be seen as an improvement on what went before, which will serve to make us, the public and we ourselves, *better than before*.

A failure to accept these principles generates the undeniable decadence of human taste. It is what Guy De Pourtalès expressed in his romanced biography of Chopin: "*The evolution of Art is no more than accepting something as beautiful today that was ugly yesterday*". All this we know. But, by mediocrity, we keep on accepting trivialities and less complicated things that only serve to amuse and not to teach. It would certainly be right, and also time, to return once again to the concert of small groups of truly spiritual people. It would also be healthy to begin once again, just as Christ did with his apostles, to teach future teachers, so that each one of them is then multiplied in a movement to attract audiences to concerts and people susceptible to taking in this type of message.

You can imagine what a concert of Chopin might have been like, having in the audience Franz Liszt, George Sand, Berlioz, and Delacroix!

8 – The Chain

We must return to Music its status of superiority, so dear to Beethoven. We must avoid deplorable performances, dubious sensitivities and circus effects (as this only runs for ten minutes, no longer) to reinstate in this Music all its nobility and lost dignity, removing it from its mass-produced level and vulgarity.

You must close your eyes while listening to Brahms' Second Concerto played by Claudio Arrau, or the magic sound of Debussy played by Benedetti Michelangeli. Remain silent, meditate and wish that such atmospheres could last throughout time and do not destroy them by shouting.

Too often, an artistic act is likened or compared to a megalomaniac political meeting. In such a place there is a collective liberation which has very little to do with Art. Of course, some artists need to be reassured. Their ego needs to be boosted. Nevertheless, they need to know that gratitude for great things does not come with trumpets or trombones, but rather in silence and in the most secret corner, the deepest most solitary corner of our heart.

We must also respect, and in fact even more, all that is rooted in the past, as in the future and the present, because what is there in this world that is not the result of a previous phenomenon? What human being has made himself entirely alone? What human being is sufficient in himself?

Can we possibly imagine Beethoven without Mozart or without Haydn? Can we imagine Chopin without Mozart, Bach and Scarlatti; or Wagner without Liszt; or Liszt without Weber and Beethoven; or Schubert, Brahms or Schumann without Beethoven and Bach; or Ravel without Liszt? I restrict myself only to our dearest masters.

The greatest novelties of Art are always explained by prior solutions and project themselves into later solutions. Nothing comes from nothing, and everything goes into the whole.

I believe that Art is explained quite simply by Life. It is a reflection of it. Existence cannot be understood without the origin of things and their death, without their time and space, but also without their *continuity*: we come from our parents and in our turn we give life to others, we complete the circle of our disappearance and as the Spanish poet, Léon Felipe, put it: *"we are on our way to God, to Hell, to Nothing, to Everything, to the Fire".*

Disappearance, without transmission, like this would be certain. And it is the same with Music. We must love what remains, the present, and above all its evolution. Like this the

Music will not die and it will be transmissible in the same way as a human being, and immortal through the Message.

But we must take responsibility for preventing it from dying   and for transmitting it every day, always aware that the terms of originality, novelty and creation are only relative. The sound, the form, the silence, the inspiration, the need to create, the rapport, the relationship, the communication, the thread, the silence, the pause, the proportion, the spatial and audio representation, *are common elements to any creator.*

This pretension of originality has no philosophical grounds: *orphan art does not exist.*

The world *was* a chain, *is* a chain and *will remain so* for ever. The most important part of our analysis, the truly vital intellectual mechanism, is to explore and understand what others have done before us. This is the first condition that will help us explain ourselves, because that is what will give us the thread to lead us back to the origins of things.

This is a prime necessity to be able to filter our soul, so that we can generate a new analysis for those who follow us, allowing them to surpass us without complexes.

BOOK III

Part one

The years of apprenticeship
  Or Salvador Dali's "Christ of Saint John of the Cross"

1 – Routine work, sound, hands, pedal, moral integrity, fingering, practice

Gauguin used to say that he painted not because he was a genius, "but that he had genius in him because he painted".

Ravel, in his turn, used to teach that *"Genius is above all the intelligence in the work; it is how to organize ideas"*.

The deduction is, then: you do not repeat the passage just to perfect your weaknesses but above all because you are seeking greater perfection.

Perfection is not of this world, but we should, nevertheless, always be seeking it and trying to draw close to it as much as possible. It is our path to Calvary.

The execution is no more than a compromise which is more or less important in relation to this model perfection, because *"I   do not believe at all that the last word of wisdom is to abandon yourself to nature, and to set the instincts free; but I do think that before seeking to reduce them and to tame them, it is important to understand them, because much of the lack of harmony that we have to suffer is only apparent and due solely to errors of interpretation"*, according to André Gide in the Preface to his Corydon.

We can always find something to say about our own performance or that of others. It is indeed a healthy attitude, when it is constructive. Sufficiency and arrogance are a brake on spiritual expansion and on personal realization. It is dangerous to believe that a work of music has been learnt just because you know it in all its twists and turns; accidents often happen inexplicably because there is no job more relative and random than ours. Nothing is ever played, nothing acquired, nothing learnt for all time. It has also been said that the greater the idea, the greater the search, and it also takes more time.

I no longer remember who said, *"Genius is 1% inspiration and 99% transpiration"*. I think it was Thomas Edison.

This intensity in work is always of value. The profit from it is tremendous.   In fact, I know of no worthwhile artist who is not   a hard worker. Just look at the following, for example: Otto Klemperer, Herbert von Karajan, Arturo Benedetti Michelangeli, Claudio Arrau; and an attitude towards work as interpreted by Gauguin: *perfect, perfect and still more perfect*.

I remember having seen Maestro Claudio Arrau, at the time of one of his recitals at the Palais des Beaux Arts in Brussels, working for hours rehearsing, hands and passages separately, his memory, the octaves of Liszt's Sonata, the trills of Op. 109 the jumps of Brahms' Third Sonata... And all that like a child: that is, full of enthusiasm and saying himself that it was still not quite right. He was then over the age of 75.

I said to him "*Maestro*, it is the work of genius". He replied, "*not yet, not yet*".

After his recital, which was absolutely memorable and formidable, he confided in me "*on that particular day, he had been playing Brahms' Sonata for 55 years in public*"!

I do not see that happening with many young people. They are quickly tired. Many books teach us that we should not work for more than 45 minutes because after that the concentration goes.

So, we should take a one-hour break to rest the brain. You might imagine that you are at your post office desk or at the Union!

A well-known pianist in Brussels used to say, "*I do not work more than three hours a day*". My response to that was rather rude: "*That is why you play so badly*". I was young and impertinent at that time.

I wonder how it is materially possible to work for 45 minutes when you have a daily program that includes the Hammerklavier Sonata, and/or Rachmaninov's Third Concerto, and/or propose Prokofiev's Second Concerto and the Sonata by Ginastera, warming up the fingers with the 24 Chopin Etudes beforehand.

Perhaps the whole problem is the need to feel like a genius, telling heroic tales that even the protagonists don't believe. That is chic and suggests, "*What a genius this guy is, what phenomenal skills he has*".

Of course, I will not dally to reply to such comments, which are stupid, unrealistic and dishonest. If you argue with an idiot, you end up becoming an idiot yourself.

2 – The return of the « tuttologists»!

One day I heard a tuttologist explaining how, in Chopin›s Etude Op. 10 No. 1, it was indispensable and imperative to change (sic) the relationship of the fingering demanded by Chopin. There was no longer any need to consider the problem of movement and extension 1-2-4-5, or 1-2-3-5, done to open the hand, but to establish a new relationship that would eliminate the tenth or the eleventh, returning to a distance of sixth, that is C, E, C, G; In other words to the relationship 4-5-1-2.

In short, this means closing the hand. In other words, doing the opposite to what Chopin demands.

Example N° 1 wrong Example N° 2 correct

A pedagogic luminary, this gentleman had not played the piano for at least 35 years, but his analysis completely undermining the problem posed by Chopin, was stronger and more inspired. He was about to explain how Maurizio Pollini could and should improve his playing. The poor fellow could not have chosen his target better…

In fact, this is called not finding problems for their solutions. All of these people talk about the Etudes of Chopin and Liszt. Since they are incapable of playing them, they are content to comment on them. This they do with a rare talent, but not a *musical* talent. Arthur Schopenhauer put it better than me in his "On the Will in Nature": "*It is one thing to teach Philosophy, but quite another to be a philosopher*".

3 – Magritte's « This is not a pipe », or « The betrayal of image"

Different to those of Liszt, Debussy or Rachmaninov, Chopin's Etudes are, so to speak, scientific. He calls a spade a spade and a shovel a shovel. Liszt wrote three types of Etude, all of them different:

The "Paganini" Etudes, where he works the "Caprices" and the Campanella (the last movement of violin Concerto N° 2 in B minor) brilliantly. He gives them different life, making them exist by themselves. Think, for example, of the gap that separates these genialities from Liszt with the transcriptions of Schumann Op. 3 and Op.10 dealing with the same themes of Paganini. However, it must be rightly said and recognise that Schumann did not understand the piano as Liszt did.

The "Poetic Caprices", or Concert Etudes, secondly, are six wonders of poetry and delicacy. Liszt turns these into a transcendental study of sonority and touch, certainly preceding the impressionism of Debussy and the neoclassicism of Ravel in their loftier manifestations. You have to think here of Waldersrauschen or of "La Leggierezza". Can you not hear the "Noctuelles" or "Reflets dans l'eau" when listening to them?

And lastly, the great cycle of "12 Études d'Exécution Transcendante", arranged in a series of harmonic relationships other than that of Bach's Preludes and Fugues and Chopin's Preludes. In fact, the arrangement of Bach's Preludes and Fugues is: C major, C minor, C sharp major and C sharp minor, and so completely chromatic.

The arrangement of Chopin's Preludes is: C major, A minor, G major and E minor, by relative tonalities and ascending fifths.

The order of Liszt's Transcendental Etudes is: C major, A minor, F major and D minor, by descending fifths and relatives, C-F and A-D.

Chopin and Bach accomplished the complete cycle of 24. Chopin in his own typical way, because he also dealt with the enharmonic relations (like Bach) after the fourteenth in E-flat minor, beginning the descent of tonalities with D-flat major and not with C-sharp major. A psychological matter within him: the expressive colour. Liszt descends only as far as B-flat minor (*Chasse Neige) because he thought to end later with another series.*

These twelve wonders were written in several versions (three) based on op. 1, dedicated to his Maestro Carl Czerny the first time. All aspects of the piano, in the final version, are examined: all metamorphoses and its pianistic and aesthetic transmutations, all the controversy on the art of playing and above all, despite immense difficulties, the natural movement for the hand that seems to run through water; speed, strength, resistance, octaves, sixths, thirds, arpeggios, scales, tremolos, trills, cadence, arabesques; the whole symphonic range of the piano, every type of cantabile and touch, every musical and poetical atmosphere, all virtuosity whether slight or strong. In short, the whole art of the modern piano is dissected transcendentally in the form of a musical painting, a style borrowed by Rachmaninov later in his own Etudes.

The Etudes of Debussy and Scriabin are closer to Chopin, despite their secondary intentions being more in the direction of Liszt. They too are less classifiable from the Etude point of view.

Chopin begins from Clementi, from the *Gradus ad Parnassum that* he knew and made his students study. Of course, I am not comparing Chopin with Clementi. Here we are talking of different planets, separated by light years. Not even jokingly can you compare these two musicians. Chopin belongs alongside Bach, Mozart and Scarlatti, these erstwhile gods. Clementi, for all his merits, remains on earth, perhaps with Salieri, Meyerbeer and Spontini, all fine musicians but without the dreams of Icarus and certainly without his wings.

Chopin's aim was to create a solution to the problems raised by his own music, and by his own creation. Therefore, he had to find a means by which to resolve new positions, new combinations, new demands and audacity without any historical references for his own music.

Indeed, I think it is unlikely, for example, to compare the *legato* octaves in his Ballad in G minor with the notes held within and forgotten systematically by almost all young pianists (and some less young, as I have already mentioned elsewhere), despite the descending melody line they establish, without studying the Etude of octaves   Op. 25 No.10.

It is as unlikely as studying the *Coda* of the same Ballad without referring to Etude Op. 10 No. 10, this *Parnassus* of pianists, in the words of Liszt: how to establish, then, the relationship between the thumbs and the joints, that is, between the right thumb and the second and third fingers, exactly as in the development of the Etude mentioned?

Can we imagine playing the Finale of the Fourth Ballad without previously studying the Etude in thirds, Op. 25 No. 6, and Etude Op. 25 No. 12, given that Chopin uses the same formulae?

Can you resolve the Finale of the Concerto in E minor, in its central development, without a detailed study of the first Etude Op. 10? You can find endless examples of such works. And, in any case, each pianist knows them by heart.

When it comes to the second Etude, the *Chromatic* for the three first fingers, Op. 10 No. 2, this seems to me to be the basis of the whole of Chopin's technique, the sublime conception of the movement of the fingers: any finger can go over any other, *above* and not *below*, ignoring the way that we were taught: placing the thumb in the scales in the same predetermined notes.

This absolutely revolutionary conception makes Chopin one of the most incredible genies of the piano: it means that each finger must be able to play in any needed position, following any other finger and on whatever key. Put away old ideas on fingering: "*no thumb on the black keys*", "*be careful where you place your thumb*", "*don't exaggerate with the fourth or the fifth*" and other similar idiocies.

We are before the Einstein of the instrument. A true Priest of the Church. Of course, like every great Lord and for every great Lord, the Etudes Op. 10 were dedicated to his friend and rival, Franz Liszt.

Chopin used to say: *"I like my Etudes played by Franz"*!

Certainly, the sacred formula *"each hand is different, so the fingering cannot be the same for everyone"* does not hold for long. In fact, I only partially agree with this proposition. After all, all hands have the thumb at one extremity and the little finger at   the other. The index finger is followed by the middle finger and everyone has the fourth finger a little weaker than the others.

The fundamental difference is the background, the culture, the music school, the temperamental training, etc. And in addition, there is the tremendous desire to be original at all costs.

I remember a teacher in a famous Belgian Conservatory, who had a mania for changing all that had been written you can imagine that he did not find Chopin terribly good, nor Liszt, nor Mozart, nor Debussy.

He had to change everything, because he had the correct option. Of course, he did not know how to play the piano.

But he taught until he retired.

4 – The tricksters

This question of fingering leads me to mention *facilitations or simplifications* on Etudes to suit the hands of each pianist and *in the name* of Music, using the argument that what counts is that it should sound good or better.

I feel that the idea, or rather the excuse, is entirely unworthy. That annoys me. The disgusting idea of cheating assumes recognizing a part of my own incapacity.

If a player scored a goal with his hand in a game of football (even with "the hand of God" as Maradona said after his goal against England), something that is strictly prohibited, it would be laughed at quite rightly.

Despite all, many teachers encourage and suggest similar cheating. How unworthy, immodest and shameful! To justify the self, one invokes beauty and a desire to serve music better.

I knew a very talented young pianist whose teacher had advised him *to avoid* crossing his hands for the melody in Liszt's "Un Sospiro", as well as the division of the arpeggios for two hands *imposed* by the composer: it goes without saying that the pedagogic aim here is to achieve a dynamic and expressive equality precisely with the movement of hands, and, to the ear, to equalize this melody that has been physically divided, *in two hands*: *the eyes see a movement that the ear should not hear.*

The teacher in question instructed that the arpeggio be played with one hand, and the melodic notes of the theme were also to be played with *one hand*: the other hand. The argument used that this sounds better is laughable and ridiculous, because it completely undermines the problem. A difficulty sought out by the composer has to be resolved and not avoided. The most regrettable thing is that the pupil loses all the benefits.

You cannot correct Chopin or Liszt, no more than you can tell Fangio, Schumacher or Alain Prost how to drive a Ferrari. Chopin, as well as Liszt, thought of our development and not of our capacity to cheat. No teacher in the world should believe he has the right to change this principle, at the risk of being treated like a crook.

Changes to the rules of conduct in the Etudes are *unfortunate and make no sense*, because they alter the problems; *unaware*, because they are suggested by *tuttologist-teachers* (and in fact I cannot see Cortot or Arrau putting up with that); *restrictive*, because they reduce the possibilities; *in bad taste*, because they aim to know more than the Masters of the piano; unworthy, because they lie.

Should there be an opportunity to help someone brilliant, although not being the pianist that Liszt was, in the best arrangement for a passage in a work *badly written for the piano*, so much the better. But to correct Chopin and Liszt in the Etudes is never justified, because there is no valid or acceptable pedagogic argument. This does no more than prove or accentuate the terrible shortcomings of these *tuttologist-teachers*.

5 – Flux and reflux

I think there is a current of *naturalness in the hand* in Bach, Mozart, Chopin, Liszt, Debussy and Ravel. The work becomes *more pronounced* in Beethoven, Brahms and Schumann. Indeed, even if *the whole is difficult* with the former, once the difficulties have been surmounted, then you might say that the hand, and even the arm, seem to be in water. The movement is natural and not at all forced. It is *fluid and harmonious*.

With the latter, the ideas are often more *complex*: the passages of Beethoven or Schumann are not models of convenience for the hands. Brahms's Paganini Variations Op. 35 inspires respect and may cause a lot of tendinitis if one approaches them *tense* and unintelligently. Clearly, we love them because they are a sublimation of Thought, as well as transfigured music. Brahms even managed to change the essence of the theme, that is: to make it more difficult for whoever was playing than for whoever was listening. His refusal of public effect, vulgar by nature, is greatly inspired here. The work is quite simply that of genius.

Composers also have different ways of dealing with the piano   as an instrument. Did Beethoven not say to Rodolphe Kreutzer: *"Your violin is of no importance to me; I am thinking of the mind"*. Of course, Bach, Mozart, Chopin, Liszt, Debussy and Ravel also thought of the *mind*.

Schumann's Toccata in another little farce for the tendons. It would be best to know how to deal with such special works as any impertinence may come at a high price, the currency being the actual muscles.

It is precisely there that one sees *the true support* of a great teacher.

6 – The great architects

Let us return to our fingerings and to the problems raised by the Etudes.

What other fingering combination would be possible for Etude Op.10 No.1, or for Op. 25 No. 12, without changing what Chopin wanted? What other substantially different fingering would be possible - without changing the notes of the chords played by   the left hand and giving them to the right hand, that is without cheating - for Etude Op. 10 No. 2 without using, for the scale, *the 3 – 4 – 5 imposed by Chopin? What other possibility is there for Op. 10 No. 7, or for Op. 25 No. 3, or for No. 4, or No. 5? Can we change radically Etude Op. 25 No. 11, or that of the octaves, legato of course, for Op. 25 No. 10?*

Chopin seems to have found in the Etudes the exact combination between mind and matter, without leaving us any particular choice, other than sharing in these wonders. Above all, he has found audible fingering: it can be heard.

For minor passages of course, we can have alternative fingering, but not essentially different. In Etude Op. 25 N° 6, for example, for the passage in broken thirds in B-flat, just before the double thirds for both hands, where the 3rd finger can be replaced by the 4 or they can be alternated. However, there is no space for a radical change. Another of Chopin's essential ideas, and also of Liszt and Debussy, is to defy the law of gravity, the weight transmitted to and directed to the keyboard, the force, height and speed of the attack on the keys. All of this refers to our complete motor apparatus: whether to the hand, the arm, the forearm and to all that follows. In dealing with these problems I am going to use the terms *consecrated* by the great masters, because it is not a question   of a *choice of words* but rather of defining concepts. Arrau, Neuhaus and Cortot used the same. For convenience, but far more modestly, I will do the same. Other terms are possible, but I think it is pointless to waste energy in saying *the same things in different words*. It is not through terminology that, in essence, we say things that are original. We must remain effective. Obviously an Etude will not be resolved until *the exact degree* to which the keys will be pressed has been decided in order to play the music, *the height of the hand* to do this, *the speed with which each finger descends*, in order to meet the metronomic speed demanded by Chopin.

That is what gives us the assimilation, the comprehension and that the *second nature* of the problem.

It is a work against *excessive weight*, because the more the key is pressed, the less speed there is to the displacement.

It is the lesson we teach our pupils, when we tell them not to play
so heavily.

7 – Sunday's Einstein

This is how Chopin demands of us a *major balance between the force and the weight of penetration on the key. It is what we could call vertical energy. We could call horizontal energy the displacement or the speed.*

We could list these principles like this:

The more vertical energy (weight) = the less horizontal energy (speed).
The greater the mass = the less the movement.
The more compact = the less lightness.

Let us look, for example, at the high-speed Etudes: Op. 10 No. 4 or Op. 10 No. 2, and Op. 25 No. 6.

The more one applies pressure, the less one travels over the keys. The more one pushes down on the keys, the less one moves.

The same problems in the Finale of Sonata Op. 35, for the little Scherzo of Sonata Op. 58, for the fast passages of the Fourth Scherzo, for Debussy's Etude for "Eight Fingers" or for Liszt's *Feux Follets.*

8 - The "voiceless" piano!

I apply the same working method for all of these works as well as for the Etudes.

Let us take the case of the *sottovoce*, for example. To begin with, we must consider what I call the *zero sonority* in order to confront the problems of *weight* or *lightness*.

Let me explain what I mean.

If we want our ceiling painted white, it wouldn't be very luminous to begin by painting it all in black and reaching white by then adding grey. Similarly, it is useless to work the *sottovoce* "fortissimo ". That would be nonsense. We should never lose sight of the final result for an instant, that is the *sottovoce*.

It would be better to begin with the idea of *minimum force* for the imperceptible pressing of the key. That means trying for a pressure on the key of no more than two or three mm, at a higher speed and above all *mute*. That is the same as saying that one plays, for example, this

Finale of the Funeral Sonata passing *over the keys without producing any sound* but *making the same movements* one would for a *real, sound performance*.

In this way we achieve what one could call a *silent speed* without *producing the least sound*.

You feel and test, then, *the resistance* of the keyboard. You feel that if you push down a key it raises the finger to the same proportion in the opposite direction and in exact compensation: *this is action and reaction*, finger, key, finger.

So, you feel the minimum necessary you must produce to bring sound to life *at its lowest volume*. This is close to a millimetre, because we *don't look for the bottom of the key, but to find the double escapement*.

The action of the small muscles of the fingers is easily perceived doing this. This is when you begin to *add* the minimum *weight* possible, that of the fingers, without in any way compromising the *silent speed*.

And so, *embryos of sound* begin to emerge, here and there, every second or third bar, or something similar to that.

Gradually, you begin to hear a few notes, very weakly, and the passage gradually reaches our ears, as in that sculpture of the slaves by Michelangelo, where the bodies begin to rise out of the marble.

This *minimum of sound* is the *sottovoce*, the *PP* of Chopin, obtained in this way from *an almost non-existent weight applied by the fingers*. However, contact with the key is absolute. There is no air between the finger and the key: the symbiosis is perfect, the finger becomes part of the keyboard, or better still, *the keyboard becomes part of the hand.*

It is a question of feeling that this type of work goes *beyond* articulation, because it would be unthinkable to *articulate* this passage as if it were "*jeu perlé*".

You cannot say that *you articulate*, because everything happens exactly as it does in osmosis or in penetration, not as in the separation inherent in articulation.

9 – Little jugglers

Another way of working this unison Finale (or any other unison), is to do it with the *hands crossed*: the part of the right hand is played by the left, and vice versa, changing one over the other.

That is, *two positions*. This means that the left hand is led also to playing the more virtuoso voice and the one most in view: the part of the soprano. With this changing of hands - because you cannot change the position of the ears – you control, from the human point of view, the upper part more, *but played by the left*. It really has *to develop*, because what you hear, in fact, is the *virtuosity of the right.*

Of course, as I have just said, I apply this to all unison. I apply it to that of the Finale of Tchaikovsky's Concerto in B-flat as well as to the second movement of Prokofiev's Concerto in G.

When you cross the hands, in theory the whole should remain *almost* unchanged, because the hands *are going to do the same work as usual*, more or less. In fact, it is not at all the case: you quickly realize that the left-hand, most often, plays *more slowly* than the right.

In all of us each hand develops differently, as does the rest of the body. We are not perfect machines and our *symmetry* is debatable. It is highly effective, therefore, to develop each hand *separately* and to make it play, *all alone*, this Finale in *sottovoce* at the real speed, as at a concert.

The supplementary work of the Finale would be, therefore, as   in the Funeral March, and from the point of view of the recital,   to make each hand work separately in real execution, in *tempo*, *legato* and *sottovoce*, as *if this had been written for one hand*, as a *finale* for the left hand alone or for the right hand alone. This would avoid the two hands helping one another, which is welcome at the concert of course.

Friedrich Gulda, that wonderful Austrian pianist, taught me *crossing the hands* in an elevator in Buenos Aires. I have never in my life heard such a Finale to Chopin's Sonata in concert. Compared to that of his recital, the others were no more than pale interpretations.

I was very young and easily influenced. So, I went to see the virtuoso to ask him *how* he did it. Very kindly, he explained it to me on the way back to his hotel. It was a wonderful lesson that I have never forgotten to this day.

I often use another working method that consists of *separating the hands* for two octaves. In this way, you can *clarify the right-hand* better for a more luminous tone in an upper octave. This produces a far more comprehensible supplementary control.

Of course, all the traditional methods for working this Finale seem to me to be welcome, for example *forte* the right - *piano* the left, and the reverse; *staccato* the right - *legato* the left, and the reverse; etc., etc., seems fine to me, *on the condition that the PP* subtlety in the work is never exceeded; only for the alternating of *F* and *P*, of course.

I leave it up to each one to find another system of study. Each teacher has a different one. The problem is, as always, its application and transmission to the instrument. So, I dare to give you a few thoughts on my method. It is not universal, of course. Any procedure that does not stray from its final aim seems acceptable to me.

10 – The sound or the tireless « Der Wanderer »

The sound cannot be conceived without resonance.

You can define it like a glance, or like the shortest route between two hearts that do not know one another. It touches points *"that words cannot reach or express"*, according to Nietzsche. The more it expands to the atmosphere, the more it is likely to reach the nerve centres of listeners at greater length, and greater depth and with more sensitivity. The more it remains in the instrument, the less it undertakes this voyage to conquer the audience. Therefore, it is essential for it to *leave* the limited spaces of the piano.

All sonority should be conceived at higher levels, to allow it to take off.

To limit it to the harmonic table of the instrument or to the penetration of the fingers on the keyboard, is to condemn it and have it resembled someone who can see no further than the end of his nose. The sound box of the piano should be, if we can put it like this, *transmitted to space*. How can this be done if you have not study with the pedal?

First of all, the pianist must want the marvellous sound to penetrate the air like smoke and not like an arrow, and for this smoke to be the richest, the longest and the longest lasting possible.

The *whitest* smoke, just as at the election of the Pope.

There has to be a hypersensitivity regarding this sonority because, with the idea and the concept of the work, this sound wonder is the essential element of any musical act: *it is what bears the Message. It is its vehicle.*

Our work at the piano is to try to *forget the key* and feel more that *we are directly touching the sound* and penetrating its mystery, just like diving naked into water without any plastic protection around us.

The path of the key should be as wide as an ocean: everything can be found there, if you know how to look for it correctly, if you know what you want beforehand and if you have the genius to do it.

You must forget the articulation of this key as an essential element, because like this you restrict yourself to receiving, more or less, the sound that the piano gives us in exchange.

I do not want only the sound *of that instrument*, but I want *my sound* from this instrument.

You cannot be better assisted than by your foot, because the pedal plays a decisive role in all of this. I repeat endlessly to my pupils: *press the pedal with your ear and your culture*, because it is impossible to create even the slightest musical tension without the pedal.

The speed of the descent of the key is also essential, because *it produces fundamentally different sonorities.*

The faster you descend on it the more the sonority is *aggressive*. The dry blow of a hammer on the chords surprises them and produces a harsh sonority, given that the vibrations take place *ex abrupto*. There is no research into that. It is almost amateurism. The *speed of this descent* must also be controlled according to the passage: if you have to sing the Trio of Chopin's Fourth Scherzo, the second theme of the First Ballad, or the first of Brahms' Fourth, the speed of descent is the *slowest and lowest* possible, the most *flexible* and the least *pesante*. If you have to begin Tchaikovsky's Concerto with a great orchestra, flexibility comes from your arms entirely, in an enormously wide muscular arc. The pressure and the rebound are of the same amplitude. The sonority in these chords must be studied to *rise upwards*. It would be silly to attach the sonority to the keyboard or to the first *sketch* produced on the piano. The ear must be lifted towards the heavens, or at least towards the last row of the theatre, towards the ceiling. Think of the great churches where resonance is the translation of cosmic space.

Each time you hold back a natural movement you are holding back the sound. Georges Cziffra, the fabulous pianist, told me during a lesson "*go there with your little finger; never contradict it*".

You must also think of deadening all movement, to rebound each time even higher, to *swim* in sublime waters, above all *not restricting* the ascending curve of the chords. The greater this restraint, the greater the rebound, the greater the control of this *double movement* (and I do stress this), the better all the voices of the chords will be achieved and the better they will be controlled. They will certainly learn not to *be equal*, given that one chord is *the addition of several different voices that produce a special colour*. Our control should channel *the different energies towards each finger*, because if the chord is *forte*, not all the fingers play with *equal* strength.

In fact we cannot imagine that in the *forte* of an orchestra, the trumpet, the flute, violin cello and double bass produce *an equal volume of sound* that one could put at 10, for example:

more specifically, if the main voice is the violin cello, this will play at 10; the double bass, on the other hand, at 8; the flute at 7, and the trumpet at 5, in proportion.

You could then say that the keys are not all pushed down to the same depth. You can in fact choose this depth if you control the pressure, following the intensities and conceptions of the voices.

The main thing is to listen to how the sound *dies out* to be able to understand how it *should come to life.*

If you consider this from the point of view of the *noblesse* of the sonority, the perception of the lowest, *weakest pianissimo,* is far more important than the perception of the loudest *fortissimo*, whether producing it or listening to it. Anyone can apprehend this harsh *FF*. Even if that person is not a musician. But to hear the *PPPP* is quite a different thing: that takes class, intelligence, hypersensitivity, grace, in short, all the major qualities.

Eduardo del Pueyo, my extraordinary second teacher at the Brussels Royal Conservatory, a superb interpreter of the 32 Sonatas, also an eminent teacher, said that in talking about force and lightness: *"anyone can play 'forte', but to play lightly is the business of a master".*
So, inequality must be cultivated.

11 - Inequality: what a fine thing!

The following must be understood *leaving a key when it reaches ground is as important as pressing it down*. Otherwise, there would never be the principle of action and reaction and, therefore, no major association would be possible.

This principle must be taught right away to children: *you push down the key and it pushes up your finger.*

This law regulates, as well, the construction of the musical phrase.

Forte or Piano does not mean *continually but globally.*

We must separate in the construction of the musical phrase the things to be made obvious, on the one hand, from the things that pass unnoticed, on the other.

We must learn *which note* determines a modulation to change the colours, *which is* the culminating point of the phrase, where it is going and how its returns.

Here we must determine the *peaks,* moving the dynamics towards them to leave *from them to the next ones*, in this way establishing a union between the *nerve centres* of the work

Above all, *this union must be as long as possible*, otherwise, we risk syllabic stuttering: sp - eak - ing - li - ke - thi - s.

In such cases what musical tension should we produce?

All of this means we must balance the *Forte* or the *Piano within them.*

We know that if something is red, all the *reds* to be found in the absolute are in fact infinite, varied; it depends on the light and the atmosphere, as well as the angle of observation or hearing.

Claudio Arrau said admirably that if one is an artist *"one cannot play two notes with the same subtlety nor with the same intensity"*. What wisdom!

Hence the platitude becomes the sharpest, most detestable enemy of the music because it proves that we are incapable of *feeling*.

If our sensitivity is limited, then it would be better not to venture into the dangerous waters of sensuality or symbolic exultation.

But of course, that may develop mainly in the work of polyphony. It is with polyphony that we learn to develop the fingers separately, to give them their true personality: they must learn to divide the hand to be able to play *expressif*, for example. This is done with some fingers only; not with the others, which play at the same time, but with a *different* touch, in the same chords and passages. Everything can be developed, but it must be done very young before vices have had time to set in.

The fingers must learn the *inequality*.

12 – Good manners

If you have to play the Finale of Prokofiev's Seventh Sonata, the Finale of Ginastera's "1952" Sonata *Ruvido et ostinato or to begin Bartok's "1926" Sonata, the attack on the key is more harsh, and so the speed of the descent infinitely faster than for the cantabile of the Berceuse, for example.*

There you are approaching a more aggressive sonority through the speed of the descent of the key. In short, roughly that would give:

A – The slowest possible speed of descent = seeking cantabile. It allows the sound waves

to vibrate with parsimony.

Result: a better nourished richness of harmonics.

It serves the passages extremely cantabile like all infinite melodies, such as the Trio of Chopin's Funeral March; the second theme of the first movement of the Third Sonata, as well as its third movement, the Largo; the exposition of the Fourth Ballade; the Mazurkas; Liszt's Vallée d'Obermann; the left hand of Ravel's Ondine in the exposition, as well as the whole work, the Pavane, Une Barque sur l'ocean; Beethoven's Clair de Lune; the Ariosi of Op. 110; the second movement of the Fourth or Fifth Concerto; the theme of the Arietta and its first Variation; the second movement of Ravel's Concerto in G; Evocacion by Albéniz; Liszt's Third Consolation; the Getragen of Schumann's Fantasie or the beginning of the Humoresque; Schubert's Impromptus; the Andante of the Sonata in B-flat, "Posthume"; its exposition; Bach's Prelude in E-flat or the Second Movement of the Italian Concerto; not to mention the works of Tchaikovsky, Rachmaninov, Debussy or Scriabin, for example. That serves to sing more, in a more relaxed way, with far more beauty, tranquillity, and softness; in short, mainly more similar to the human voice.

B – Faster speed of descent = seeking to play more brilliantly or more bitterly.

Striking is drier and more determined.

Result: a sonority less rich in harmonics but clearer because shorter. Favours "jeu perlé".

Haydn, Mozart, Beethoven when young, Mendelsohn, Weber, Chopin in many of his Etudes; Bach in his motor Preludes; Liszt as virtuoso in his Second Transcendental Etude or in the Fourth Paganini Etude; Debussy's Toccata, that of Ravel or that of Prokofiev; certain of Chopin's Preludes and Polonaises; certain passages of "germination by the fingers" by Rachmaninov; Ravel's Alborada del Gracioso, the Tombeau de Couperin, and so on.

C – Very fast descent = seeking sonorities that are harsher and more rigid.

An energetic and almost violent striking of the chords. Result: more vertical, angular sonorities.
Bartok in his First and Second Concerti and his « 1926 » Sonata; Ginastera in his «1952» Sonata; Finale of Rachmaninov's Third Concerto; Fugue in Barber's Sonata; *Rudepoêma* by Villa-Lobos; the Finale of Prokofiev's Seventh Sonata; *Trois Mouvements de Pétrouchka* by Stravinsky; the central part of the *Corpus Christi* by Albéniz; Manuel de Falla's *Fantasia Bética*; the central part of Ravel's Concerto for the Left Hand, and so on.

To this we must add an enormous, almost infinite, variety of touching, finger angles, the contact of the fingers or the pad of the finger with the keys, the curve of the hand, the force or mass of attack, different heights, etc.
In this way sound as we conceive it is produced.
If the conception is wrong the sound follows this poor approach. On the other hand, the mind corrects the defects more confidently than the muscles.

13 - « Des pas dans la neige » by Claude Debussy

It is amazing to see how we continue to play with the fingers tensed as at the time of Czerny, ignoring the lessons of Chopin and Liszt. Marie Jaëlle, the favourite pupil of the Hungarian teacher, was right in what she said. Eduardo del Pueyo taught this suppleness of the finger as something fundamental for the touch on the key, for the beautiful sound.
If you want something *très expressif*, the *contact with the key must be more supple* and the clash of *a hard element* with the ivory or the ebony must be avoided. The harder or sharper the contact between the finger and the key, the harder and sharper will be the sound. The ear should refuse such sounds, which are closer to noise than to music. By just extending this finger the sound becomes more human, more caressing.

So it is imperative to use the hypersensitivity of the finger pads: they must be made more sensitive, more intelligent, more aware, more sportive, more ready to leap; as well as calmer and more relaxed so that they may like to remain on the key for longer.
The touch must come to life, by using the last joint on each finger, but not hardened more each time.
It is, along with our eyes, the most sensitive part of our body.
An excellent exercise is to place the hands with the fingers just touching gently, as in the position of prayer, but without the palms touching. You then make very supple movements by varying the inclination of the fingers; you loosen all the finger and carpal joints while

thinking of the desired sonorities: cantabile, brilliant, light, heavy, etc.

The *up - down* work of these fingers must be felt as an expressive element of prime importance.

Imagine, for example, that you have the most powerful Ferrari in the world. If you remove its tires it is immediately useless. Our fingers are the tires of that Ferrari.

They determine the sound and its beauty, because it is there that the symbiosis with the keyboard is produced and the real contact between the two becomes reality. It is through this contact that we feel the Music. The greater the subtlety, the greater the expressivity, just like touching the hand of someone you love. That is when you truly feel the nerve endings of the finger; something impossible to feel when they remain hard or tense.

So, we can understand the premonition of Chopin: *"The whole (he meant the arm, the fingers, the wrist, the elbow, the shoulder, all the muscles in general) should float as in water. There are no angles, but only circles. Everything turns in every possible direction, because this whole constitutes an ellipse."*

14 – Gliding

Suppleness should be *acquired from within us* and not by executing useless movements without first *controlling* them in the brain. We should also approach the keyboard with our soul. We must love it: it is the keyboard that allows us to make Music. It is for us to change it into an *ocean* or into *a little stream* with no future and no pretensions.

Suppleness, being relaxed, the sensation of *returning* to a normality in the execution (*controlling muscular relaxation and tension*, in the words of Liszt), the action and reaction of the muscles in executing passages full of intricacies, complexities, should, therefore, be done *as ordered by the brain and not by external movements*.

It is useless to move the elbows to *show* that you are relaxed if the brain does not order this movement. Relaxation flows just as the blood flows through our body. *It cannot be achieved by non-recorded movements. You must work consciously on this relaxation*, like solving a problem and not as if it were a factor foreign to us.

We all react in the same way to the difficulty because in the mind there is an *alert system* that, one way or another, influences muscular behaviour in all of us. Feelings of fear, worry, anguish and nervousness, *do no more than to aggravate this tension*.

A good teacher must find the way to channel these energies positively according to the capabilities of his pupil, because he is the first to know that *there are no muscular problems that are not caused by psychological situations*.

Just as in psychosomatic illnesses, playing the piano correctly originates in the psyche of each individual. As a result, we cannot be *the healers* of the piano. We should accompany our pupils like spiritual fathers and understand the deep-rooted causes of the problem and not the superficial ones.

Teaching means being open to the needs of the pupil.

15 – Touching the keys differently ...

An excellent exercise is to place each hand separately on *Chopin's notes*, that is, E, F- sharp,

G-sharp, A-sharp, B (or C, according to others).

Then press the pedal and try to produce fifteen (or more) different *touches* for each finger, with different expressions: *piano, mezzo piano, forte, energico, sottovoce, lyrique, chanté, brillante, grandioso*, etc.

This gives a very close delimitation of the sound. You can really feel it at the fingertips.

You hear it in *each movement.*

It is a remarkable awareness *because you can determine in advance the desired sound, intellectually and emotionally.*

And how many young pianists are able to listen to what they produce?

Listening to a sound means *accompanying it until its total extinction*, until regretting that it is no longer there.

Young pianists today are in too much of a hurry: they produce tons at high speed. *They do not know how to enjoy the sound.*

Localizing and *becoming aware* of the double escapement are equally essential. At this moment, between the escapement and the bottom of the key, *our decision is made. It is the moment of truth.* It is there that the sound is produced. It is like witnessing the birth of your own child. You can see how someone *comes* into the world.

The quality of this last descent must be particularly careful, because if we jerk it, the touch and the chords will be surprised and the resulting sonority will be hard, as explained above. If we drop on the key too slowly, the chords, in this case, will not react. This won't produce any kind of sound.

It is important to have this descent on the key planned in the mind just as a pilot plans the flight of his plane. Listening to the sound means *understanding it*, as you understand a human being: knowing when it is *in form, in poor form, sick, energetic*, knowing what its curve is, that is, how it rises, its apogee and its definitive descent.

16 - … otherwise it is too late!

Our problem remains therefore the conception and production of sound, because once *it has come to life,* we cannot change it. We can no longer reach it or correct it. Any possible action on a sonority that has already been produced will damage *the following sound*. This is why it is so important.

It is almost impossible to separate it from the technical or mechanical work, because it is like the blood in our body. Without it no music can exist; it is the essential element. The educated ear plays an essential role here, not just in terms of volume or quality, but mainly in terms of *good taste*, excellent *training*, education, respect and an understanding of styles.

This appreciation of the problem of sound has differed over time. For Bach nothing was more normal than transcribing a violin concerto for the keyboard, or four violins for four keyboards. Perhaps what truly counted in his eyes was the idea, the pure expression, the relationship of spaces, the volume, the line, without the sound being a sensual element, contrary to Beethoven and Mozart, who did not find writing for the piano the same thing as writing for a quartet or an orchestra.

But it is above all with Chopin, for whom the piano was *his soul and the sonority of his instrument was his life*, that things changed fundamentally. You cannot imagine the Fourth Ballad transcribed for an oboe or a clarinet!

17 – Mild impertinence

Among the Romantics and later musicians there is identity between *sonority and work*. It is impossible, for example, to imagine Chopin *without melody*, or of imagining Debussy with the sound of Bartok. That would be like looking at the Mona Lisa dressed in a monokini. *Neutral sound cannot and should not exist for our music*. It cannot *be made asexual*. This sonority serves to translate a thought, to incubate it in silence before existing, to love it during its existence and to weep when it is no longer there. We must accompany it to the end.

We should not only work *the sound*, but above all *on my own sound*. A pianist with a disagreeable sound is a bit like a terrible voice singing opera. That quickly becomes tiresome and the audience begins to reject it.

But how, technically speaking, can we produce this *cantabile*? How can we produce this *clair de lune*, and these thirds or *cantabile* octaves?

It is extremely difficult to teach that without having ever played the piano. This is why I only believe in *pianist - teachers*.

18 – Adjustments

The sound palette has a whole kaleidoscope of infinite subtleties. This means that adjustment has to be made to all the different aspects of speed, penetration, tranquillity or nervousness in the manipulation of the keyboard; synchronizing with the foot, with the pedal; listening to the difference produced, not there where we are, seated at the piano, but making our ears travel to the end of the hall; feeling the resonance of the instrument *going up and never down* (Georges Cziffra said to me one day "*Feel that the piano resounds and never that it sounds*"); imagine the lines that the sound curve produces, always *circular* and never *angular*; see it as we do the stars in the sky and avoid seeing it only as a relationship between my notes and my hands; feel it as the goddess of Beauty and Thought, not only as the *transmitter of the execution*; wish for the music to represent *us* and reveal, above all, the work we are interpreting at that moment.

It is said that a computer one day calculated the different types of volume and touch produced in the playing of Ravel's Gibet by Walter Gieseking. Everyone knows that Gieseking was a genie of sonority, but the results produced by the computer are no less incredible: more than 250 different sounds!

19 – Enter and leave: I leave suddenly!

For me, what is fundamental is the moment of attacking the key and its contact with the finger: *at this moment* there must be *two* movements.

One plunges into the depth, determined in advance, of the key, and reaches its bottom, cantando or brillante.

The other is to leave the key, propelled by the ground towards the new articulation.

These actions and reactions guarantee muscular relaxation. The pressure of the finger does indeed block the hand and the arm   in the depth of the keyboard. When you press a little too hard, the results are felt up through the forearm, and this blockage, and abnormal tension in the upper muscles, *becomes the initial cause of tendinitis.*
These two movements are like a propelling exit towards another key.
Also, the more my *mass* increases, the more my elbows move away from my trunk. Like this they discover their autonomy and as a result their freedom.
To understand that, you only have to begin Liszt's First Concerto or that of Tchaikovsky, with the elbows *glued* to the body, as we mentioned when speaking about relaxation, to discover the paralysis that this implies. In other words, the freedom and the return to the normal state are the done thing.
The best way to get *there is to practice in pianissimo* and do not use disproportionate force. Nothing is gained by studying *fortissimo* for hours apart from breaking the chords and wearing out the muscles. Study in a calm atmosphere, rest and constant relaxation will be the *life insurance* for our muscles when we are working.

We do not ask an athlete who is running a hundred metres to try for the world record whenever he is in training. Overexerting the muscles can be very harmful. Always think of your arms in *water*, as Chopin recommended.

20 - « The Cathedral » or the association of the two hands of Auguste Rodin

The hands are wonderful instruments and symbolic of what we are on earth. We must cultivate this love for harmony between them as an illuminating symbol of the spirit. We should study their more elegant movements, as well as their more distinguished and aristocratic movements. *They are the tools of the soul for our work.* In fact, all you have to do is look at the magnificent work of a Rodin. He called these hands "Cathedral". In his work they are in a position so moving that they have come to symbolize the beauty of the spirit. They point towards Heaven with a magnificent lyricism and simplicity. They are elongated, supple and perfect.
Rodin felt a great love for the hands. Just think of his works such as "The Hand of God" or "The Hand of the artist". Each time, you find his two favourite themes: God and the couple, both giving life.
The hands constitute to an extent *the enunciation of our work.* They join in incredible ballets, extraordinary miracles, endless caresses and harsh blows. They allow us to communicate with composers and the public in carrying messages, like true Messiahs.
They develop each finger like a much-loved child, full of affection, love and spirit, like the Archangel Gabriel. The children learn to talk among themselves, to listen and above all to respect. The love that these hands show their children is so great that they would never want to ill-treat them or in any way punish them. We must strive for the harmonious growth of all our children and help them to understand their determining, irreplaceable role.
These hands must be kept in constant contact with the mind and spirit because without them nothing is possible. Even Art would die.

21 – Ballets full of wonder

All movement should be considered as a return to the thumb, because it is the action of prehension that is constant in life.
It is this movement that brings to me all else that exists and that puts it in contact.
So it is a circular path taken by all the other fingers towards the thumb. Everything evolves towards it, in this way completing the dimensions of the height of the hand on the keyboard. It is well known, for example, that two chamber musicians look at one another to breathe together before attacking a piece. The four fingers must do the same thing with the thumb and in moving towards it, because the whole sense of balance of the hand, its whole stability and importantly all its sensitivity depend on this: think, for example, of the coordination of the chords.

We must also study the topography of the keyboard. We must know how you go to and return from a black key: prepare the hand in the diagonal towards the thumb, which is shorter because it has one less phalange, or towards the fifth finger, which despite its three phalanges, is shorter than the other fingers.
We must also determine the direction in which we are playing. Mixed movements are not at all welcome and can cause terrible accidents. In the rotation, particularly, we should go either towards the thumb or the fifth finger, following the natural movement of the forearm.
The thumbs will be essential in the double octaves, for example. What I mean is in the parallel octaves, where there are only two octaves, each one played by one hand. But there is also the third octave, that played by the two thumbs at the same time, which is without a doubt the leading octave between the two hands, since it is this octave that gives the balance as in the fuselage of a plane. Another fundamental movement is, on the one hand, the arc that must be formed between the brain, the neck, shoulder, the whole arm, the wrist and the fingers, and on the other, the arc that comes from the Earth, our reference element, that fully sustains us: this is the arc formed between our feet, our legs, buttocks, waist and backbone that connects us to that other preceding arc. These two arcs, after all, are no more than one symmetric or extended arc.

So, here are the two *major* confrontations: on the one hand my brain and on the other the Earth. The waist is our hinge. The extremities of the third and second metacarpals should be as high as possible. They are the summit of the hand at the piano.
In this way we can add to the sound box of the instrument in the space of the sound box of the hand - *the true human sound box in the depth of the hand.* It is there that the sound must resonate for the first time, *in the depth of the hand.* It is from there that it draws all its humanity. In this way the hand takes on three dimensions: *height, depth and extension.*

Another important aspect is the different role played by each finger. Our index finger has the soul of a searcher in that it seeks out the direction to the right or to the left. It is *our aerial* and determines the bearing we will take, and it makes the hand wind its way in its search relentlessly. When the hand is open everything turns around it. It is the central axis, the heart and its most sensitive centre.

Chopin turned the index finger into his messenger. He gave it this exact role of the *ideal, perfect centre for the hand*, or *its musical heart. This is the soul of his technique.* It is the most refined finger, the one that has a preference for everything. It is the one with which we choose to *feel something*, It is the most *expressive* finger of all.

The big finger, the clumsiest and *least refined*, it is the *physical centre* of the hand. It has a lot to do, but compared with the index finger, it is nothing. Even so, it helps essentially in the fast passages. It can also replace the thumb in an accent. Sometimes, we give it expressive tasks, which it performs with dignity. However, the index finger and the ring finger, both *finer* by nature, prove to be more suitable for these requirements.

The fourth finger is the poor relation of any pianist. Chopin complained to God for having given him a *large nose* and a fourth *stupid* finger. I do not know what he did about his nose, but for his fourth finger he found some incredible solutions and fingerings. Attached to the third by nature, this finger is very sensitive, innocent and almost vulnerable. I love it very much because it is full of goodwill.

With regard to the *major commanders*, the thumb and the fifth finger, we could say that they are *the towers* of the hand, of the arm and of almost our whole *upper* body. I no longer remember who said it that *you could kill a man with the fifth finger*, proof of the strength of which it is capable.

The fifth finger is indeed very strong and independent by nature. It is able to imitate or replace the *piccolo* in an orchestra with eloquence, style, clarity and brilliance. It always makes itself heard. The thumb is the king of the hand in terms of strength, support and decision. It determines, as in the gesture of the Emperor, *life or death*. Without it nothing can be done.

It is said that once Liszt cut his finger slightly while shaving but despite this he managed to play Beethoven's Fifth Concerto with only *nine* fingers, as Paganini did for his recital, using only *three* chords on his violin (it is said that his instrument was ruined).

Certainly, Liszt was not missing one of his thumbs!

The role of the thumb is fundamental. *It is a leader.* Suffice to imagine Ravel's Concerto for Left Hand to realize that it is the true soloist of the hand and of the music.

I will talk about fingering later, but I tell in advance that for me, as for any other pianist, *all fingers are of equal importance. We must use them all on any key.* However, we must distinguish the *different expressivity* of each finger. Clearly if the melody is to begin with eloquence, sensitivity, agility and evasiveness, you avoid beginning with the clumsier fingers. You allow the more *expressive* fingers to act. The same goes for a passage that begins forcefully. In this case, the *expressive* fingers are to be avoided and these notes will be given *to the chiefs of the hand* or to their replacement, our dear third soldier.

I think that sonority depends on the will of the artist, on his desire for the infinite, his imagination of symbiosis; it means accepting, above all, that a key can descend to hell or, with a few millimetres more or less can rise to the Heavens.

22 - « When the colour has attained its fullness, the form has reached its plenitude »

Can we possibly imagine not using the pedal in our work?

For example, you study the second theme of Chopin's Sonata Op. 58 *without pedal*. This is fine when learning the notes, but after that what is the point of working dryly? Is the aim not to obtain the finest melody in the world and to recall Bellini?

We should really feel a long breath, *legato*, pure, moving, almost from another world. Think of the human voice, *touch the sound without using the hammers of the instrument*; feel the finger penetrate directly the sound and even the Music. How can you do that without the pedal?

This is the same as Titian, van Dyck or Vermeer of Delft *making sketches* for their portraits by painting witches or the fearsome wild Baba Yaga!

The pedal not only improves the sonority but also *creates all the aesthetic drama*. How can we improve the sonority without the strict, in-depth, constant work of the pedal?

23 – The secret liaisons of the *legato*

I have always claimed that the Nocturnes of Chopin or of Liszt, apart from being magnificent works, are true *studies in cantabile*, slow and melodic studies, studies in sonority. They are, above all, *extraordinary studies in legato*.

This legato is not just a physical question on the instrument but a mental issue: one should produce a sound that merges into another. Above all, it must be richer in harmonics.

If I *connect* two fingers and I do not *think* of producing *these two sounds that are richer and more harmonic,* these two fingers will never be entirely *legato*, despite all my physical contact with the instrument

Chopin used the *gliding* of the same finger for *legato* and this gesture on the part of such a virtuoso only reinforces this idea, *that it is not a question of physical legato but the legato we hear.*

Look at his fingerings for the Trio of the Funeral March, for example. He saw *legato* as a breath, as an acoustic element, as harmonic *richesse,* as a sound result to be obtained *to imitate the human voice* in space and *not as an emergency liaison on the keyboard.*

So, I make no difference in learning Etude Op. 25 No. 7, for example. A double dialogue, with different sound plans, voices that respond, lovers the talk and agitation in the central part makes this work *one of the finest Nocturnes.*

The certainty of the real *legato* must be conceived precisely, not only based on combined fingerings, but also on the *symbiosis of sonorities*.

24 - The pedal, the *legato* or the soul

This work of the pedal seems to me to be fundamental. You do not ask a baker to make bread without dough.

Basically, the correct use of the pedal does not depend only on the pianist, but also on the acoustics, the instrument, a concert hall and/or on your surroundings, among a thousand other things. You cannot use the same pedal in a *dry* room, for example, and in an enormous cathedral. The age and the technical condition of the piano also demand a different use each time and impose different changes to this pedal.

It depends above all on the ear, sensitivity and intelligence. This is why I said that you could not use the pedal without culture and imagination, and *without being aware that the foot has a touch like the fingers*. The foot is their equal.

Pressing down on the pedal by *two, three, four or five millimetres, or completely,* is determined by the conception of the work, the hypersensitivity of the foot, the balance of an ensemble according to the desired musical tension, the condition of the piano and the hall where the music is being played.

The pedal should be considered as a supplementary key, and   it must be used to obtain the best sonority. So, it should not be pedalled as you do a bicycle, that is, *pedalling without listening for the need to modulate.*

The movement of the dampers must be watched carefully because even if the pedal is pressed by *a millimetre* they are activated. The pedal is already in action at *this minimum distance from the strings*. It is highly recommended, as a result, to wear shoes that are comfortable and that have soles that do not block out the sensitivity of the nerve endings of the toes.

It is also recommended that *the inclination* of the feet in operating the pedal should be developed: to engage this pedal, it is one thing to glide over it (with the technique of the foot gliding over it without pressing it) and another to bear down on it with kilos of strength from the leg.

This means that the light touch must be studied so as to avoid heavy pressure at special moments, in a *cantabile* for example.

I tell my pupils constantly to *press the pedal with their ears and show that they are cultivated.*

25 – Squaring the circle, or the arguments of the sophists ....
   No, rather the philistines

Of course, there are *insurmountable* pedals, the case with Beethoven, for example.

Everyone knows the problem with the Waldstein Sonata or Sonata Op. 31 No. 2 in his *recitatifs*, in the first Movement.

It must be said that Beethoven, followed later by Liszt with Ludwig Bösendorfer in person, contributed to the evolution and the technical revolution of the instrument. Without his demands and those of Liszt, we would be reduced to using far less performing instruments than our current Steinway, Bösendorfer, Yamaha, Fazioli or Kawai.

You could deduce from this that current instruments no longer allow for Beethoven's pedals. One could also respond that each Beethovenian pianist has not dared to change his pedals. I do   not recall Schnabel, Brendel, or particularly Arrau, or Pollini, changing the composer's intentions.

The idea is, obviously, to have a bass *in the sense of something ideal*, whether this is in the Waldstein or in Op. 31 No. 2. It must be glimpsed in all its poetry and in the mist, in order to give the colour of an *aurora*; that is, to give the idea of the birth of light at dawn and not at *midday*; or to give the idea of doubt, in the other D minor Sonata. There should be no controversy over the virtues of *tonic and dominant* and to slightly raise the problem intellectually. Try first of all to use this pedal *without thinking of others*, without thinking of criticism and without thinking of the audience. All alone in your studio, close your eyes and let your muscles *flow through water*. Relax, feel that the earth is dropping away from you, let yourself descend to dawn, *offer no resistance to Beethoven.* You have to *learn* how to do this before getting into controversy. *You have to bring down all the psychological barriers.*

You are in good company, with the great pianists. In any case, it is Beethoven, and you, now, who are right and not the audience, nor the critics, nor your colleagues, in fact no one else. Take the risk, for the love of God. Do not let anyone tell you what you should do. Make your own mistakes, on your own!

If you do not feel you are able then you must *negotiate* and find

justification for the problem raised by Beethoven.

The first excuse is that pianos no longer sound the same in our day…

The second is that the sound volumes of instruments are different. At the time they sounded less…

The third is that Beethoven was deaf and could not hear the din made by this pedal…

The fourth is that this pedal affects the clarity of the work: so, it is not at all pure…

The fifth is that… words, words, words….

The six is… words, words, and even more words…

The most important solutions and justifications are those of knowing if you are ready *to solve this problem or not, and whether you are able to or not.*

I like to say that I have enough to do dealing with my own errors that I have no time for the errors of others. I am too conceited to even think of copying errors made by colleagues. If you have poor intellectual intentions, if you are lacking in spirit, to begin with, you should not play Beethoven, because, despite everything, his principal message has not been understood. I advise such people to interpret only Diabelli.

There is nothing more disgusting, more miserable or more regrettable than being intellectually dishonest.

You can be mistaken, you can be wrong, but *to be mistaken* for dishonesty is beyond me and it is a discussion in which I really do not want to take part.

26 – To know or not to know …. that is the question

Returning to Waldstein, the idea is not at all *cumulative*: you do not need a pedal to increase the resonance, as could be the case for the first movement of the *Appassionata*. As in *Clair de Lune*, the pedal is almost *Impressionist*, and I choose my words carefully. *It is obvious that Beethoven was aware of the overlapping of harmonies,* otherwise how do you explain *the harmonic exceptions* in the Symphonies or in the Quartets? Orchestras and quartets have no pedals!

What we need to know is how to make *such exceptions* for the piano, because we should not draw conclusions from our incapacity.

It is clear that Beethoven's pedal is poetic, evocative, immaterial, *but it is not at all harmonic.*

The whole should not be seen *in the light of mid-day but glimpsed between shadow and light.*

It should be hinted at, dreamt off or *idealized at dawn.*

The real problem is the right-hand, because it is that hand that makes the noise and not the bass pedal. In fact, try to hold down this pedal *without playing the right-hand*: the sonority, like this subtly, almost ideally, mingled, *if done with the required delicacy,* is delightful, extraordinary and visionary.

The original pedal can be *modulated* with the touch of the foot, that is, *worked,* obviously, precisely there where it is felt it *should* be changed. What is important is that the dampers never reach the strings, under any pretext, and so the bass is lost. *The ambiguity should be preserved.* At dawn *pure* lines are not distinguished, but one imagines them rising out of the mist.

Just think of the five Cathedrals of Rouen by Claude Monet and you will understand why the pedal of the Waldstein is one of the *picturesque* touches of genius of the work, and long before French paintings.

In Op. 31 No. 2, the Tempest, it is clear that the intention of the composer is to keep the anguished interrogation of this terrible bass chord. It is this bass that should go on being heard *like a threat* while *the voice* tries to give a response to this strange interrogation. In other words, in speaking of *the transmission* of the principal message, the chord must be present, held, sustained, deaf, and the recitative, *con expressione e semplice,* is played almost on the double escapement.

On the other hand, if you want an *average* result, achieve it without the pedal… You will achieve *miserable poetry and an immense vacuum* in the atmosphere. Like this you will please the purists who do not understand essential things. The result will be worthy of a pharmacist, because everything will be weighed and controlled, but without genius.

However, the artist must follow his decision, *his extremism* and his idea until the end, and not just to please those who do not know, *but to educate them.*

27 – My terribly sensitive foot

As I said above there is *a touch of the foot.* I like to repeat this. *Our foot feels the pedal* like our finger feels the key. So, we should work our feet as we do our fingers *at different depths*, which produces from the pedal's different sonorities. To a great extent it is our feet that produce *the musical tension* because, without them, the final effect of the sound is not achievable.

The mechanics of this pedal, in a piano in a perfect state, is extremely sensitive, and it also reacts *to attempts* to put pressure on it. So, it provides us with a palette with a wide range of colours. But it can also ruin everything, even when the fingers are *playing well.* I love telling my pupils to think of the great painters at their easel when they use the pedal. I usually take Raphael as an example: his colours and his lines *form the unity of the ensemble.* The perfection of the *outline* of his characters is extraordinary. They are not separate elements but are always in perfect balance. You could indeed say that *it is pure Mozart,* as certain aesthetes like to think. Too often, the pedal is pressed not like Raphael but more like the painters of a building. Yet it is the pedal that gives colour and life to the execution. It should be pampered by the pianist like a well-loved girl.

It can and should be used "en continuation", even in the Fugues (without affecting the counterpoint, of course), to avoid a dry, sapless execution. Busoni gave the same idea to his pupils.

I do not think that you can play *expressif* without the pedal. That would be quite useless, in any case one of the major tasks of the pianist is to make the instrument, dry by nature with its poor, short sonority become a singing, miraculous *voice*. I believe that not even a Benedetti Michelangeli could have done it without the transcendental use of the pedal, which in fact he did, admirably. *Little touches* on the pedal also highly recommended. Sharp, rapid touches, *a millimetre* in depth, are possible thanks to touch on the pedal and the hypersensitivity of the foot.

It is recommendable for female pianists, but also for male pianists who admire the US Marines, avoiding *insensitive* footwear, even if elegant. They become a *barrier* between the skin and nerve endings of the foot and the pedal.

I recall a wonderful execution of Debussy's Etudes by a Japanese pianist whom I adore, Mitsuko Uchida, wearing dance pumps for a better feel of the pedal and giving a magnificent sonority to the Etudes.

Of course, everything is still governed by the ear. It is the ear that suggests other thing than the *camouflage pedal,* at the critical and difficult moments in our recital.

There are also major differences between what are called *harmonic* pedals and *poetic* pedals. Take Ravel's Ondine, for example. If you use the harmonic pedal during long bars (to cover the irregularity of the right-hand above all), you will not hear *an Ondine* make her declaration of love and her lament, but *a choir of Ondines* in the marketplace. I do not think that this was Ravel's intention. The choice is imposed by the poetry of the passage and by its conception, not just by the harmony, because this is but one of the decision elements.

As to the left pedal, its role is, I think, eminently poetic. Everyone knows the romantic definitions of this pedal, such as *clair de lune, évaporation des sonorites*, etc. When you play on only two chords (and not just *una corda*, literally), *there is a change of colour in the instrument, regardless of volume,* because the hammer does not hit the three chords fully but restricts itself to two of them. It is not a matter of sourdine, *but simply another sound.*

Ravel did indicate, for example, on the last page of *Scarbo: "Sourdine mais forte"* … And according to Rubinstein, *you can play forte with one chord and piano with three chords.* It is difficult to understand that after the advices of great masters, *we still do not understand.*

BOOK III

Part two

The Old and the New Testament: Bach's Preludes and Fugues and Chopin's Etudes

1 – The art of speaking in two, three or four with the greatest of courtesy: quite simply, Bach

The study of counterpoint and polyphony is perhaps one of the most civilized and finest expressions of all Music. Here you learn to listen to others, to be other than always the main protagonist doing all the work yourself. In Mozart's words, *"There are no servants in Music"*. Everyone, all parties, all voices and all instruments are indispensable.

Due to its development, the Fugue imposes *a brake* or a mental discipline on whoever plays it. It is one of the most fundamental links in the teaching of music.

Here you learn to think, to listen, to control and to forge a convivial rapport among all the parties involved in the music, to divide the hands not like a pianist but like a duo, a trio, a quartet or a quintet: each finger can symbolize a different instrument. The left-hand is not always content with alto, but may begin to sing, assuming the role of the soprano of the right, and vice versa.

All the parties are at the same time soloists and accompanists, and this in the same work. This is how the search for different timbres in each finger is produced.

Bach provides a great lesson in modesty and humility. *"When I play Bach, I am at peace with the world"*, said Neuhaus. Another great musician, cellist and orchestra leader, Pablo Casals, used to begin his day by playing two or three Preludes and Fugues on the piano to listen to *"the harmony of the World"*. The great pianist Sviatoslav Richter, thought that, *"one should make of Bach a form of mental hygiene"*.

Of course I share all of these wonderful ideas: the order, the rapport, the balance established between registers by Bach, the relationship between dynamic volumes with no more development than to be in *two, three, four or five* pure voices; the economy   of expressive means; the concentration of contained passions; the resemblance with the Universe; the symbiosis between man and God; the modesty; the desire to glorify the Lord; the absence of all egoism; respect for the hand, the ear, the heart and the mind... (I could go on for pages), turn *"Das wohltemperirte klavier"* (the Well-Tempered Clavier) into the true Bible of every musician. God in person seems to descend into our midst and to speak to us. It is the *nec plus ultra* of all human musical creation. It is, in a nutshell, one of the supreme peaks of human thought.

The Fugue, particularly in *his solution*, is deliverance.

I think that Bach organized Music for us for around two hundred years, asking for nothing in exchange but the *Glory of God*.

Later, Franz Liszt was to change this order by introducing through the *major thirds* the destruction of the dominant and the scale by tones, well before Claude Debussy, in the Melody "*Der traurige Monch*", dedicated to Franziska Ritter, the niece of Richard Wagner. Hence he opened the door to *Wagnerian disorder*, that was passionate, ardent and extreme, creating atonalism (not only in his Bagatelle without tonality), the vague and the atmosphere for Debussy, great virtuosity for Ravel, mystic expressionism for Scriabin, along with Chopin and Schumann… and all this without mentioning his influence on all the other Russian, Spanish and Nordic composers. Liszt, like Bach, asked for nothing in exchange. To all this new Music, we must add Chopin, *the harmonist*, of course.

Below, in the left hand, the first tonal scales of Music, in Liszt's Lied.

The world, or rather the gap, that separates Bach from Liszt is, I think, not as big as it appears.

The purity and desire for God, the solidity of ethics, recognition of one's own faults, following the   example of the greats, the desire to be completed by those similar, the incredible humility - Liszt   defined himself, despite being the greatest pianist in history, as "*king of the smallest* " (I have not heard that often from current day pianists)-, the artistic fertility, the influence, the generosity, the confidence in the Judgment of God, the desire to serve others, the love of transcriptions, such as those of Vivaldi, Wagner and Verdi, for example, turning them into being brothers rather than antagonistic artists, or into a favourite son, if you like…

Of course, there are differences, particularly in the sensuality, but they are rather the reflection of a different epoch rather than a fundamental artistic dissimilarity.

Besides, Bach was exceptionally sensitive to *changes in tonality*. The Fugue in B minor of the First Volume, where the twelve tonalities are examined, is a perfect example. This aesthetic point fascinated Liszt.

First, we must *wonder* what would have become of the Western Music without his unconditional support for this *temperate system*. Bach was in fact the first to feel, through this tempered and tonal division, the colour of each harmony, what made it special; its personality, its resonance and vibration. Look at the *brilliance* of his D major, for example, in the Preludes of the two books. Or look at the *obscurity* of his B-flat minor, a funeral tonality for Chopin. It would be difficult to wish for anything more *stunning* for his epoch than the Prelude in D of the Second Volume.

Liszt is, at the same time, a multifaceted artist, even if there is a good deal about his work that is still not well understood. He is not just the rutilant artist, but also a composer of religious music, which is almost more important than that written for the piano (except for the Sonata in B minor and his other major works). The public does not yet know his great Oratorios and Masses: what we have been *sold* is the image of the composer of the Hungarian Rhapsodies, also magnificent. Although they are not comparable with the later philosophical Beethoven Sonatas, of course, but they can be compared with his Polonaises, Fantasies, Rondeaux or Preludes, for example. We find that even Beethoven is also capable of *slipping* into the popular world.

The so-called *serious* side of Liszt has not yet been thoroughly examined by either Musicology or Aesthetics. The intellectual dishonesty of men means that History constantly creates *misunderstandings.*

I will have the opportunity later to return to Liszt, because any pianist in love with Beauty could not do without him, creator of a harmonic reference, a halo, poetry and a resonance absolutely unknown and non-existent before his time.

Could a piano *sound* any better, for example, in *"Les jeux d'eaux à la Villa d'Este"* or in the *"Petrarch's Sonnets"*, as a *singing* instrument?

We are in the world of *Ondine* or of *Une Barque sur l'océan* of Ravel, where beauty, sensuality, virtuosity, ecstasy, sound idealism and the unreal coexist. For me, Liszt is rather like the Leonardo of Music, because he too thought that *"nothing is finished, but everything is incomplete; someone else must finish what I have only begun"*. Art for Liszt is *a becoming* and not a definitive work.

But let us return to Bach.

God is his inspiration and it is through Him that Music is transmitted to man here on Earth. *This power of the ascension of the work* must be *felt*, because it was written *to glorify the Lord* and not for *the instrumental virtuosity of men.*

The innocent discussion that consists of knowing whether these works can be played on the piano or not shows the failure to understand the wishes of Bach himself, because limiting the Preludes and Fugues to the clavichord were to him *a restriction*. He left *the choice of the type of keyboard to use* up to the performer. Again, this is proof of his intelligence.

The piano is, by nature, a keyboard instrument. The interpretation of the Preludes and Fugues on the piano seems to me perfectly legitimate. Amen.

The French and Italian influence is remarkable on his work. It is moving to note how Bach was able to assimilate them with his Germanic temperament. However, care must be taken *not to exceed* the necessary dose of ornamentation, because the beauty of this Music lies in *its actual line of Bach* and not in *our makeup*. Practicing Bach appeals to our intelligence quite remarkably: nothing can be played without the mind, organization, science, symbol, controlled passion, mathematics and without the right dose of *rubato* (based far more on dynamics than on a rhythmic deformation), without the comprehending the text as *volume and relationship of spaces*. And in particular, nothing can be played without religiosity.

This *whole* is organized like the vital functions of the human body: nothing exists *in general*. Nothing exists if it is *not explained*. *Everything* has a Cause and, therefore, an Effect.

2 – The Fugue: or the art of perfection Analysis of the Fugue in C minor of Book I

Claudio Arrau defended rightly that the practicing of the Fugue was important for the musical brain of the pianist: either this organization would strengthen his memory *forever* or leave it feeble and less able to perform because of the lack of discipline and control. Reasoned study of a Fugue will, therefore, be an essential task in teaching Music, although there are different ways of learning it, of course, some of them good and others bad.

The work and practice of separate voices, and not of separate hands, are fundamental. I am against the *harmonic* sight-reading, if we can call it this, of a fugue as a learning system, particularly *when one reads the whole without any idea of the counterpoint*, as if it were the first movement of a sonata. The *harmonic* analysis of a fugue is something else, as we shall see below.

I am against studying with the hands separated, effective for the harmonic system. It would assume here negligence in the ordination of the voices.

I am also against the system that consists of playing one voice and singing the other. Let us leave the singing for the singers and keep the piano for the pianists. The fact of *singing with one's voice* prevents the ear from controlling the tiny defects in imbalanced sound.

However, I have a method for the *rational* learning of a Fugue. This is not an exhaustive description, but it does give an idea of the work to be accomplished.

For reasons of space and clarity we will examine the Fugue in C minor of Book I, because it is *simple* and lends itself admirably to this purpose.

For convenience, I will give the analysis done by my friend and colleague Warren Thomson, a distinguished Australian pianist, Director of the Sydney Conservatorium of Music and Artistic Director of the Sydney International Piano Competition, in his excellent edition of Bach's Preludes and Fugues. I praise his unadulterated edition, with a comparison of copies of original texts incorporated, the facsimiles, the history of the work in question, avoiding the fingerings so as not to influence the phrasing. His analysis of each Prelude and each Fugue is done separately.

It is a dual pleasure to see the text of Thomson *laid bare*, complete, and to compare it directly with the text of Bach, without going through the convoluted, false comments of editors and revisers who in their wisdom always give the originals, which is doubtful! Here is an edition produced by a great musician with no intention of imposing on others views in which reality *exceeds fiction.*

Here I borrowed part of this analysis with his permission and friendly approval.

Fugue in C minor, Book I

Thomson explains, "*This is a tonal Fugue, and in the Answer the fourth note is changed. It is a merging of French and Italian styles, done in a light-hearted way*".

Exposition: Subject in Alto. Bars 1, 2 in C minor.

Bar 3 in G minor with Answer (tonal) in the Soprano. Countersubject in Alto.

Bars 4 and 5, in C minor, *Codetta.*

Bars 7 and 8: Subject in the Bass, in C minor. Countersubject in the Soprano.

Section of development, modulations: bars 9 to 26. Modulations towards F minor, B-flat and E-flat major.

Use of part of the Subject: the head of the theme, imitated between the Soprano and Alto. Countersubject in the Bass.

Bar 11: Subject in the Soprano, Countersubject in the Bass.

Bars 13 and 14: material from the Countersubject in the Soprano. Bar 15: Subject in the Alto, Countersubject in the Soprano.

Bars 17, 18 and 19: episodes with material of the Subject in the Soprano and the Bass. Countersubject inverted in the Alto.

Bars 20 and 21: Subject in the Soprano, Countersubject in the Alto. Bars 22, 23: imitations between the Soprano and the Alto with material from the theme, Countersubject in the Bass.

Bars 25 and 26: progressions towards the Recapitulation. Recapitulation: bar 26 to the end.

Bar 26: Subject in the Bass, Countersubject in the Alto and in the Soprano.

Bar 29: Tonic pedal and *Coda*, Subject in the Soprano. Bar 32: *Tierce de Picardie.*

First, thoroughly analyse the Fugue without the instrument, and then decide the fingering for each note.

The fingering should be chosen depending on the decided phrasing (errors from improvisation of fingering must be avoided because in the final execution of a fugue they cost dearly). Then *each voice must be fully transcribed, if possible, in different coloured inks.*

Lastly, the fugue *must be copied in its entirety maintaining these selected colours for each voice as this will show up the autonomous voices just as motorways are highlighted on roadmaps.*

The construction of the Fugue must be built up carefully in all   its details, even the tiniest ones. Having done this, you begin the study of *each voice* separately just as if you were studying the part of the violin, the viola or the cello.

In this work of studying the separate voices, respect for the final fingerings is essential, and I repeat this readily, so as not to create bad habits by mentally recording negligent fingerings. This is why it is imperative not to learn the work within a harmonic system, as *this is a disorder to be avoided* at the risk of producing a disastrous cacophony. You cannot play a Beethoven Trio if each instrument does not thoroughly understand its part.

What could be simpler than practicing *two instruments at a   time*
for pleasure? You should play:
The alto and the soprano. The alto and the bass.
The bass and the soprano.
And this is done by heart and following the respective instruments. It is only at this moment that *all the voices should be brought together.*

So, we could say that we have studied the Fugue to our full capacity and not by *reading* it more or less successfully.
This little scheme gives an idea of the *complete function of a Fugue as a mental discipline.*
This in no way removes the musical pleasure from the point of view of expression, because without order Music would be chaos.

3 – The 48 Perfections of Johann Sebastian Bach or the art of drawing closer to God

Now, with a few words on each Prelude and Fugue, classified according to the families of tonalities, as in the order established by Bach, we are going to broach a number of issues.
This is of course a personal view: the aim is to transfer, to suggest *to pupils a vision* and to inspire *a reaction* from them, without wishing to impose my artistic views on them.
And I repeat, the lines that follow aim principally to encourage personal conception, stimulate ideas and to develop the principle that each artist is unique and different.

Comments on the "48"

3.1 – Preludes and Fugues in C major

Both in choral form, these preludes do, however, differ greatly from one another: that of Book I, without doubt Bach's best-known Prelude, is arranged according to specific registers. Although simple in appearance, it does explore some daring harmonic regions without the slightest ornamentation and in an *immobile movement* based on broken chords of three and four notes.
In his serenity, Bach is capable of achieving cosmic order. Chopin no doubt thought of him when composing his first Etude Op.10, giving it an extension of four octaves. It is particularly wonderful to see how the simplest lines get far closer to the truth. It is a moment of *supreme order.*

That of Book II, written in *expressive* style like a *toccata*, forms a magnificent four-part choral ensemble: it is a quartet of sages recounting the absolute truth.
The whole is serious but fluid. The balance is superb. The dynamics impose themselves

because everything develops in the most logical way. Towards the end, the demisemiquavers return to calm; *the whole remains impassible.*

The Fugue in Book I, for four voices, is a masterpiece in counterpoint: very *legato* and complicated, it is written in a continuous *stretto.*
Drawn, extended, as difficult for the memory as for expression and very austere, the parsimony in *divertimenti* allows Bach to go to the essential. The Fugue ends acutely, perhaps symbolically to show the intention of the ascending path towards God.

That of Book II is jovial and sparkling; good humour enlivens it. Its appearance is almost *virtuoso* and brilliant; its three voices are in contrast to the severity of the Prelude. It is *a sparkling festive occasion.* The bass notes towards the end give it a joyful air and they should be emphasized; here you need to spring and bound joyfully.

3.2 - Preludes and Fugues in C minor

The Prelude in Book I is authoritarian and serious: a comparison with a virtuosistic *toccata* is too easy.
In the definitive version (because there is another one), Bach added the central *Presto,* in the character of a brilliant improvisation. *The march is implacable, relentless.* The *Adagio* is reminiscent of certain passages from the Chromatic Fantasy. After this *Adagio* the return to the *Allegro* is more sapient and less agitated. Everything seems to return to a more serene climate.

That of Book II brings to mind an Invention for two voices and sometimes adopts the expressive arabesques of an *Allemande.* It could also be the expressive *Courante* in the Second French Suite, for example. More thoughtful in nature, but without ever losing its elegance, it *does not seek out the impact, but the pure line*, with no rush.

The Fugue in Book I is an amalgam of French and Italian styles, in three voices, as seen in the analysis. Its carefree development, almost positive for a minor tonality, is *charmingly logical.* Everything seems to flow, untrammelled. The octave pedal is not that of the organ, but a gentle point of support for a Fugue that consumes itself.

The Fugue in Book II on the other hand it *is a model of religiosity*: it develops in three voices, apart from the central part where it develops in four. It reveals its contained, piercing suffering. *There is a continuous tension throughout.*
The metric changes of the theme are magnificent in bar eight. The *Coda* gives the left-hand painful *stretti*, almost desolate. Its theme was announced in the Prelude.

3.3 - Preludes and Fugues in C-sharp major

The Prelude of Book I is luminous, meridional and light. The grace of its central part knows no limits. The broken chords hint hidden melodies, like bringers of glad tidings. Even *its virtuosity is dissimulated because it is so light.* The alternation with the left-hand is absolutely delicious. This prelude is reminiscent of *a spring* spouting out of the earth.

Written in two parts, the Prelude of Book II is far *more contained and severe*. The suspensions of its syncopations make for an *expressive and poetic* programme. They do not really bring light and its second part, an *Allegro*, sinks into a grave register. It contrasts tremendously with the Fugue.

The Fugue in Book I, for three voices, is elegant, relaxed and suggestive. From a distance it resembles an odd *Minuetto*, although in common time, because of *its character of dance*, not because of its form. The themes are presented delicately and seem to be danced by fairies. Its pirouettes are distinguished and suggest high flying *gallantry*.

In three voices, that of Book II is, contrary to its Prelude, *piquante* and spirited, with the airs of a *Gavotte*. Its *shorter values are full of optimism and caprice* and the fast movements at the end, like the descending arrows of scales, suggest that this cheerful idea, of a *brilliant finale*, is just right. *You could compare this to a carefree, versatile little girl* who is also full of charm.

3.4 - Preludes and Fugues in C-sharp minor

The Prelude of Book I leads to *regions that are sublime, resigned, pious and suffering.*
A true perpetual motion develops within contained calm giving a glimpse of a *hidden, but fervent, passion*. Any sentimental interpretation would give a false idea of the meditation that infuses this magnificent work. Its expression is *sublime, contained and introverted.* Care must be taken to maintain a discourse that is equal, profound and full of hope. This is the really great Bach.

The character of the Prelude of Book II is also austere, but livelier than that of Book I. *Its ornamentation is rich and part of the melodic line*. The movement is almost pastoral, and Bach takes pleasure in developing its themes in a rounded way. The three parts each speak their role in turn, independently. Chopin was particularly fond of this Prelude. You can almost feel the echoes in the second part of the Trio of the Scherzo in B minor, in its ornamented arabesques.

The very long Fugue of Book I, for five voices, is rich and complicated, with two countersubjects and triple counterpoint, reminiscent of *a religious meditation on a tremendous grief.* The movements in quavers *spread an idea of desolation.* You get the feeling that you are *watching an immobile procession.*
It has seduced many musicians and pianists. There is magic in this pain, almost spiritual regeneration and true purification. It is one of the most sublime moments of the "Well-Tempered Clavier" as a whole.

That of Book II, for three voices, is almost a *Gigue* in its rapid character. Its *control is difficult, its turns brusque and its pirouettes sharp.* However, it is very convincing and efficient because its power is very effective. Nothing seems to stop it, like a *perpetuum mobile* that will only find its solution at the end.

3.5 - Preludes and Fugues in D major

The Prelude of Book I is a *diabolical divertimento* that is very difficult to play: its *cabrioles would later inspire Chopin* in his Etude Op. 10 No. 8, in seeking the axes. Those of Chopin move through the keyboard, contrary to those of Bach that remain almost motionless. The formulae are the axes 2-3-4: it is like a distant comparison between the preludes in C major and the First Etude. The left hand seems to play an eternal *pizzicato*. A few bars later, an imitation, preceded by a pedal note, makes the passage riskier. A brief and very brilliant final scale and *arpeggiato* chords animate everyone.

The Prelude of Book II, a true masterpiece, could serve as a Prelude to a great Partita, to the Fourth in this case. It is written in the form of a Sonata in two sections. The play between the imitative artifices of the motifs is absolutely incredible. You can breathe the health, the athletic strength: *it is like a superb firework display, a musical waterfall*, in which the steadiness of the musical discourse, its Word, leads us into the realm of the splendid. *A major articulation is welcome* in order to give this page all its splendour and brilliance.

Sometimes reminiscent of the French Overture, the majestic Fugue of Book I is imperious and in four voices. There is often a temptation to overload the sonority and *to double* the bass notes at the end, but this would be a mistake because it is not music for the organ. Care must be taken to avoid an interpretation *less severe and more romantic* in the episodes for the soprano in bars 9 and 10 and the same in the bass, in bars 17, 18 and 19. The voices with the themes, on the other hand, very severely articulated. *The magnificence of this Fugue leaves one speechless, its movement is grandiose.*

The Fugue of Book II is serene and in four voices; it is full of *stretti*. In *its deeply calm procession*, it sometimes resembles a chorus. The counterweight made against the activity of the Prelude is remarkable. The fugue is *Olympian*, and nothing seems to detract it from its peaceful, but profound, destiny.

3.6 - Preludes and Fugues in D minor

There is a vague resemblance between *the natures* of the two Preludes. The attachment to the character of the D minor and its general atmosphere is almost the same in both cases.

That in Book I, in its technique of chords in broken arpeggios, transmits a slight sadness. You must discreetly sing the lower line when it no longer provides *the accompaniment*, for example, in the sixth bar and those similar. It is wonderful to see how Bach combines certain *descending and ascending* aspects of the theme. It is reminiscent of Greek lines. The addition of a third voice at the end is masterly.

The Prelude in Book II is a work of inversions, suspensions and additions in the melodic cells of more *cantabile* elements. The *pedal* passages are important: a rhythm of steel must be maintained, and the *intention* of the principal note prolonged. The Prelude dies away in the last notes.

The Fugue in Book I is for three voices. It is sage and not too agitated. Bach often uses *stretti*. His countersubject is *expressive and well developed*. Episodes derive from this. The trills are not easy, particularly for the synchrony of the longer ones. However, they should be measured and incorporated into the general discourse.

The Fugue of Book II is in complete contrast, starting with its theme: *the triplets are turbulent and the scale extremely expressive and almost painful.* This is a Fugue for three voices. Its countersubject is also *agitato*. There is no sensation of tranquillity throughout. It tries to settle down, but the climate remains unstable.

3.7 - Preludes and Fugues in E-flat major

The Prelude of Book I is probably the *oddest* in the series. Apart from its beginning that takes the form of a *fantasy*, it is more reminiscent of a *double fugue*, serious and severe, than a Prelude. This is a very particular point in this Book I, because you get the impression of playing *two fugues* in E-flat. It has to be dealt with in *pure polyphony, without the slightest concession.* However, the form is very original and is almost close to choral music for the organ. It is immensely beautiful.

That of Book II *is a spring of water and flows in a sublime moment of goodness.* It could even encompass St John the Baptist. Without the slightest impediment, like benediction, this Prelude fascinated Chopin in the perfection of its lines: *it is almost an Impromptu and* is quite marvellous. The lightness of its little ascending scale at the end is a delight, as is the descending passage that ends the work. You need almost to smile to play it, *infused as it is with an extreme abnegation.*

The Fugue in Book I, for three voices, is *sparkling*. It is very active, eloquent and optimistic, and *good humour contradicts the severity of its Prelude*. Busoni wanted to play the Fugue of Book II with the Prelude of Book I, much closer in nature. With all my respect for such a great musician, I do not agree with him because it is this grandiose dimension that the fugue brings to *its* Prelude which seems to me to be the interesting thing.

Serious, the Fugue of Book II spreads into four voices. It is highly ordered and is a masterpiece in Counterpoint. Even when it is not *sonore*, you get the impression that *something transcendental* is about to be revealed. You must not hustle it but rather find *the lines* in order to oppose its vertical dimension. One should seek the proper *tempo giusto*.

3.8 - Preludes and Fugues in E-flat minor and in D-sharp minor What is there left to say?

We stand before one of Bach's *greatest moments. This Prelude from Book I touches on the unbelievable. The analysis makes almost no sense and is useless for such a visionary work that announces the tragedies of the Music to come.*

Written in pure French style, in an Aria sustained by arpeggiated chords, this Prelude expresses what we might call the pure suffering of Music; its movements can be compared to a violin legato, or better still, to the voice of a man facing his destiny, conversing with God.

And there is no need to describe such a miracle as *you can hear the divine rapport*. Silence proves to be the most talkative.

The Prelude in D-sharp minor, in Book II, written in the enharmonic equivalent, it is vast and long. It is one of the more complexes of all the "48". Almost an Invention in two voices, it sometimes *seems simple*, but only in appearance. It is difficult for the precision. It is very similar to its brother in A minor of the same Book and includes similar figures. The work of *denudation* is intense as it involves a *pure conversation* between superior minds.

The Fugue of Book I is also written in D sharp minor and is in three voices. Its development is exemplary: its *stretti*, augmentations, inversions, and a thousand and one artifices of counterpoint made it adorable to Chopin, Liszt and Wagner. With such references, there is little else to say.

It is one of the most *complete* in the whole collection. The *fluidity, religiosity and almost the repentance of man*, are all very clearly present. In all of Bach's work, this fugue is one of the most beautiful moments, together with *its* Prelude.

The Fugue in Book II, in four voices, *is very solemn*. Bach speaks frugally, unhurried. Calm, he knows precisely where he is going. This is a difficult Fugue for the memory and is a test of concentration and contained beauty. It is not at all sophisticated. It is *economic* and does not do too much. It is a fine theme, a beautiful Fugue and a sublime moment of music.

3.9 - Preludes and Fugues in E major

The Prelude in Book I is a true Pastorale. It is elegant, light, fluid, fine and without wrinkles. Conceived as if being part of the French Suites, its voices are pure, *and transparency is its most outstanding element*. The ease of the semiquavers is superb: they roll like pearls on marble.

That of Book II is entirely imitation. In its central part, the bass becomes more independent. *Although flowing, it is relatively well detailed* and above all it should not be hustled. It has its own logic. It is fluid and beautiful. Interestingly, Bach places this Prelude and Fugue at the end of his manuscript.

The Fugue of Book I is active, in three voices and there is not a single moment of rest in its semiquavers. It seems to flow in a flash. *Brilliance and decision* are the order of the day. Its difficulty should not be underestimated as the slightest lapse is indefensible.

That in Book II is completely static. Written in four parts, it caused Neuhaus to say
"With it you are witnessing the creation of the world". There is not the least sign of virtuosity:

the whole is calm and Olympian. Its major elements are its logic, precision and interiority. It is rather like a chorus, a *cantata* movement or almost a *Motet*. Very far from a piano demonstration, it is quite simply pure. It has to be *comprehended* rather than played.

3.10 - Preludes and Fugues in E minor

The Prelude of Book I is an Italian *aria;* it is sustained by a monochord movement in the left hand. The theme develops thanks to the right hand, in the soprano, *with pure beauty and in an uninterrupted breath.* The ornamentation is rich in trills that show how Bach wanted, with his own divisions in the figures of short values, a cadence, if not strict at least in good order. Later he incorporates a *Presto* section into this Aria, where the melody halts and the monochromy of the left-hand awakes in animated movements that shall serve the development of the Fugue.

That in Book II is a very long Invention in two voices. You could say it had been inspired by the Sixth Little Prelude of the same tonality. *Its pace is serene, restrained, with no agitation and no cries.* Prolonged trills, whether for the left or right hand, contradict moderate movements. Here there is a climate of serene beauty.

The Fugue of Book I is the only one in two voices out of all "the 48". This is more like a *Fughetta.* Its subject appears to arise out of the development of the Presto of the Prelude. *It is sparkling, articulated and animated.*
The writing is virtuosistic, as if Bach had thrown himself into a *little demonstration* just for his pupil, *as if he had improvised* in the magic of the moment. It is a brief, delicious moment, full of good humour and sometimes rhythmically malicious, as in the descending scales where you need to avoid drifting into another metrical division.

The Fugue of Book II, in three voices, *is rhythmically far more sought.* Its meter is not simple particularly since it is 2/2 and not in 4. It is a high voltage rhythmic exercise, and not at all evident. Its theme, extremely long, demands considerable mastery. It is   a rare moment in "the 48", because it is a much-worked Bach, sometimes *baroque.* It is difficult to discover anything natural in the discourse hidden in this strange rhythm. But it is there.

3.11 - Preludes and Fugues in F major

The Prelude of Book I is a charming Invention in two voices, with long supporting trills, in the most perfect style of a brilliant school exercise. Its *limpid beauty, transparency and even candour,* make this Prelude a charming *musical moment* for its grace, light virtuosity and enchantment. The perfect technical equality is not evident. It is not as easy as it looks.

That of Book II is an extremely developed Prelude. Far more melodic than its *brother* in the other Book, it has a remarkable polyphony, often in five voices. The whole resembles *circular,* without end, because the cadence *is not an end here, but the   start of something else.* The forms are more ambitious than those of *a simple Prelude.* Its major quality is the transparency of its polyphony, in view of the complexity of its counterpoint as well as its *smooth flowing savoir-faire* and absence of any hindrance.

The little Fugue in three voices in Book I *is a true dance.* Its whole composition is carefree: it is light, without major ambitions, but attractive in its good humour and delicacy. No ulterior motives are necessary to make it authentic.

That of Book II is a Gigue, the themes of which are sometimes interrupted. It is one of the least severe Fugues of the "48", but very difficult. *Its cabrioles pose many problems;* its construction should not be overlooked in view of its hybrid nature. The long pedals in the bass make it even more impish and mischievous. It is a brilliant moment that shows us a smiling, optimistic Bach.

3.12 - Preludes and Fugues in F minor

We come back into another of these severe and solemn moments in the "48". The Prelude of Book I *is an aching, languishing lament.* An expressive polyphony runs through it and makes the *quartet* obscure and difficult to deliver.

It comes from one of the exercise books for his children, in this case Wilhelm Friedemann, but the transformation brought about by in the definitive version makes it a true *masterpiece.* It is a burdensome music that sometimes seems to make no progress. We must respect this *march* despite it indicates a certain *fatigue* in its accomplishment.

That of Book II is a *moment musical* rather than a Prelude, and it is interior and scorning the least pianistic *effect.* The naive passage with the semiquavers is moving in its sadness, or rather in its melancholy. Moments of extreme delicacy are appreciated. It follows a clear, pure line, like a true *prelude* to something. It vanishes in a cadence of quavers (and not crotchets) as though *afraid of remaining.*

The Fugue in Book I *is a moment of anguish in its chromatic and suffering theme.* Its development is so important that you ask yourself where Bach may arrive. The laments indicated are already presented in the theme itself, which is difficult to express. *The climate rarely calms down* and the pain, sadness and solemnity will not easily leave this disturbing Fugue.

That of Book II is far lighter. Its character is more that of a dance and its homophony sometimes surprising. We might believe, particularly considering its Prelude, that this page might have served as a *movement* in the *Sonata form* of the age. Whatever the case, *the charm, warmth and spiritedness* of the work, as well as its simplicity, make it an *unpretentious, agreeable musical moment.*

3.13 - Preludes and Fugues in F-sharp major

The principal qualities of the Prelude in Book I are elegance and delicacy. This is a true *Pastorale*, which is quite exquisite and fluid. *She*, rather than him, spreads like an Invention in two voices: its development is so simple that it encompasses the miracle of *pure line*. I am ever tempted to say that Raphael in person *assisted* Bach in its design. You get the impression of looking at one of his Madonnas. Its execution should *be linear, pure and without the least exhilaration.*

That of Book II is also in two voices but is far more complex and ornamented: *its style resembles more French lines*, or perhaps those of the Overture. It has a double theme, one being melodic and the other in the purest counterpoint. At the close, in its cadence, it becomes more *harmonical. Its execution should be fluid*, without any exaggeration in the tempo. *The wonder of it is revealed in its melodic arabesques* incorporated into a line without breaks

The Fugue of Book I *is charming, delicate and full of disarming purity*. Its three voices follow one another and intersect in sheer delight, without drama. Its episodes with *articulation in two notes* are delightful in their expressive logic. One listens with a smile of disbelief. Thank you, dear Bach.

That of Book II is, on the other hand, far more complicated: its execution is less easy and *more controversial*. Its character is also more *interrupted*, the ornament introducing the theme being already a surprise. A *more sprightly* movement would be welcome. However, its three voices are a very clear even as we pass from one surprise to another and remain in awe of Bach deploying his *savoir-faire*.

3.14 - Preludes and Fugues in F-sharp minor

Severity is the main characteristic of the Prelude in Book I: its non-indulgent imitations make us imagine immediately a religious fugue. Despite its style of *Invention*, the implacable logic of its movement does not permit us the slightest *coquetry*. The tempo must be *lordly, concerned and contained*. We do not feel so much that we are *playing but introducing a subject on which to reflect*; it shows us the stoical side of Bach.

With the Prelude of Book II, we open, once again, the gateway to the sublime: the suffering of the theme gives us a glimpse of Bach's Passions, heartrending and begging God. It is obviously one of the great moments in his work and an absolute masterpiece. Its three voices dispute *the beauty and the piercing moments of sadness*. A painful pause becomes one of the most disturbing interrogations: the little passage that comes back into the theme is worth more than a thousand explanations and a thousand pages of other music. *The rubato here is strictly banned*. It would be *obscene* in such a moment of truth.
The forces must come from within, from the acceptance of destiny and the most accomplished spiritual starkness: we must thank God, and Bach, for giving us the privilege of taking part in such a communion.

Einstein described the Fugue of Book I as "*his most beautiful equation*". It is in four voices, *austere and solemn*. Nothing seems to hinder its steady progress and its implacable logic: it is one of the most perfect of the "48". Its inversion in the contralto, from bar 20 on, is inserted masterly, without affecting the religious line that guides it. The same feeling is felt in the bass, in bar 32. The greatest economy is required for its interpretation: no sign of *divertimento* but rather an *unwavering expression and inescapable character* are to be desired.

That of Book II is one of the highlights of the "48" and the only triple fugue in the whole series: one might say a *crucifixion.* It is, perhaps, the link between the "48" and "the Art of the Fugue": the combination of the three themes reveals Bach's art in all its splendour. The episode of the semiquavers seems to give movement to the themes less inclined to move, *and more likely to remain in a state of suffering*. Its execution, like that of the Prelude that precedes it, should be *elevated, sublime and inspired*.

3.15 - Preludes and Fugues in G major

The Prelude of Book I is a model of virtuosity and lightness, alternating between fixed and displaced positions. It is constructed like a *toccata* in Italian style. It is illuminated by a constant smile. There is light throughout. Undeniably, *sunshine illuminates it throughout its development*. It is sparkling, *radiant and radiating* Bach. Supreme control of digital technique is required.

That of Book II is less brilliant and more based on pedal notes. You cannot put too much trust in the *'exercise'* aspect, because although when this is Bach's design, it is more an exercise of mind and not one of form. It's discreet charm and episodes in scales give it a touch of ease and grace.

The Fugue of Book I, in three voices, has *the character of a Gigue: brilliant and full of surprises*. Inversions are the order of the day and a dazzling execution is desirable. It is written similar to that of the English Suite in D. Bach uses the artifices of counterpoint to a glittering effect. It closes by calming which is enough to charm us.

That of Book II is also in three voices. There is a family resemblance between this Fugue and the Prelude of Book I, which could prove Busoni *to be right*. The work on the arpeggio is remarkable. *An almost staccato character gives it a carefree air*. The scale running through it at bar 62 is a surprise and only accentuates its joyful, coquettish character. This scale finds its delicious match in the penultimate bar. This is almost a lordly wink.

3.16 - Preludes and Fugues in G minor

The serious nature of the Prelude in Book I brings to mind *something important*, perhaps a Symphony or an Overture in Italian style. There is a vague impression of choral with the pedal trills and a sensation of *non-movement* sets in quickly. Imitations, more emotive than real, are presented in all voices, giving an idea of *culmination*. Any romanticism is to be regretted. Dignity must prevail in executing this magnificent page.

That of Book II is a Largo. Bach *himself demanded it*. It is incredibly beautiful: you could say a phenomenal development of that in Book I. A dignified march, both imposing and grave develops in a rhythm that at the least is obsessive. There is harmonic economy. It gives the impression of *emotional stability and almost monochromy*. This is a *severe, austere, inflexible* and almost authoritarian Bach. *Sure* of his subject, nothing detracts him from his route.

The Fugue of Book I is a remarkable composition, considering that it is in Bach's *early style*. Its very brief subject is composed with *incredibly* very little material. Bach achieves a *triple stretto that almost plunges into emotivism*, but the whole remains more severe.

That of Book II is interrupted by pauses in its subject. Repeated notes give it an air of spiritual condensation with identical sonorities. Despite that, Bach manages to create *an atmosphere of movement*. The work is difficult to play both technically and psychologically, because it is not as *rich* as those similar to it from the point of view of musical material. The march in thirds is proof of this. The meeting of chords in bar 73 breaks slightly the *stoical climate* of this strange, but extremely seductive, work.

3.17 - Preludes and Fugues in A-flat major

A sonorous, proud nature, like the sound of bells, gives the remarkable, bursting Prelude of Book I the qualities of a revelation. It is written in two parts; the second, in its development, becomes more *expressive* with its constant movements. An air of *proud dance* emerges which in some way recalls Italian dances. The motif is in different ways illuminated more than developed, but at bar 35 the calm returns and the figures become more benevolent.

The Prelude of Book II is more ample and difficult to hold. It is rich in rhythmic variations (at least four) and demands well-founded assurance in its execution. *Its motifs are fluid, almost in the form of melodic arabesques.* It is also a serious *moment musical* but with hints of considerable sensibility. A *lucid* air comes through. The whole seems ordered by a superior mind, which is indeed the case!

The Fugue of Book I is *deeply introspective*. In four voices, it seems to close up in its intervals, which inspired Beethoven for his first Fugue of Sonata Op. 110. A climate far more serene than that of its Prelude allows it to unfold with *parsimony and tranquillity*. Its beauty resembles a delicate goddess. Its inversions are expressed with more *peace*, calm and pacifism than its Prelude. Its *nobility and elegance* are unshakable.

That of Book II presents inverted intervals in relation to that of Book I, but its theme is far more ample, more developed and better spaced out. Its countersubject is different in that it is chromatic, but its *tempi*, on the other hand, are almost the same. Written in four voices, it is a transcription of an earlier Fugue written in F major. It seems that it existed with its Prelude in this tonality. It is more in harmony with its Prelude than its sister in Book I. It is also a *confident, poised and peaceable goddess*.

3.18 - Preludes and Fugues in G-sharp minor

The Prelude of Book I opens the doors to two magnificent works in both Books. Its character is impregnated with *a certain sadness or at least with a deep melancholy*. It is written in three strict voices, in the style of a Symphony. There is not a single bar without the motif: all its possibilities are examined. To complement the first, a second motif is associated with it, as a countersubject, and it becomes very *cantabile* in the second section. The tonality of G-Sharp Minor acquires its disenchanted colour that is found again in the Fugue.

The Prelude of Book II is equally *flowing, but in a different manner:* it is extensive and deploys a vision in its form that is at the least astonishing. A mix of Prelude and Sonata for his children Christian and Carl Philippe, almost a demonstration of Alberti bass, reveal Bach in a moment of grace. It is *sensitive, gracious and distinguished*. Its ornamentation is discreet and aristocratic.

The Fugue in Book I *is serious and suffering*. Its chords, more than its voices, in bars 8, 9 and 10, *suggest premonition and the unexpected*. Contrary to the formally severe style of a Fugue, they determine a kind of more anguished phrasing. It is the right character for this extraordinary work: *there is a condensation of despondency, almost a depression* that classes it among the finest in the series.

That of Book II, on the other hand, is more fluid and lends itself to different interpretations of its *tempo*: it can either be played fast, it is then not in sharp contrast to the Prelude, or contained, and in this case it is *almost like a trio of woodwind instruments*. I tend to prefer this second interpretation because it is precisely in this slight contrast that it finds its unique beauty in completing its Prelude. Whether fast or slow, it remains no less *a spring that flows endlessly*.

3.19 - Preludes and Fugues in A major

The main characteristic of the Prelude of Book I, a superb miniature, is its resemblance to a fugue. There is no doubt that it could be included in the series of Symphonies in three voices. The true devices of counterpoint used by Bach are all quite simply masterly. You might say that it is a mind game cultivated in *triple*, following the laws of its combinations. *It is full of grace and malleability*.

The distinctive sign of the superb Prelude of Book II is that of *a magnificent Pastorale. A fortunate source,* it bears the mark of its brother the Prelude in the E-flat of the same Book, nothing disturbs *this caress* to the ear, the fingers and the mind. Constructed as a Symphony in three voices, *a supreme fluidity guides it as well as a celestial delicacy*.

The Fugue of Book I, in three voices, is *spiritual and sometimes brilliant*. Its theme bears a succession of fourths, as in the Beethoven Fugues of Op. 110, but more relaxed in character.

It is not at all easy *because its turns of phrase are often unforeseen*. Bach makes no real recapitulations. The end is more of a hint of a non-accomplished return.

The little Fugue of Book II is a transformation of the theme of the Prelude, but rhythmically enriched. In three voices, it also seems to be an invention in three parts. Marked by its *very brilliant* character, *any heaviness is absolutely out of the question.*

3.20 - Preludes and Fugues in A minor

This Prelude of Book I gives the *impression* of being infused with *tranquillity*. Despite its prolonged chords, its development is almost always in two voices. The sporadic episodes in three parts only go to anticipate the more organ-like nature of the Fugue.   It does not try to be complicated and moves frugally, without much bother.

That of Book II, written in two voices, *is a masterpiece in counterpoint and gradual tension*. It is constructed in two parts: *that of the development achieved with extraordinary apprehensions* if we consider the economy of the means used. The chromatism of the counterpoint presages disquietude. The alternation is magnificent. Possibilities of colour are presented throughout; although to abuse this would be to contradict the spirit of Bach, more centred on relationships and volumes.

The Fugue of Book I is a didactic exercise of the first order. Here Bach makes *thorough use* of all possibilities and devices of form and counterpoint. You could say that this is a fugue for the organ, in view of the *coda* with its pedal note, the A of the bass, in the form of suspension. It is very long with its 87 bars. Perhaps it is not the most inspired Fugue, but it is no less of a feat to interpret, from the point of view of construction.

That of Book II, in three voices, *is grandiose and almost heroic*. Its imposing, majestic theme reveals a remarkable state of grandeur. It is traversed by great scales that give it *an air of unimagined virtuosity*. Tremendous precision is required to execute his work because *the inner* voices are not easy to perform. The scales   are tainted by true disarray. *The final impression is august and majestic.*

3.21 - Preludes and Fugues in B-flat major

Brilliance is the main characteristic of the tonality of B-flat major, and this in both Books. Just think of the Preludes in D major.

The Prelude of Book I is a model of the slight form of the *toccata* of the 17th century. The rapid Scales, changes in *tempo* not indicated in all editions for the chords, *despite Bach's own writing in one of the manuscripts*, give it an air of *healthy, radiant improvisation.* A great energy emerges from these chords and breaks into these scales. The work demands *fantasy and joy.* Italian inspiration is very clear here.

The Prelude of Book II is in a *pre-Sonata* form, with an exposition, a development and a recapitulation. The extension of the *Coda*, which is decidedly masterful, surprises. The expressive character *is always present,* and Chopin was to take it up in his *rapid melodies.* In view of the importance of this Prelude attention must be paid to the precision of the attacks in two hands, required to preserve a counterpoint as perfect as possible.

The Fugue in Book I *breathes pleasure.* Written in three voices, of Italian inspiration, like its Prelude, it flows like *a fountain and spreads joy. It hovers over the keyboard with enchantment.* The most perfect equality in a *non-legato* is required.

The Fugue in Book II, in three voices, is a veritable *Minuetto.* You could take the risk and interpret it as such, given that Bach himself indicated certain articulations slurring two notes, a fairly rare occurrence for him. *At every second tranquillity emerges* and nothing seems to contradict its logical, smooth progress.

3.22 - Preludes and Fugues in B-flat minor

Now we move into the four sublime moments, true high points   of the "48": The Preludes and Fugues in B-flat minor, which are among Bach's best compositions.

The Prelude of Book I is *an imposing, obscure, heartrending march, full of suffering.* It is in the character of a great choral work. Its *harmonic* richness is impressive. The expression should remain *severe, austere and without the slightest complaisance.*

Each note and each chord seem to be expressed by God. *All the voices participate in this communion* and are part of the solemnity of the moment. The fermatas at the close accentuate the pain that overwhelm this work with grief.

We might consider the Prelude of Book II as one of the greatest compositions for the keyboard composed by Bach but it can   also serve as an example for other instrumentations, for a Trio, for example, because *its sonority and its drama* often exceed the limits of the keyboard.
It is in the form of a Symphony in three voices and extremely developed. *Rigour and severity are in order.* Bach handles all the purest aspects of counterpoint with accomplishment. Its balance is fabulous, just as its continual density. Not a shadow upsets the clarity and *deep transparency* of this sublime moment in the "48".

One could define the Fugue of Book I, in five voices, as the perfect example of a *stretto,* from the point of view of construction. Everything pales before a demonstration of such depth. It could almost be *an immense choral* work that continues the climate of the Prelude and *that leads us into divine spheres*, close to the Lord. The theme is *piercing, just like a lament.* The passage in D-flat major brings a fleeting balm. But the suffering is too close to the theme of the Crucifixion and traces of the Passions are clearly present.

The incredible continues in the Fugue of Book II, in four voices and very expansive. Its execution, although rarely practiced by pianists, *is almost always hailed as a performance,* because its success is not always guaranteed beforehand.

Very accomplished from the point of view of construction, it could be part of the Art of the Fugue, that Bach began precisely at that time. *Majestic without being heavy*, its clarity of construction is radiant. A feeling of *great nobility of spirit* comes over us after its execution.

3.23 - Preludes and Fugues in B major

The delicious Prelude of Book 1 is touching in its simplicity. Calm and serene *it should be played with extreme generosity*. Nothing should strike or trouble its confident development. Written as a very simple Symphony in three voices, it returns constantly   to its theme, in the same style as that of its brother, the Prelude in G-sharp minor, of the same Book. It moves agreeably in all directions, accompanied by a second *motif* of *great gentleness.*

The Prelude of Book II is, *on the other hand, of very moderate virtuosity*. It is based on a *motif* of scales that respect one another's space: they cross very rarely and avoid intermingling. A sort of Alberti bass is also present. Sometimes, it could be called *an exercise in play or work*, almost *an apprenticeship.*
At bar 35, distances of ninths accompany the second motif in the post-Bach classical manner. The idea is healthy. It assumes clarity of mind and an almost pragmatic need for form.

The Fugue of Book I is in four voices. Just like its Prelude it does not seek to upset but rather remains *in a cantabile, serene discretion*. It is fluid and elegant in character. The movements of the scales by contrary or parallel movements are a pleasure. It exudes *amiability, modesty and mellowness*.

Its big sister in Book II is more expansive and also in four voices. A fine set of intervals in minims, at first in thirds, then in sixths and to conclude in crotchets and quavers in a descending scale, add *an amiable but majestic allure* to the theme. It would be difficult to call this work *a double fugue*, although certain secondary *motifs* might suggest this. In the development, the movements of the bass are important and rarely rest. It feels *like a relaxation* after its preceding Prelude.

3.24 - Preludes and Fugues in B minor

The extreme, although strange, beauty of the Prelude of Book I is compensated by the serious nature of the Prelude of Book II, of which the Fugue has coordination problems in the trills; it is not easy to play. However, that of Book I *is extraordinarily visionary.*

The Prelude of Book I is an *Andante, established by Bach,* just like the *Largo* of the Fugue. Written in three voices, two of them - the alto and soprano - talk to one another and complement one another. The bass abstains from this dialogue but moves in a phenomenal counterpoint with remarkable independence. The non-legato on the left is a good counterpart to the legato of the other two voices. The climate is tense, serious and not very loquacious. One feels that Bach is assailed by philosophical and religious preoccupations. He frowns, but the superb sound of the Prelude is like none other.

An *Allegro, determined by Bach*, is the movement of the Prelude of Book II. The *tempo*, in 2/2, *shows some concern as well but is livelier than that of Book I*. It is constructed with an Invention in two voices of grave beauty. The connection of the two voices is remarkable as they continue and intersect one another. A feeling of *starkness* is indispensable, despite the atmosphere that is rather more that of negative lyricism.

In four voices, the Fugue of Book I is, as mentioned above, *visionary*. Bach also established the phrasing in his manuscript. The heart-breaking character of this Fugue is incredible. Bach announced almost one hundred years of harmony. What am I saying? 200 years!

The expressive dissonances are fabulous. Genius flourishes here in a timeless aesthetic-historical panorama, free from the practices of the age. Bach is ahead of his time. The paths engaged by this Fugue are incredible: it deals with the twelve tonalities! Beethoven, Chopin, Liszt, Wagner, Debussy, Schönberg, Stravinsky and Webern are all there, although only in the antechamber.

It is an end *without an end* to Book 1, and *the beginning* of the music of the future. This Fugue *is infinite*. The phrasing of Bach demonstrates a greater vision than mine. He says: "*Fine. Soli Deo Gloria*". Let us leave him with the last word.

Even more brilliant and difficult, that of Book II, in three voices, *has the character of a Gigue*. Its theme sometimes moves in octaves adding a robust nature to this last page. Its development, although not too long, *gives an idea of soundness, exuberance and stability*. There is no manifestation of grandeur at the end but the certainty of a justice of tone.

The end of the "48" is an enigma. In fact, there is no end, *but rather the principle of entry into regions that were once thought to be impenetrable*. Bach leads us towards God, just as Mozart or Beethoven were to do later, but with such a renunciation of himself that he seems to be a divine instrument before whom any musician becomes a true *aspiring* candidate.

The diversity of musical, religious, aesthetic, formal, volumetric, spatial, pastoral, gallant, polyphonic thought, of counterpoint, inspiration and creation obtained by Bach bring more than musical genius to mind; in reality, he is a true apostle led by God to man, not to the Glory of God, *but for our own consolation.*

BOOK III

Part three

*The Etudes of Chopin ... or the « 24 » works of Hercules ...
and the wonders of the world*

On the whole, the Etudes were very much in fashion at the start of the 19th century, that is, at the dawn of the *discovery* of virtuosity, displayed by the great stars of the piano of that time: Mendelssohn, Chopin, Liszt, Thalberg, Clara Schumann, Hiller, the young Brahms, and others.

The new *humanist* position of musical aesthetics that centres of the artist at the heart of the problem needed virtuosos to fill the music halls, more and more concerts focused on a *soloist*, keyboard legends in fashion, romantic shocks of hair and fingers faster than those of the old masters unable to play three notes in a row.

Clementi and Czerny approached the problem by creating a whole literature that was dry and musically deplorable, boring and without any vision of how piano technique would eventually evolve. It was, and still *is, a source of martyrdom* for whole generations, a repetition of old formulas without any thought to the obvious needs of the new age.

What indeed had been created that was new since Beethoven, Mozart or Weber? We cannot refer to these fine old masters as *conquistadors*, because if we had continued to play with that technique, we would never have known Rachmaninov, Horowitz, Arrau and other Michelangeli.

At a time like ours, when we have absolutely fabulous pedagogical material, the schools still insist on giving such Etudes to children instead of helping them find Bach, Mozart, Mendelssohn, Chopin or Liszt. *This is certainly the best way of putting them off music for life.*

The argument that *musically it is too difficult* has not being valid for a long time. It is the argument of teachers who do not know how to select, either due to fear or ignorance.

Mendelssohn wrote incredible Etudes, true *pearls,* in which the Music is the *centre* of the problem, dealt with by a master of the piano. This was already a revolution.

But the Etudes of Chopin and Liszt are *historical cultural revolutions*, because thanks to them Music has been opened up to an entirely new possibility, which is both expressive and instrumental. It can be summed up as follows: the new musical conception, that of Chopin, Liszt and Brahms, was such that it demanded new techniques to be accomplished.

All three, Brahms a little less, were the founders of a new way of handling the instrument and they forced piano makers to exceed all expectations. The entirely new conception did not just include finding faster fingering but also *new timbres*.

It was this devil Paganini, *because of him* the piano had to imitate the violin. So it was this Lucifer of the violin who began the great evolution in piano technique. The other personality was this devilish singer, Malibran. She made the composers imagination run to making the piano imitate human voice.

So, it was two musicians who were not pianists that gave rise to this evolution in piano technique, and *timbre and sound* became musical elements in their own right.

The sophistication of playing was to be fundamental for the new musical expression. The principles of Bach, *joining technique with expression*, were to be once again in vogue. We know that Bach thought that counterpoint should help the pupil to make his instrument *sing better*. Both for Chopin and Liszt, Bach would be the God of Music.

We do not compare an Etude by Chopin or Liszt with the formulas of the age: the search for expression is so colossal there that *form is adapted to needs.*

Imagine, for example, the Etude *Chasse Neige* by Liszt or the Etude known as "revolutionary" by Chopin. The theme and the programme music, as in the Etude Mazeppa, reflects the desire to express sentiments that are patriotic, heroic or lyrical; the state of soul that is in pain, passionate, troubled, dramatic, violent, joyous or comical; natural storms assimilated to accompany these passionate and personal dramas. In Liszt, for example, they take on unexpected metamorphoses.

Nevertheless, they were not always well received by the public at the time. We know that in Italy people laughed at Liszt's Concert Etudes. It was the same at the La Scala in Milan. We know that on his last trip to England, Chopin played some Etudes that went completely unnoticed.

The development of the form, simple in any case, deploys firstly the exposition of the problem: its technical formula and the modulations present the most heated moments of technical and expressive transformations. The recapitulations culminate in the psychological aspects of the virtuoso knowing how to make the last thrust of his sword. This will be either in the sense of the fireworks of virtuosity or in the obscure and tortuous expressive sinking of the work played.

There is a vast amount of literature on Chopin's Etudes. Sometimes it is very good, even excellent, like that written by Alfred Cortot or that of Abby Whiteside. My contribution here is to outline some brief considerations (they do not replace a course) on these 24 masterpieces, which are true musical morsels of pure genius and my companions throughout a life of music and teaching. I do not think I have spent a single day in my career without turning to them, if only for 10 minutes or so.

I think that there is nothing more formidable for the piano than playing the two series together, Op. 10 followed by Op. 25.

As far as I know few people in the history of the piano can boast of having completely managed to *master all of them* with the same ease. Playing one superbly does not mean that you will master the other. It is like changing a level, if we consider them as a whole. But we can take things in *hand* with courage so that we can study them wisely, patiently and philosophically.

We shall thank Chopin throughout our whole life.

1 – Family stories …Preliminary caution!

Chopin's Etudes, and we have already spoken of the aesthetic and musical wonders that they represent, form *a true family*: there are brothers, brothers-in-law and cousins.

The arpeggios, chords, intervals and scales are all related to one another, which leaves us stupefied.

It will be difficult to imagine that Chopin only dealt with isolated problems. On the contrary, he found how they were *related to the piano*, which had never happened before him. In this way he opened the gates is to all modern, sensitive, artistic, beautiful, sensual and all-embracing piano technique, or rather continuing on from Bach, the *difficulty of musical expression* without being able to detect the limits and pick out the problems.

So, we will talk of them in *families*, after a few basic considerations. First, we must find these families, and then study them together, remembering that their difficulties and their solutions in execution communicate with one another.

They support one another mutually, complementing one another and developing together. *In being interconnected they are almost dependent.* One Etude often finds *its solution in another.*

It serves absolutely no purpose to exhaust the muscles and tendons by working them *fortissimo* for hours, a poor approach that will only hide the true tactile sensations.

Working intelligently, without exceeding *mezzo forte*, helps even more particularly if it is prolonged. The work *in minimum sonority PPP* proves very beneficial.

You should manage to detect the slightest subtleties and the smallest muscular movements by developing *internal control* and not by *external appearance*. Do not become drugged by powerful sonorities that, in practice, do no more than distort reality and serve only to provoke tendinitis.

As in any work, a good working *tempo is not the possible speed of the fingers, but the identification by the brain of each note, each movement, each displacement and each structure.*

It is useless to study them without thinking of the final sonority, particularly in the Etudes *cantabiles*; without understanding the musical and aesthetic sense, as well as the relationship of timbre within each work. The pedal is all-important for these Etudes. They have been readily compared with the Nocturnes, works that I call the *etudes of legato and cantabile.*

The sound, *this path that is the shortest between one heart and the other*, is the final, supreme and absolute objective of one work and the other. As a result, the technique is none other than that: *a base* from which to take off into the superior regions of the Music. At all times we must remember that since the technique comes from the mind - let us recall Liszt - any mechanical work must be *made sublime* in view of its definitive results. *The mechanics alone make no sense:* they do not and should not do anything but serve the Music. That is why, and only for that reason, the mechanics are there.

Another thread to follow is the dissociation of problems: we must now how to give each one of them a specific role. They should serve to liberate us and not to create additional hindrances.

Emotional disassociation is also of capital importance. For example, we have to be able to play an Etude without the help of the other hand, not by exercising it separately as in a preliminary work, *but mainly by eliminating from the technical exercise the thematic aids that may hide the real problems of each Etude.*

Of course, this means that we should be able to play only the left- hand of Etude. Op. 10, No. 12 in *tempo* and expressively, *as if the work had been written for this hand alone.*

Or it could be for the right hand alone, in tempo and expressively, for Etude Op. 10 No. 5 or the Etude Op. 10 No. 2. This means also being able to play Etude Op. 10 No. 4 eliminating all the chords and passages that do not involve the semiquavers.

In all cases, *a well-accomplished result is necessary without the emotional aid of the respective themes.*

We spoke of that when dealing with possible solutions to the Finale of the Sonata in B-flat.

Chopin, as the excellent polyphonist he was, teaches us and advises us to separate the voices: *the double notes become simple to make the distances more flexible and to obtain separate speeds*, voice by voice, region by region. On the other hand, the simple become double *in order to understand the distances and the melodic expression contained therein.*

So, the first intelligent thing to do is to eliminate all the mechanical work *separate* from the musical aspect, reducing it to a strict minimum and *applying it, preferably, to the true objectives* of the Etude on which are working.

The difficulty raised must be understood, as well as *the nature of the problem* aiming to solve it *scientifically and artistically*, using the intelligence and not only *parrot-like repetition.*

If we forget the supreme objectives of Art, we will fall into ridiculous situations in which muscular concerns will determine spiritual concerns.

We will end these considerations by quoting the thoughts of Alfred Brendel, in his comments on Busoni: "*The pianist tends endlessly to put mastery of technical difficulties before musical meaning. Now, there is no technique that has resolved all problems, because the true problems are not of a technical nature, but of a musical nature. Busoni is the greatest defender of Liszt's formula "technique as a support to the idea".*

Not even a comma can be added to these very wise words.

2 - « The Holy Family with a Lamb» by Raffaello Sanzio
« The Holy Family with the Infant John the Baptist" by Andrea del Sarto
« The Holy Family with Saints Anne and Joachim » by Diego de Pesquera

I think that the families are formed as follows:

1 – The Etudes for the arpeggios:
   Op. 10 No. 1, Op. 10 No. 8, Op. 10 No. 12 and Op. 25 No. 12

2 – The Etudes for the broken arpeggios: Op. 10 No. 5 and Op. 25
   No. 11

3 – The Etudes for the double notes and their basic Etude:
   Op. 10 No. 2 (this constituted the base for the whole of Chopin's technique), Op. 10 No. 7, Op. 25 No. 6, Op. 25 No.

8 and Op. 25 No. 10

4 – The Etudes for the phrasing:
Op.10 No. 10, Op. 25 No. 4 and Op. 25 No. 5

5 – The Etudes *cantabile*:
Op. 10 No. 3, Op. 10 No. 6, Op. 25 No. 1, Op. 25 No. 2 and
Op. 25 No. 7

6 – The Etudes of extension and more fixed positions:
Op. 10 No. 4, Op. 10 No. 9, Op. 10 No. 11, Op. 25 No. 3 and
Op. 25 No. 9

It is possible, and even certain, that other groups can be found.
I have grouped them like this according to their degree of relationship, to find in this the corresponding solutions (at least those I believe) and not isolated solutions.

2.1 - The first family
Four Etudes for the arpeggios: Op. 10 No. 1, No. 8 and No. 12; Op. 25 No. 12

I will now begin to examine the Etudes with arpeggios.
The first great working principle is to understand the problem and to solve it by *augmentation*.
What I mean by that is *augmenting the difficulty*.
But not in the sense of Leopold Godowski, that is, creating another type of problem through other difficulties and through other Etudes, but *augmenting the same difficulty with the same Etudes*.

Of course, I am not discussing the right of a great pianist to provide musical literature as copious as his on Chopin's Etudes. That would be a masterly lesson that, no doubt, would have served many pianists, but I prefer to follow in the traces of Chopin, more modestly.
Alfred Cortot said admirably, "*Do not work only the difficult passage but the difficulty contained in it*". I would add, with all humility, *augment the difficulty without affecting the nature of the problem.*

Let us take the example of the first Etude, Op. 10.
The right hand must move over a distance of 4 octaves, by opening and closing it.
In the meantime, the left-hand determines the solemn, profound and grandiose octaves in a great choral that also predetermines the choice of the colour and dynamics of each arpeggio that it develops. The role of this left-hand is, therefore, eminently musical, while that of the right-hand is to confront what are often uncomfortable displacements. It struggles in all positions. It is on the razor's edge all the time and risks accident or a slide at each note and at each octave.
Clearly, as in Etude Op. 25 No. 12, the thematic sequences must be organized, for example, by 4 or 8 bars, in order to understand that the arpeggios are not separated but coordinated in groups or in themes, just as in Bach's Preludes.

It would be technically more difficult, as a result, to augment the problem by accomplishing it *in 6 octaves and not in 4,* following the score by Chopin excluding the left-hand, carefully guarding the essential difficulty of the right, but beginning two octaves below.

As with athletes, this will be training *according to Chopin*, in   the same course, on 6 octaves instead of 4. Of course, and by deduction, the Etude will be 50% more difficult.

When this principle of augmenting the difficulty is mastered, the Etude should become easier when it is played in the normal position of 4 octaves, *then with the support of the bass*. It will be at least 50% simpler by inverting the order of work.

The transcription for the left-hand, in symmetry, it is an important aid.

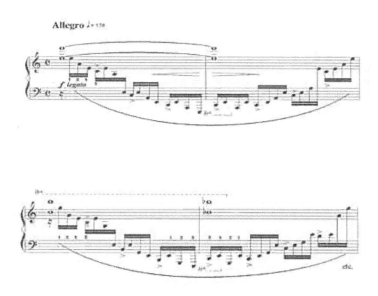

Another (well-known) principle is *to modulate it each day in a different tonality*, in the whole chromatic scale (from C major, C-sharp major, D major, E-flat major, etc.)

This is not a pastime but an intelligent way of demystifying the difficulties that we run into with certain arpeggios. So, at *each modulation the "odious" arpeggios change place.*

I attach to this work, which is complimentary and parallel to that preceding it, the greatest importance because to a great extent it eliminates the mechanical concept referring to a particular arpeggio, for example the famous C, E-flat, A-natural, E-flat, the difficult descent E-flat, A-flat, E-flat, C, or that of E-flat, B-flat, E-flat, C-natural.

By comparison every arpeggio becomes difficult because the positions on the keys are changed.

Bar 1

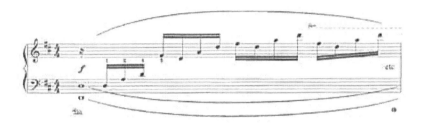

Bar 31

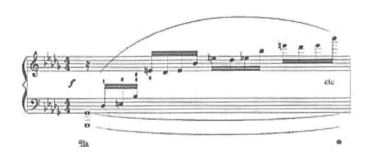

There is not a single hand in the world that does not suffer with such positions, even those of the great pianists. But these positions were designed for that: to be *works of art and pedagogy and not to be made easy.*

The arpeggio in question (to each its own) remains difficult, of course, but, by comparison, it is not the only one, *considering that the other positions in other tonalities make it more accessible.* It's almost like not being afraid in a large aircraft. You feel better seeing more people around you.

Every teacher has his own working methods for the Etude, either by intervals (in two out of two notes, or in one out of three, or in three out of one), by sections, by rhythms or by accents… *But the essential thing still remains fixing the axes, that is, the two central fingers.*

If you begin with the second finger well in place, clear, defined, isolated searching like an aerial - and the same thing for the third or fourth, according to the case, in the descents -, the said arpeggio will be better determined and clearer for the brain. And certainly, it will be much clearer and precise then if you drowned stupidly in the *FF* sonorities, in the absence of minimum control, in a pseudo- execution of the whole without the slightest dynamic or structural construction.

A mental line of axes is therefore highly recommended, because it recognizes the topography of the said arpeggio.

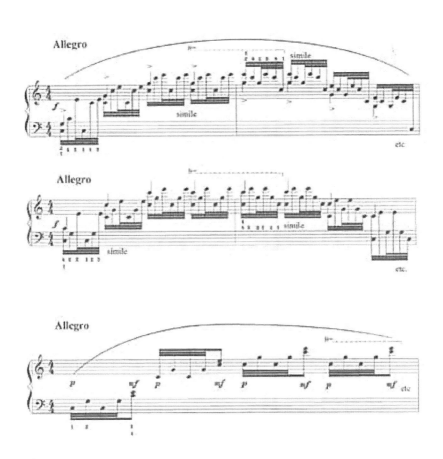

The speed of Chopin, 176 per crotchet, is not accessible to just anyone, but not just the negative side should be considered when you cannot do something. On the contrary, it is better to develop our means to achieve our maximum.

It is said, "*The metronomes weren't written by Chopin*". Who "invented" them then?
I have read, in a so-called *traditional* edition, a tempo of 104   per crotchet! "*According to the tradition of the great Polish interpreters*" (sic). May I have the names of *these great interpreters*, please? Not the least argumentation or mention of names on the part of those interested, of course, but rather aesthetic whims and a recognition of impotence, quite simply, *sold in the name of tradition.*

This Etude remains very difficult for small hands and the eventual changes of fingerings or *facilitations* do no more than distort its difficulty.

I refuse to speak about it.

Nothing is gained from forcing or changing Nature: you always lose. It is far better to try and understand it. The positive thing to do, for these very little hands, is to study this Etude in *PPP*, to avoid the tendinitis that it could cause, by trying to make something of it that can be *much more helpful than all sorts of little tricks that lead nowhere.*

The gain to be made from inter-digital extensions is formidable.

I apply the same principles of augmentation to Etude Op. 25 No. 12, in C minor, the big brother of the first of Op. 10. It is also based on a choral in the first notes of each bar, which are sublime and imperious.

The augmentation of arpeggios by 3, 4 and 5 octaves is highly profitable. It is clear that in these two brother Etudes the control of each note remains fundamental. The slow work, as the control of fingering combinations (five - thumb; three - two; thumb - five, per octave, etc.), as well.

On the other hand, *nothing can replace the effective control on the axes*, that is, control of the second, fourth or third fingers, as seen in Op. 10 No. 1.

I have "invented", for my personal work, this exercise of *topographic recognition* using *accents* on the seconds - thirds:

Allegro molto con fuoco ♩=88

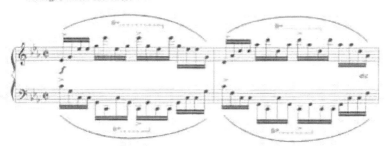

Allegro molto con fuoco ♩=88

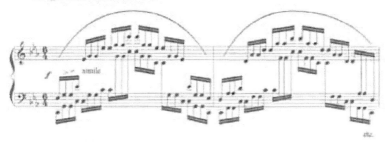

Allegro molto con fuoco ♩=90

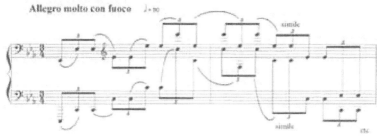

Multiple working methods are possible for this Etude.

For example, hold one octave in the left-hand and, quickly, make the arpeggio with the right hand. Or hold the last note on the right, in the form of an octave, and quickly make the arpeggio in the left hand.

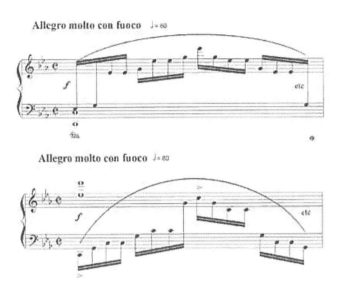

The definition of its sublime choral seems like the first musical thing to do, considering that *otherwise you cannot determine the corresponding touch for each arpeggio.*

It is, therefore, indispensable to reduce the volume, *although not its expressive intensity,* of the second note, the one following the thematic note and, a little less, of the third note. This then allows for the expansion of the first.

An effect similar to this:

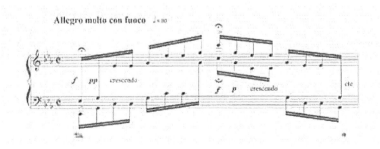

The fact of opening and closing the hand at each octave constitutes a problem for recovering the positions in the following octave, as in Etude 10 No. 1. As a result, *the work of this axis reveals itself to be once again essential*, because the *legato* between 5 and 1 in changing positions (the inverse for the left hand) remains an illusion; it is better to close the hand as little as possible and leave it almost in a *profound portato* at high speed.

Control of the distribution of weight is as follows: thumb right hand, second right hand, thumb left hand, second right hand. This makes it possible to reduce the extension of the spans falling necessarily on the parallelism of the arpeggios.

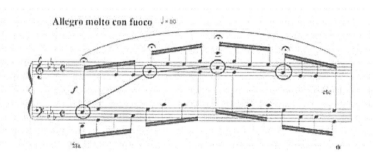

Another indispensable way of working is to study the first 3 ascending groups and the 3 descending groups of each bar (inversely), by adding the first note of the following. This means that changes in the direction of the arpeggios can be made at the same speed, but with restricted control.

In this Etude, one feels more than in any other the need for grandeur, pathos, a close a cycle, a finale. The work is eminently aesthetic. In this way the mechanical aspects can be developed and influenced with more certainty. *Thanks to this spiritual demand.* Special attention must be paid in conducting the melody of the choral, and particularly its dynamics. In the long arpeggios, just before the development and the recapitulation, the notes corresponding to the *guiding* accents must be observed. Editions contradict one another in their placements.

Before the recapitulation, it is clear that the melody should be presented like this:

In all the last measures, Chopin reaches *FFF*, which is rare for him, placing accents every 4 notes, as if the sonority was failing him.

There is a feeling of apotheosis, or a triumphant spirit, like that of a conqueror. Perhaps he is responding to the idea of *close of cycle*? Whatever the case, we have here a work of art of the greatest magnitude.

We will now speak of the third close brother to the preceding two, the Etude Op. 10 No. 12, known to audiences as the *Revolution Etude*.

Of course, we are all aware of all the stories surrounding this Etude, Prelude 24 in D minor and the Scherzo Op. 20 No. 1, in B minor: "*It is the fall of Warsaw, the despair and the military impotence of Chopin*", etc. The imagination of artists has produced films, novels and studies on the subject, and Chopin was presented to the public as a weak, pale, sickly youth.

So be it!

It is clear that these three works, the Scherzo, the Prelude and the Etude are more like hurricanes than *moments musicaux*. Chopin's technique is unleashed with maximum tension. The instrument seems to be on fire, and to be consumed; flaming tongues of sound rise in spheres from which violence, fury, disarray, defeat, anger, bravery, vehemence and injustice are present at every moment.

There is not a single moment of calm. Neither the pianist nor the listener are given time to breathe.

The force of the fingering demanded to execute this Etude Op. 10 No. 12 is almost inhuman. And this is at a speed of 160 per crotchet.

Of these three Etudes examined, virtuosity leaves ennobled. Hence the preparation and reasoning required to achieve this muscular possibility, without which we remain only with words: we will *speak* about the Etude like the *tuttologists* and remain incapable of playing them.

The terrible arpeggio that hits the piano, at the start, the ninth of the dominant (G, B-natural, D, F, A-flat) shows no sign of the slightest weakness.

The impact is right there: strong and fast.

As always, we must have faith in Chopin: the accent falls on the axis. It is indeed the second finger that is *charged with producing the force*. The roles of the 4-3-1 will be to produce the speed, dividing the hand, once again, according to Bach.

So, they will play *less strongly* in the articulation and will go *less close* to 'ground' in penetrating the keyboard. This, of course, will be in proportion to the general dynamics

In much of the development, from bar 29, the demands on the axes, the second fingers, remain essential. They must be worked in both directions, in inverting the groups.

The scales in bars 33, 34, 35 and 36 are true missiles in sharp descent, while the arpeggios, in contrast, flame upwards to the heights.

They must be divided like this for the work: ensuring the *bass octaves* and the other higher *octaves-broken chords*, in positions of *two octaves*.

b)

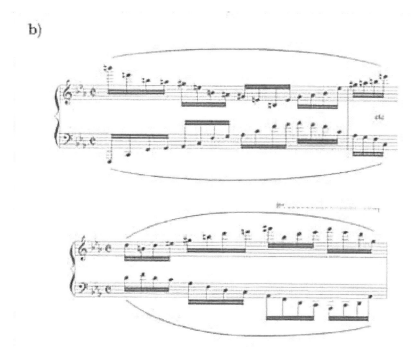

For the little chromatic formula, presented four times, the first in bars 17 and 18, the fact of beginning to play it more *piano* removes much of the real difficulty, and has the advantage of giving it expressive strength. It is mainly its extension that is worked.

Once again, I repeat that I believe far more *in the articulation that comes from the keyboard, than that which descends on the keyboard.*

I think that any exercise should depend on this touch. It would not be very intelligent to think of developing the speed using any other.

Clearly the extension of the arpeggios should be increased as in the Etude Op. 10 No. 1 and Op. 25 No. 12.

The statement made by the right-hand is tempestuous, moved and violent, and it demands strength in the curve of the hand as in the dome of a cathedral, in this way ensuring the human resonance of the palm of the hand, indispensable for the continued pathos of the passage.

You have to be ready for the leap between the G octave and the D chord, the G octave and the F chord (at the re-exposition the highest note is G, please: this fault has been corrected a thousand times, bar 45: the chord is therefore F, G, D, G and not F, as the first time).

The neighbouring position between the first axis and the second must therefore be established: 2-3 (E-flat, F) to 2-3 following (F, G).

The second is easier because the axis 2-3 (E-flat, F) is replaced by the thumb in the F and the G.

It is easier if the duration of the axes is held for a little longer, for example for a dotted quaver.

The statement of the octaves in the theme is in steel: I recommend fingering 5-5 for the white keys and 4-4 for the black, so as to waste nothing as force and to add that of the arm.

In bar 57, a famous *poetic concession* is permitted to everyone, although I think it is ridiculous: the two octaves G and C are semiquavers *and not quavers*.

Violence is the main characteristic of this Etude and not convenience.

The subtlety of *FFF* is also presented as the end of a first cycle, as it is at the end of Op. 25 No. 12.

This must be the crowning of maximum expression by a youth aged 21 able to produce such a counterpart of 24 crown jewels to the Preludes and Fugues of John Sebastian Bach, his all-time God and his great model.

All that is required is to listen again to earlier piano production, the Etudes written by other composers at the time, Liszt apart, to revere Chopin in his handling of the instrument.

When did the piano ever sound like this before? No more is required *to place Chopin in the Pantheon of the greatest.*

We now need a few words on the other Etude of arpeggios, Op. 10 No. 8, in F major. This is another way of handling the arpeggios. The three big brothers - Op. 10 No. 1, Op. 10 No. 12 and Op. 25 No. 12 - are, as already mentioned, true cyclones on the keyboard. This one is, however, full of elegance and nobility, with some delicious cascades, a very lively false *Coda* and a brilliant ending in which *arpeggiated* chords seem to announce Etude Op.10 No. 11.

Allusions to pentatonic scales are made with a good humoured left-hand that recalls the mischievous, pleasing side of Chopin.

The modulation in D minor changes the atmosphere a little, without letting it fall into the dramas of its brothers. The virtuosity remains refined, slender and without any torpor or heaviness.

Fingering is symmetrical in the groups in the opposite direction, and once again the work of Chopin on the axes will be fundamental. *An excellent exercise will be to fix them to recognize the topography of the terrain* on which we are operating.

The work of extending the arpeggios remains fundamental, as does carrying the whole Etude over to F-sharp major.

You must also exercise displacements of the thumb combined with the axes of 2-3 and 4, ascending and descending.

The elasticity of the passage is fundamental, and exercises of this type will help achieve this more quickly.

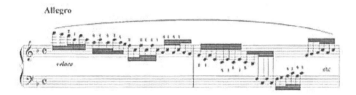

From bar 48 the relationship axes 3 - thumbs is inverted. Chopin examines the other extreme, that is axes - fifth.

The same exercises as before must be done carefully.

This demands not only an inter-digital extension of the hand remaining parallel to the keyboard, *but also turning on the axis of the third finger in this way giving it almost two surfaces.*

In the central part, this type of exercise is recommended in order to fix the axes.

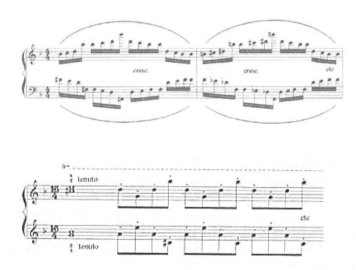

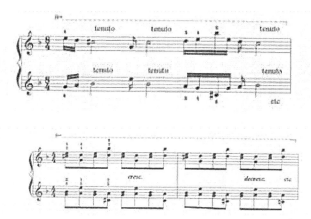

In the highly eloquent false *Coda*, distances are reduced but the passage of the thumb remains fundamental to almost each group:

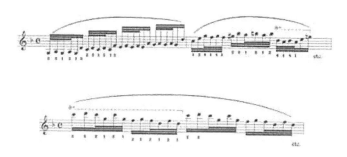

However, the left-hand loses its good humour and calms down in these polyphonic passages. It ends by becoming suspended in an elegant, irresolute chord of two superimposed fifths before rushing off *con brio* across the keyboard in exemplary brilliance. This melancholic doubt was no more than transient.
Work like this:

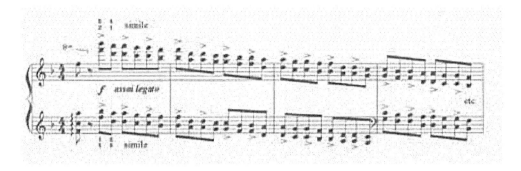

For the final chords, exercise as follows:

A serene joy flows throughout almost the whole of this Etude, with only a few moments when it changes but not to true sadness. The wonder of this pianistic juggling is remarkable, and it makes this Etude one of the favourites with young pianists who are anxious to show what they know with brilliance and a light touch.

2.2 - The second family
Two Etudes for the broken arpeggios: Op. 10 No. 5 and Op. 25 No. 11

Let us now look at the small group of broken arpeggios, Op. 10 No. 5 and Op. 25 No. 11. They constitute two opposing worlds. One, the infinitude representing mischief and good humour, Op. 10 No. 5; and the other Op. 25 No. 11, is pure drama, because it is close to the displeasure of the big brothers in Op. 10 No. 1 and 12, and Op. 25 No. 12, with the addition of an epic dimension of great nobility.

The Op. 10 No. 5 is popularly called the *Etude of the black keys* and is a wonder in lightness. Here Chopin uses incredible genius in applying only the black keys and the pentatonic scale, as a result. It is useless to look in the literature on the earlier piano for such an example of black key use.

Of course, this Etude has to be transposed to G major, using the white keys, to get extraordinary results (and not just to please the editor of Schubert for his Impromptu in G-flat, Op. 90 No. 3, also transposed because it was too difficult to read). Care must be paid to the development, where the arpeggios demand opening the central fingers to keep the hand in perfect tranquillity.

Repeat the extensions to make your hand flexible. Prolong the extension of the arpeggios to make them more accessible.

The work of double notes is heartily recommended because the problems with variable distances should not be overlooked at all. You must remember to work on *staccato-legato*, and vice versa. Movements of the thumb demand the greatest subtlety in the wrist,

as well as extreme elasticity in the different openings. The thumb moves after the 2, the 3, the 4 and the 5, in a remarkable grooming of the right-hand demanding at the same time the greatest balance in these displacements.

Chopin demands covering three, four octaves, or more, in risky movements, *always maintaining a serious legatissimo* and constantly displacing the thumb. The touch should be designed starting from the keyboard and avoiding, above all, wide articulation. Here too the speed depends on it.

The *staccato* work of the fingers is welcome because it starts *from the key* rather than *going to it*. Here we try to develop a clear, brilliant and sometimes incisive touch; burlesque at all times. Take care to employ only finger *staccato* and not heavy *staccato*, that will do no more than impede the finger work. This has been known as "jeu perlé".

The technical formulae in the composition of the Etude are not always the same, however. But… if one understands then all is well.

Central controls must be maintained in measures 27 and 28 and double the leaps with octaves, to bring them back to the thumb.

In the *Coda*, the thumb movements must be combined with pseudo-trills or mordents, and alternate brilliant fingerings with moments of caution, particularly in measure 75 throughout the whole descent. This is a moment when accidents can happen.

The rise in double first notes in measure 79 should be dissociated into simple notes to obtain the same speed as their companions.

In principle, the double octaves are in the same *tempo* as the rest. As for Liszt's Sonata or in Tchaikovsky's Concerto, you must separate the thumbs playing the *third octaves in the passage*, that between the two hands, in order to make them independent.

The left hand is an example of lightness and phrasing. Avoid the *"soup"* pedals and go for the *light* ones. They must be used according to the phrasing *in two* and not for harmony, without impeding the burlesque aspect of the thematic line, particularly on the third page in D-flat major.

You must ask yourself about the effect produced by this Etude on a public used to following, sometimes with difficulty, the dominant, tonic relationship. What an aristocratic quip, burlesque but refined and, at the same time, what a superb exercise for this *black hand*!

Lastly, let us look at Etude Op. 25 No. 11, in A minor.

It is almost immoral to define this work as *an etude*. Its dimensions, its rises, its grandeur, its drama, its amplitude, its vigour, its epic side and its warrior qualities make it seem more like a cataclysm than an etude for piano. Its similarity with the Scherzo in B minor is striking, as is the way of dealing with the arpeggios.

The theme, with disarming economy, is composed of only three notes. They are very homophone and almost *detached from the world* in the first exposition, which is quite bare. They do not predict the hecatomb that will fall from the heavens. To say that this theme is a glorious march is true, but that would be too simple. Chopin examines it in many tonalities, but this march seldom loses its expressive force.

For several seconds, when it *moves* to the right hand, the broken movements in the left-hand evoke a phantom on fire. This confrontation with the theme, closer and more visible to us, is terrifying.

The music is expressed with fury and violence. It agitates and suffocates. A slight breath in A-flat major, followed by E major, makes one long for something that does not exist, because the imperious octaves in the left-hand break the dream.

The hands then confront one another savagely until there is a deep cry, heard twice. Muted repetitions precipitate an implacable scale towards the lower register that relaunches the Etude towards its fatal outcome.

The warlike exaltations have the last word: the theme asserts itself in a grand resonant choral, in *FFF*. But a violent scale, like *the winter wind*, sweeps the piano leaving no trace of life behind.

It is the type of work that takes the breath away.

One wonders how Chopin could be considered *pale and weak* when we listen to such works. His force is titanic. He was certainly sickly and weak, but it is not for that he composed *only* charming melodies and delicious mazurkas. Like so often, the truth is found elsewhere. It certainly raises a crucial problem: should we always identify the works with the health of those creating them, or with their personal characteristics, or should we look for and detect what they wanted to say?

However, despite all this, we must address the technical problems involved in this pianistic epic. Of course, it cannot be resolved with a tiny articulation. Major means must be used because the Etude will make us pay dearly for the slightest failure or weakness. We must begin by making the fingers much stronger. To this end, much *staccato* work is required. The work of distance between intervals is essential.

We must observe the reversal of the fingering for the extreme notes of the chromatic descent of Etude Op. 10 No. 2. It should be assisted using a precise rotation movement as far as the end, without it being too pronounced because it could compromise digital action.

Allegro con brio ♩=♩

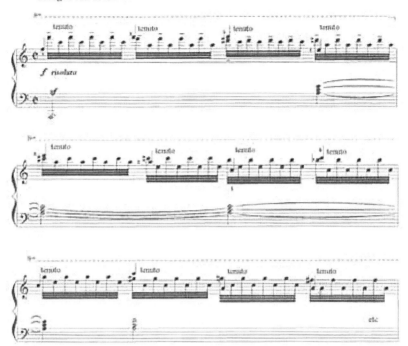

Allegro con brio ♩=♩

Allegro con brio ♩=♩

118

Whenever the passage moves to the left, in measure 42, take care to obtain the same speed for the left hand as for the preceding right, *given that you must work with one finger less*; we are now playing only 1-3 and 2-5, without the 4.

I suggest this *insolence to the ear* to make the speeds equal: exercising both right and left hands with the same formula, at the same time, apologizing to Chopin for this impertinence.

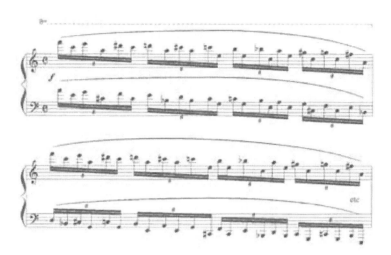

After, the chromatic designs of the broken arpeggios spread over three octaves, displacing the thumb according to harmonic needs. I recommend this work of very effective *localization*: exercise starting from the thumb, sustained for longer.

From measure 17 on, open intervals are not always good for small hands. This whole section must be transcribed in triplets of double notes just like a *toccata*, if possible duplicated by symmetry of the left hand, alternating with the work of the broken arpeggios. This must be done, of course, each time the problem appears in different tonalities.

After these flurries of the left hand, take care to avoid making too effeminate an interpretation in the modulating passages in A-flat major and in E major. These are serious introversions, of deep gravity, and not reminiscences of agreeable, dreamlike voyages. We modulate, with the *arpeggiati* chords in F major, E minor, D Minor, before relaunching a more distant atmosphere on the seventh chord. Everything becomes suspended while waiting for the E of the bass.

The two passages in symmetry in *FF* will be articulated at full steam, with implacable vigour. The work of double notes, as in *con bravura* of Etude Op. 10 No. 3 is necessary here. I do not risk becoming seen as presumptuous in recalling that in the repetitions F- D - E, G-sharp, *quaver plus pause, to count the measure well.*
Each teacher knows something on this point.

The *Coda* should begin with a muted sonority and minimal articulations to stretch to the major *exposé* later on, when Chopin demands it. The tradition of holding the pedal on the last F of the theme in the left, before the rise of the left hand, and to resolve it in the six-four chord seems to me excellent as a musical conception. Obviously, if we play a false note, we must relinquish this monumental pedal.
In popular parlance it is known as the *emergency pedal*. However, it is worth trying it, particularly if we have a resonant instrument, and if we are up to it and in good form on that particular evening.

Different editions give for the great final throbbing in the left hand a B, in the fourth bass, the others A. I prefer the B because it corresponds to the theme. I recognize the possibility of increasing the sound by the repeated note, but, quite simply, I am not convinced by it. I remain faithful to the B of the theme.

In general, the left hand must pay attention to playing 4 against 6, and not 6 against 6, as it is usually heard.
The *diminuendo* demanded by Chopin must be *impressive* and not *impressionist.*

I recommend open fingering for measure 11 in order to keep the 2 on the E and reach the D-sharp *legato* with the 3 in a real axis position.

For measures 18 and 19, practice shows that the fingerings retaining the axes are the best. Besides, they are Chopin›s and they help hold G and B-flat with the same fingers as in the successive chords.

For the octaves of the development *an arc in steel* is indispensable, particularly when they open in the opposite direction to the arpeggios.
Pay attention to the *crescendo* to avoid any ridiculous effect.

The devastating discharge of the final scale must be done *in tempo*. Do not begin too much in *PP*. This is an out of place effect in such a work. Let us try, rather, to enjoy all the benefits of such an odyssey. We are unlikely to find it again easily. It underscores the Etudes as an almost unrivalled sublime moment.

2.3 - The third family
    Five Etudes for the double notes and their basic Etude: Op. 10 No. 2, Op. 10 No. 7, Op. 25 No. 6, Op. 25 No. 8 and Op. 25 No. 10

We must now get into a very large chapter on the Etudes, because the etude with the double notes is fundamental for Chopin the teacher and for all of his music.

In fact, Chopin created a base of fingerings for this whole sound edifice, whether in thirds, sixths, octaves and other polyphonic intervals, symmetrical or parallel.
I have already said that the octaves, so dear to Liszt for other reasons, with Chopin are frequently *polyphonic*, and therefore *legato* and *cantabile*. The sixths and the thirds have the airs of hidden melodies, vague perfumes and fleeting memories.
Playing well the Etude in Thirds means, almost, listening to a delicate *glissando*, like an evaporation of material. The elegant *toccata* in C major, the seventh Etude of Op. 10, suggests a petite *valse brillante* in its central part. It is delicate, spiritual and capricious. The division of the hand here is superb.
Op. 25 No. 10, the Octaves, is, on the other hand, a test of strength. This Etude devastates the piano.

The Etude in A minor, Op. 10 No. 2, is the great *commander* of this whole legion. It expresses no excitement, nor does it produce any bother. It is rarely *forte* and seems to have no courage. However, like all things that are truly difficult, it does prove to have disarming simplicity. It is almost nonchalant. If one heard speaking the Liszt of *Feux Follets*, one would say *dolce* and *innocente*. Just like an ephemeral goddess, it very rarely shows its beauty. It is also the most difficult to grasp. Like its brother, or son, the Thirds, it seems to vanish because it is so light and fleeting. It is a challenge to the law of gravity. It is immaterial.

Many pianists consider it to be the most difficult Etude, and rarely can true success be claimed, that is, completely and without *any cheating*. Certainly, any simplification in playing it is in order. But once again, I refuse to talk about it, because this is not the aim of these comments. If you want simplifications, you will find plenty of them in far too many books, but not in this one.

The first problem to solve it is the uninterrupted scale and the muscle fatigue that it causes. As a result, it is recommended that you learn it apart from the rest. No pianist in the world can contradict this. *Its difficulty lies in being the theme.* This is its principal role: it is not a support for a melody, *but a melodic design that is weightless, fleeting and self-sufficient.*

Its subtlety demands that we find the precise weight, although with such evaporation, it is *almost impossible to speak of weight.* It would be far more appropriate to speak of *non-weight. The working method without sound* is fundamental here and highly recommended. One must be fully aware of the *minimum pressure* required for the keys.

I follow a symmetrical path for the left hand that seeks the same benefit as that indicated by Chopin for the right, in an exemplary uproar. The aim is not to detract from Chopin's exercise and not to imagine yourself as a Sunday composer, but to *make this Etude equally useful for the other hand*, not through the musical result but through *its identical elementary mechanics.*

Once the scale has been *mastered (?)* the chords must be added just as Chopin arranged them; that is, *without changing the position of the notes in the right-hand with assistance from the left, just like beggars.*

It is better to begin with the thumb alone, first of all *staccato.*

After, with the second finger, without the thumb, which is far less easy, also in *staccato.*

Of course, the decomposition of the chords seeks considerable benefits given that their movements are so similar to *the finger movements*, and mainly *they are incorporated in the speed.*

The contrary must also be done, that is, *maintain* these chords for the exercise. This will make them *less malleable* and will allow the hand to play in a more fixed position, something that should develop the finger muscles and so make them more independent.

The expression in this scale is magnificent.

In what other Etude, by another composer, can a scale, deprived of its melody, its dynamics and change of colour have such an atmosphere? You might almost believe that *air becomes substance* through the notes on the paper. But there is no doubt it is, for its sound representation, more *an evaporated substance*. It seems to exist beyond reality. You are tempted to say that the Music is pared back to the minimum because there is no opulence there at all.

Too much force is fatal, even in infinitesimal scale.

For this, the chords of the left-hand should leap like fairies without really much pressure, but rather like *remote references*, that can only go to accentuate the *vague character* of the work. They must be studied with the wrist raised, as though floating over the keyboard and without going to the depth of the keys. Consequently, one should avoid bringing the fingers down in too vertical a position on the instrument. Choose rather *the technique of a caress and so avoid heavily striking the hammers*.

This is the basic fingering to be used for the other Etudes in the group, given that the fundamental principle is the position of the three upper fingers of the hand in the chromatic scale. Replacing the fourth finger to a fifth, for example, on the white keys, may sometimes be justified.

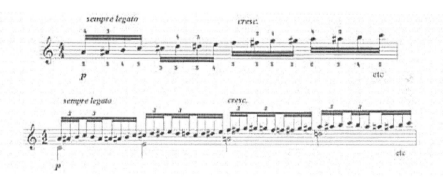

This *non-articulation* brings to mind the effects of the *glissandi* in Ravel or in Debussy, in the evanescent passages, for example, in the *glissandi* of "Voiles", as though the miraculous touch of Debussy had already been *foreseen* by Chopin.

The general character of the Etude is found in the elimination of any abusive span in the movements of the fingers and in the assurance of maximum contact with the keyboard.

The ethereal, the fluid and extreme virtuosity will underlie thoughts in the detailed analysis of this page and shall improve our understanding of Chopin and the immensity of his unbridled vision.

We will remain in the same context for the Etude in Thirds, Op. 25 No. 6. We are used to hearing more of an exercise than a work of art. Nothing could be more deplorable for such a work. We could say that here the effects of *crescendo* are clearer than in Op. 10 No. 2, although much less obvious than in the Etudes in Sixths or in Octaves. *The secret, the elegance, the vapour and the perfume are* decisive elements in these two works, the Chromatic and the Thirds. *The bravery, heroic impulse, the strength and the impetuosity* are the components of the other two, the Sixths and the Octaves. As a result, the articulations are higher in the Sixths and the Octaves.

Let us now look at Etude Op. 25 No. 6.
There are five elements to be considered in the Etude in double thirds:

1 - The trills in double thirds.
2 - The ascending and descending chromatic scales with the *legato* in the fingers that correspond: upper when the scale is ascending, lower when the scale is descending (the same thing for the diatonic scales).
3 - The scales and the diatonic groups.
4 - The broken scales.
5 - The thematic designs in the left hand.
There is no need to say that special and separate study is required for each item.

The first thing to do is to invert the formula for the right-hand for the left hand, as in Etude Op. 10 No. 2. This is fundamental.

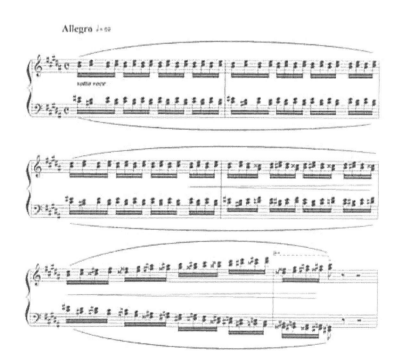

Now let us consider the trills. First, we must decide whether the fingerings are parallel, crossed or combined, given that the positions of the trills are not the same.

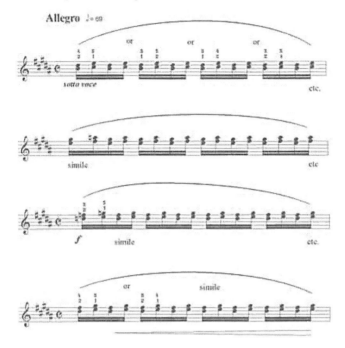

Perhaps for the trill D-sharp-F-sharp and E-natural-G-sharp, the fingering 2-3 / 1-4 or 5 is the most comfortable. So why not adopt this fingering for all cases? Exiting this position is extremely simple. You only have to slide the thumb from C- sharp towards B-natural.

a - Either we employ Chopin's classic;

b - or we slide the second finger towards the white key, in what we call the modern pianos.

There is another very personal fingering used by Godowski, but it will be better to use the others, left to us by Chopin and Liszt.

For the fingerings for the descending diatonic scales we also have some historical choices. The best solution is to avoid continuous changes because *they take time and* slow down the general speed of the Etude.

For example, in bar 11, if we compare these three fingerings:

One requires less position changes than others. Of course, considering the *diminuendo*, the one seeking the fewest changes would be the more logical.

The fingering must also be observed in the other large diatonic scale in measures 47 and 48: the descending repetition of the thumb on the keys E - D is, I think, slower than the fingering 2-4 and 1-3, which is far faster.

The general work of the thirds and the double notes certainly - trills included - is far more prolific and effective *providing movement synchronization is ensured.*

In fact, this is the only solution. Just as you work the simple notes by associating them with other similar notes forming double notes to understand the distances, that is the intervals, one must dissociate the double notes and make them simple, in order to develop the speeds impossible to achieve because of the hindrance of a poorly adopted synchronization.

The *crescendi* and the *diminuendi*, in short, the dynamics as a whole, are of tremendous technical and musical importance in the passages of this Etude. As a result, in this work of breaking down double notes into simple notes *the same nuances must be observed*.

In regard to the broken thirds, in measures 27, 28, 29, 30, 31, 32, 33 and 34, in the passages in C major and in B-flat major   the internal movements remain fundamental, of course. The same goes for the work of the extremes.

If we *exercise an ascending rather than a descending control,* the passage becomes less prickly.
This means controlling in measure 27 the thirds G - B with C - E, E - G with A - C, etc. The same work goes for the rest of the passage.
The fingering combinations for the passage in B-flat are more difficult than in C major, given the black keys. To each pianist his own.
The two fingering alternatives are the most reasonable:

The left hand is at the heart of this work.

Its fundamental design must be seen as an expression of melancholy, almost of sadness, as *if not joining* the whims of the right-hand. The latter moves easily throughout, in positions that are sometimes a caper, while the left hand appears, disappears and then vanishes and is rarely joyful. Therefore, the fingers driving the themes must be discreetly clarified, sometimes in a troubling expression and sometimes in an even more disturbed expression.

It seems that Chopin was phenomenal in executing this work. It would be impossible to imagine anything other than that. Chopin often played the two first Etudes of Op. 25 with that in Thirds.

Did he find some relationship between the "touchers" of these Etudes? Or was it the secret harmony that made him prefer them to the others? Whatever the case, the sonorous wonder of this Etude in Thirds is more striking when it is execution is *full of delicacy*. If, on the other hand, it is weighted down, it will be less effective. It is like a meteor, distinguished and aristocratic, that crosses the sky and breaks up quietly, almost without trace. Above all, there is no need to demonstrate or explain the work it has demanded of us. A gesture from the great Lord proves necessary to play it in its true spirit.

Now we come to the Etude in Sixths, Op. 25 No. 8.

It could be considered as a severe movement for the right-hand, uninterrupted and hypnotic. Apart from the four final, triumphant chords, the right-hand does not change interval one single time: it is the severe and implacable sixth. The hand does not stop to draw breath until it arrives at D-flat major for the *Coda*.

We think tenderly of the arrangement of Etude Op. 25 No. 2 by Brahms, who loved Chopin with good reason, for sixths, thirds and other intervals. The difference with Brahms is that Chopin always found *the exact tempo* for his themes. Brahms did too for his own music, but in his arrangement of Chopin's Etude we find neither the tempo of the Thirds, nor that of the Sixths, and above all not that of Op. 25 No. 2. It is a work of composition that the British might define as *interesting*.

It is terribly difficult *to arrange* a theme by Chopin or Mozart. They are so perfect in themselves that they prevent other musicians from doing better. Moreover, Liszt, in his Sonata for piano and violin on the second Mazurka, or Rachmaninov, in his variations on the Prelude in C minor, knew something of this.

Op. 25 No. 8 is perhaps "*the most Etude of the Etudes*", although Chopin succeeded, despite everything, to give it a changing character by moving it between *mezza voce* and bravery.
The interest lies in the interpretation of Chopin's melodic trait, in its curve. Clearly if it is interpreted *a la Clementi*, the Etude loses its expressive value *which is, precisely, the malleability* in the execution of the sixths and their diversification between the extremes of delicacy and impetuosity. Detailed work on the separate voices must be ensured, the target being the definitive speed.
Gliding fingerings are indicated in several editions.
But I remain sceptical over this passage in particular; I use this, coming from the master Del Pueyo.

The work of separate voices should be done each day, until the moment when *the finger articulations are reduced to a minimum*. It is advisable to do this in both directions, beginning first with the thumb and then with the fourth.
I repeat that so the development of the speed is tremendous, avoiding the tensions that the distances might cause.
It goes without saying that for measures 19 and 20 the left hand, also playing the sixths, will do the same work.

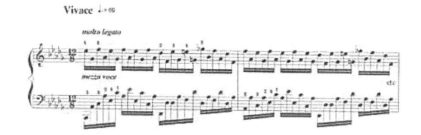

For the chromatic scales I think that the basic fingerings of Op. 10 No. 2 are best, here more open (or too open) for small hands that must - nature demands- glide the thumbs.
I recommend this fingering for the grand final scale.

When it comes to the left hand, although it makes intervals spanning the tonalities, it also makes some little leaps, in *tempo*, which makes its mission more delicate.
It is better to divide these three exercises:

a)   Study only the intervals, without the leaps, as in   the right-hand. This must be done applying the same principles of division as for the right-hand.
b)   Study the leaps adding octaves to reduce the distances.
c)   Consider this leap as *the first note* and never as the note of arrival.

Legato is absolute in both hands, except during the leap in the left. We should note that the repetition of the thumb of the left-hand makes the physical aspect of the *legato* impossible. In these cases, it is better *to connect the possible voices*, that is, the lower notes on the left and the higher on the right, as specified for the Etude in Thirds. It will be the same case in the Etude of the Octaves.
On the whole, we could say that the *legato* of double notes is possible in the acoustic result but not always *in the physical reality*, given that *we must play six notes with five fingers.*
Whether it is with the classical fingering or the modern gliding fingering, one finger must glide, whether it is the thumb or the index finger. Whichever it is, the *legato* is, as already seen, *a question of producing a longer sound and, according to the judgment of the ear, one that is richer and more harmonic.*
The Etude in Sixths brings up the interest in the harmonious development of the hand, given that they work continually in double notes and, as a result, reinforce the inter-digital muscles making the fingers more independent and more solid. The pianist begins to feel more powerful when he is able to succeed in this Etude without the slightest error.
The malleability and shaping of the open passages, give the pianist a *savoir faire* without the usual melodies and harmonies. This seeks out a less classical musical discourse, but one is not prevented from discovering *an agreeable musical work* if one knows how to search in the hidden substance.
The profound work of the Sixths brings an additional musical pleasure if you understand the

true nature of the problem they put before us.

We now come to an examination of Etude Op. 25 No. 10, the Octaves.

The term *etude* is here once again and incredibly weak way of describing the music that Chopin proposes and imposes. Rarely does he unleash such fury on the instrument. A colossal outbreak strikes the keyboard: it is without name until the fifth measure, when we recognize the tonality of B minor. Raging, frustrated double octaves, wanting to join with other voices or with other chords, move across the instrument to the extent that we think it must explode before the end of the passage, at full and dazzling speed. It compares with nothing in all the earlier literature on the piano.

The explanation is simple: it is not an etude but rather a *work of grandiose, epic, Homeric art*. The choice of the polyphony of octaves is once again unique: each finger is a soldier armed to the teeth. It installs a superb musical fresco that is Herculean, proud and almost haughty.

It is inaccessible to many pianists because its *honest* barriers to execution are almost insurmountable. Chromatic passages contradict diatonic passages: blocks appear, and you could say that you are witnessing a labour of Hercules. The octaves then separate in contrary, *ferocious* movement, to meet again in a low register with a strength uncommon in Chopin. An imperious cadence plunges us into a nervous silence of maximum red alert.

You might imagine anything, but such a melody.... such a guileless song...

It could be defined as contemplation: the sonorities are at the zenith, zephyrous, diaphanous. The tonalities are also often strange. Chopin is adrift in polyphonies in four voices, in intermediary melodies, in repetitions that are not what they seem because they are always varied with genius.

In this obsessive persistence, its length being unnoticed, he shows *his sense of unrivalled musical psychology and his understanding of the resistance of the ear of those who were listening.*

The whole plunges into a long, very extended pedal on the dominant ninth, loaded with woes and tensions, which leads to an intensified recapitulation, whether in drama or dynamics. The *piu forte possible* is attained. The lava flows from this volcano, at this moment, exposing all the cracks in this devastated keyboard.

Clearly to execute such a work a range of preparatory work must be undertaken in order to strengthen the finger muscles that must be, poor things, assisted by those of the arms, shoulders, back and the entire body.

Although the Etude in Octaves is not within reach of everyone, as mentioned above, every self-respecting pianist must study it. Executing it, without any *cheating*, is almost a record. The fingerings are almost impossible for all hands: the *legato* demanded by Chopin is probably the major difficulty, because it requires muscular capacity to resist, while fatigue undermines that capacity even before the end of the first major exposition.

In fact, one of the major tricks is not to respect the *legato*, but to leap and to use muscles other than those demanded *by* Chopin, with a pedal camouflage studied and administered. But....

The initial work to be done is therefore to study the extreme voices on both sides, following the basic model of Etude Op. 10 No. 2, in order to obtain a profound *legato*.

The study of the broken octaves, in both directions, is highly necessary, always keeping the extreme voices in *legato*. They will build up the resistance of the muscles in the forearm.

For the first sustained notes, in measures 5 and 6, a separate work for voices is demanded, particularly that for the higher voice. It must be done in absolutely *legato* and holding the central note. Of course, when studying the thumb alone with the sustained note there will have to be complete relaxation of the muscles of the forearm and upper arm. Repeating the thumb several times will help this need by avoiding its separation from the key.

To do this a absorptive movement without *staccato* is necessary. Clearly applying this working method to similar passages will be welcome for all the problems raised by this Etude.

When practising, anticipation of the thematic voices will help relax the muscles that must connect the octaves and isolate the elements involved. Always study by large structures in order to develop endurance. Do not be afraid of the dissonances in bars 17 and 18. Rather support them, because they are disturbing elements, like cries of distress.

From measure 21 on, the *sforzandi* on the third quavers must be respected. There is still crescendo!

But this *does not permit you to begin in piano* the octaves A-sharp, on the right, and C-natural on the left: *this is a crescendo that begins with strength from the start*. The fact of playing in

PP to begin it goes only to reveal our fears. However, the Etude will help us develop more confidence. So, take heart.

It is essential to study the thumbs, guides in these dazzling measures, particularly when the octaves separate in *FF*. You have to recognize the topography of the keyboard.

The cadence before the central part is authoritarian, without *ritardando*, and almost violent. You have to take a deep breath before plunging yourself into this central gentleness. The *fermata* and the long-sustained note so precisely for this purpose!

The nerves must calm down and relax; the muscles must again receive *oxygen*. The austere indication given by Chopin, *ben legato*, speaks for itself. There should not be too many languid outbursts in the exposition of the theme: this is a warrior resting and not a young girl sniffling.

The alternation of melody, counterpoint and polyphony should be highlighted as an essential element: we should understand that these elements are not conceived *as rubato passages* but rather try to demonstrate the precision of Chopin's inspiration.

After the *fermata*, four measures further on, *the theme of the tenor is of capital importance throughout four measures, as is that of the contralto four measures later*. This continues until the re- exposition of the enriched theme, where Chopin reintroduces the principal recapitulative melody.

It is preferable not to change the hierarchy of the voices in this long central part to make it *more interesting*: it is already superlative. The only thing that would be achieved by doing this would be to spoil the musical integrity of the Music. It would be better to develop and enrich the *toucher* to safeguard this Olympian calm. The contact of the fingertip or the phalange with the key must be complete but guided by a thread of steel. Contact between the thumb and the key is, on the other hand, shorter and with less pressure. Contact of the central fingers, provoking other themes, must be deep like the voice of the soprano: full and serene. It should be possible to feel the length of the pressure on the keys.

In the large pedal on the F-sharp, the tenor must be presented like a dull threat, while the soprano will concentrate, without being too visible, before unleashing the final catastrophe. The melody then becomes harsher.

The weapons must be recovered for this *Coda*, which seems less tiring because it is shorter. However, the muscles must be oiled so that they can achieve this *piu forte possible*, without any conventional *ritardando*, but with a splendour and an apogee worthy of the work.

This is a moment of *conquistador* for a pianist, because he emerges from the impossible dream and finds himself back on earth after a fabulous conquest, given that it seemed that this limit was unachievable. Then, and only then, can you raise your sword in the direction opposite to that of Damocles. Perhaps, we should thank the heavens for our safe passage through all of these traps and for an unblemished exit.

And now let me say a few words to describe the opposite in Etude Op. 10 No. 7. The key aspects that describe a completely different type of execution are elegance, aristocracy, flexibility and lightness. In fact, Chopin's savoir-faire here is remarkable. Quite correctly this Etude has been described as *the finest toccata of Romanticism*. Double notes in constant *piano*, vaporous liaisons, insinuations by the left hand, particularly in the central part, make it seem to be in flight, fleeing the sonorous masses of the Octaves Etude.

The sudden rebounds between the intervals of thirds, sixths, seconds, sevenths, fourths, fifths, majors, minors, diminished and augmented, give it an enchantment close to magic and leave us puzzled confronted by such a miracle.

As if this were not sufficient, the central part also surprises us with its dreamy reminder of a valse brilliante, which should *"be danced only by countesses"*, according to Robert Schumann.

This whole climax of seduction does not prevent Chopin from making it an entirely unique etude; the hand never ceases from opening and closing in astonishing flexibility turning on all the axes. This is without doubt one of the most extraordinary aspects of the genius of Chopin: the perfect symbiosis between mind and matter; the height of artisanal talent and musical aesthetics.

Replacing the second finger by the thumb in the lower voice, with a perfect *legato*, only goes to accentuate this work of genius.

Preparing this marvel demands, first of all, learning the two voices separately, by giving them the most delicate *legato* and a melodic movement in the higher notes as in a rapid melody.

Another fundamental approach is to learn these voices in *broken movement* until achieving real speed, or *true digital vertigo*, which will mainly help to command the greater distances, such as the major sevenths, for example.

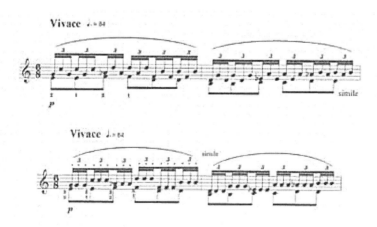

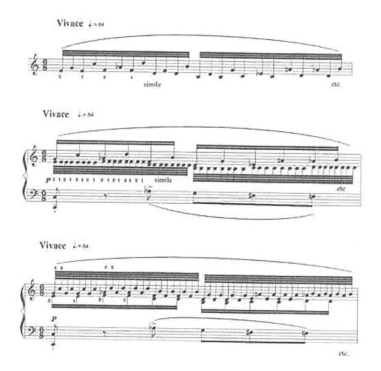

The position of the wrist, scarcely lower than that of the hand, should avoid any wasted effort. *The articulation is more imagined than real.* Avoid all stress and any excess of sonority.

The left-hand also demands extreme delicacy. Avoid over- accentuating the delicious little supports on the third or on the second quaver. *It is more a question of sophisticated humour than accents on notes.*

Further on, in the central part, from measure 16, phrasing is conditioned by the subtle touch of the resonance pedal: *it must be raised at the third quaver of each measure and replace it at the next quaver* to discreetly highlight the cheeky little valse and the sustained notes further on.

Do not over-accentuate the octaves or the chords on the left. Any overcharge is superfluous and unwelcome here: Chopin demands brilliance and not vulgar blocks of sound.

The final *crescendo*, where one of the notes disappears, is articulated a little more brilliantly but without exaggeration, in order to retain the idea of distinction that adds flavour to this moment of grace. The work of breaking it down into triplets helps to relax and lighten it.

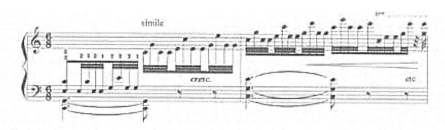

The last chords assured resonate rather than sound. Certainly, this is no place for the anxiety of second-class virtuosos. This is a moment for smiles and happiness.

2.4 – The fourth family
Three Etudes for phrasing: Op.10 No. 10, Op. 25 No. 4 and Op. 25 No. 5

Let us move on to an analysis of the Etudes for phrasing.

We will begin with Op. 10 No. 10, "*this pianists Parnassus*", in the words of Franz Liszt.

Chopin demands different phrasing and articulations in the first 16 measures of the work, just as he did in Etudes Op. 25 No. 4 and No. 5. We have here, once again, *a study of the joint possibilities of supporting the hand and its cantabile division*, using, of course, the thumb and the fifth finger.

It is very clear that all work we do on this Etude, even during practice fragments, the phrasing indicated by Chopin will be respected to the full as well as the rhythms marked *by two* or *by three* quavers.

The elegance of the work, its lightness and its distinguished sonorities are more reminiscent of an undulating Impromptu than an Etude. But this impression is not confirmed: it demands a great deal of work because the control exercised by each part of the hand is severe, and any loss seems like a rude attack on the general sonorous atmosphere. The aim of these three Etudes is precisely to develop this dual control of the hand for the phrasing, either on opening or moving the thumb.

Etude Op. 10 No. 10, gives the impression of floating in water or gliding on air because there is no impediment, no break and no interruption. There is a moment of *relative bravura* in its central part, but it never exceeds *good manners*. The *climax* is moderation, careful execution, refinement, fluency and *the virtuosity that scarcely shows itself*.

The return to the theme is delightful, on the pedal of the E-flat, and the little leaps also increase the distances. *No sign of excitement or agitation* should be given. The fact of writing continually alternating the thumb and the sixth gives an impression of musical stability that must be retained without interruption. Above all should be savoured, enjoyed and its delights felt; in fact, you can almost revel in the *elegance* that flows through it.

The first task is, obviously, to divide the difficulties. The etude of the constant fingering 1-2-1-2-1 for the lower voice must be learnt in order to obtain the speed for the *less rapid* fingers.

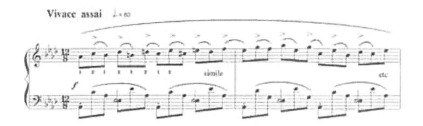

A similar result must be obtained for the sixths by combining the possibilities 2-5 and 5-2. Inverting the formula of the Etude seeks advantage in fixing the axis of *the second finger in relation to the thumb*. Fixing the second finger serves to make the remaining octaves more flexible. *A totally staccato work* fundamentally encourages the lightness of the final execution, just as the work *in chords (and in octaves)*.

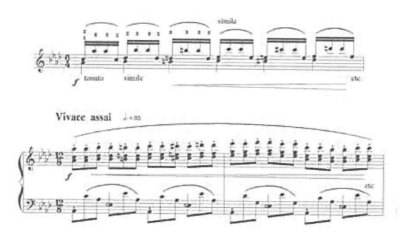

The three notes must then be combined by playing them in triplets, against the two of the left hand, throughout the whole Etude, so as to develop *the general speed limited to the fingers*.

Displacement by chords is beneficial for the central cadence in order to give authority to the displacements. Extension over several octaves on the keyboard is also very important.

Constant formulas are also there for the left hand. *The principal axis is, however, the fourth finger*, but the aerial value of the second is essential. An attack by a heavy thumb must also be avoided. Octaves must be added for the perilous leaps on the E- flat of the bass.

140

Of course, the same exercises must be applied to the final measures where Chopin adds some chords and some thirds.

It is very useful to transpose this Etude into A major.

A tranquil hand is essential to interpret this work; the wrist should not be the only reference, but rather a subtle rotation of the forearm to obtain a magic atmosphere.

Let us now move on to Etude Op. 25 No. 4, another true marvel: the technical stroke of inspiration is unique, and its verticality does not manage to hide all the melodic arcs that it involves.

The left hand, which leaps without stopping, is full of impishness, and is roguish and malicious. And is extremely difficult moreover. There is a whimsical *atmosphere* to this work. It could also be one of the great Preludes. Being able to achieve a melody with chords, sometimes detached, sometimes a bit *legato*, other times fully *legato,* is a challenge. It shows how Chopin knew his themes from within and not just their formulae, no matter how brilliant they were. Changes in phrasing are the order of the day, as in Etude Op. 10 No. 10. You cut, you connect, you accentuate, you hold more or less, to end connecting definitively the whole to fall into a Neapolitan cadence. A terrible chord inversed over the tonic, of a seventh on B-flat, comes to rest. The melodic derivation towards the A major does not entirely manage to illuminate it.

The rhythm must be well established, which is not at all simple. It is the rhythm that will determine the expression of the chords. It must be presented as *an obsessive rhythm on the fifth finger of the left hand but controlling the melodic system on the weak part of the tempo on the right, also on the fifth finger.*

This melody is often held, and its lower part turned into intervals that maintain the expressive, formal contact with the rest of the Etude.

As in Etude Op. 10 No. 10, the formulae demanded by Chopin should never be abandoned, because the playing and its differences are the fundamental aspects of the musical development of the right hand.

The difficulty of the left hand demands some initial training.

We should *compare* this formula with Etude Op. 10 No. 9 and study it in triplets or in four notes, according to the case. This will bring maximum flexibility to the muscles. This work is done in the direction demanded by Chopin; the opposite direction is also highly recommended. This means *inverting the intervals to give the thumb independence.*

Agitato ♩=160

The study of the fifth fingers forming octaves in the real position is fundamental for fixing the leaps and above all *mentally reducing* the distances. This allows you to calculate these distances and to reduce their psychological consequences.

Also exercise by displacing the leaps to a lower octave.

Isolating the fifth finger of the right hand - *its anticipation during the practice* - helps a better choice of desired melodic quality. Of course, each pianist will find other working formulae to alleviate the lower fingers. Above all, it is the thumb that is difficult.

The fact of repeating the chords several times, but very lightly, helps to make them more flexible.

The more obscure atmosphere of the central part does not allow for any *rallentando* as in a freer work.

There is a distant resemblance between this Etude and the Prelude in G-sharp minor, from the musical point of view. They are not the same formulae, of course, but the somber character of the two works has greatly assisted my personal execution.

The *Agitato* speaks for itself, as does the angular nature of its rhythm. The accentuation, which is never conventional, causes clashes and upsets a stable audition. Furthermore, the final cadence is a model: a spiritual collapse seems to follow this preceding deployment of energy. Desolation confirms this: the work is suspended as in a big question mark and is never truly resolved.

You might say that there is no response *to it*.

Now a few words on another small marvel, that of Etude Op. 25 No. 5, in E minor. Chopin has rarely written anything so spiritual, light, poetic, distinguished, full of gentle melancholy, dreamlike and almost fanciful. It seems to have wings and to smile in a charming *scherzando*. After some brilliant, but light leaps, it plunges into a central part with a malleability reminiscent of Vermeer, so perfect are the lines. It emerges into a melody with a very pure, serene line that is scarcely agitated. This *agitato* is far more the result of the modulations than the real charge of the musical message. The final cadence, with its insistent *appogiatures*, flows in superb trills that spread into an apparent *FFF*, because it is far from the *piu forte possible* of the Octaves Etude in both character and volume. You could say that Chopin plays with the dynamics as with fire, but without burning himself. There is nothing here that will allow for an accumulation of rude sonorities. This *FFF* is brilliant and illuminates the keyboard like the halo round a star.

In the meantime, the left-hand amuses itself in ballets and little *cabrioles* full of good humour. It is sometimes in *contratempo*, but always gracious. In the central part, however, it commands a more profound, although lighter, melody, which is much more serious, but without becoming dramatic.

The dissonances caused by the *appogiatura* are to be savoured. They should neither be emphasized nor hidden, but rather *naturalized.*

The work of phrasing is as intense as for the preceding Etudes, Op. 10 No. 10 and Op. 25 No. 4. For formulae are demanded here by Chopin.

As already mentioned, here we must take care not to change   the phrasing into caprices or commodities, particularly in the penultimate variation, in crotchets, *where less scrupulous editors have dared to change Chopin's fingerings, destined to link the soprano and to glide the thumbs in the lower notes.* Such procedures are unacceptable because they denature the Etude.

In fact, so are Chopin's *methods (phrasings are three, four* if you count the central *cantabile* part):

1. *Scherzando* in quavers and semiquavers with arpeggiated chords in the left-hand.
2. *Scherzando* in quavers and semiquavers with the movement of the left-hand that follows the right.
3. *Scherzando* in quavers and semiquavers with accentuated notes on second beats.
4. *Scherzando* with the same notes and in quavers on the right.
5. *Crotchets held in the right forming a melodic legato soprano!*
6. Quavers on the right and on the left. The whole is
7. *legato.*

The fifth variant or third phrasing, that of the black keys, demands connected fingering, therefore not the same as what preceded.

That of Chopin must be used, of course.

All the differences must as well be emphasized.

The fundamental work is to play 2-1 separately in the right hand, in preparation for the definitive execution. The intervals must be broken down by forming triplets.

It goes without saying that the thumb is not *staccato* and that despite Chopin's indication of *leggiero* - referring to the touch on the key and not the duration of the notes - *the lower line must be followed without the gaps* to which less careful pianists have accustomed us. However, in the crotchets variant, *Chopin imposes the legato*, as already mentioned, *as well as the gliding of the thumb, still not staccato.*

Chopin's nuances vary from piano, *dolce* to little *soufflets*. By deduction the first leaps are not as noisy as those of the re- exposition, where they are in *FF*.

You must absolutely avoid *the mistake* in the central part *of falling into languish*. If you look at it without hindsight, metronomes indicate 184 for the crotchet in the first section, and 168 for the second. Therefore, there is no space to make so many differences in *Tempo*. A flowing feeling must prevail.

The *ben tenuto* of the left hand indicates the depth to which the keys must be pressed, with the phalanges well placed on the keys, against the *leggiero* of the right-hand, which spreads well-shaped, distinguished arpeggios, without the least heaviness. The addition of octaves does not mean forcing the passage. The effect on the ear is already more profound without adding too much volume.

The semiquavers do not fundamentally vary the expression of the accompaniment, but they add a fabulous sensation of completion.

The first thing is not to articulate them too much, but to make them merge into more intimate atmospheres, because the protestation of the preceding octaves and chords becomes calm and diluted.

Study by breaking the groups down into four or five notes.

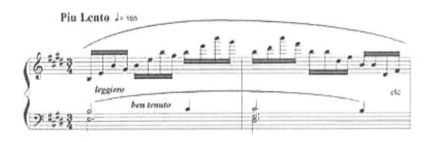

An added note completes each chord in the recapitulation. Its character and its phrasing remain unchanged, although Chopin always manages to vary something. The final *crescendo*, towards the great leaps, is the most important thing.

To draw a parallel with the central part, the voice of a cello, in measures 126, 127, 128 and 129 takes its place solemnly before the *appogiatura* that changes into trills. These trills gradually prevail and do not let it open out. Once again, *con forza* do not be brutal but brilliant, in order to illuminate this rise of the arpeggio which will superbly close this gem among the Etudes.

2.5 – The fifth family
Four Etudes cantabiles: Op. 10 No. 3, Op. 10 No. 6, Op. 25 No. 1, Op. 25 No. 2 and Op. 25 No. 7

And now we come to the Etudes *cantabiles*: Op. 10 No. 3, Op. 10 No. 6, Op. 25 No. 1, Op. 25 No. 2 and Op. 25 No. 7.

We will examine them together, considering the similarities and interdependence of problems involving sonorities and styles.

First, we must differentiate *the pure speeds from static or melodic speeds*, that is, *the different speeds* in the fast Etudes or in the slow Etudes.

We will speak, for example, Op. 10 No. 6

Its unique meandering makes us think of this inescapable attraction that creators have for this *motionless continuity.*

They are seduced by *this non-movement, or by this perpetual motion,* or quite simply by the obsession. Think only of the Bach's First Prelude (and there are very many more), Beethoven's Moonlight Sonata, the last variation of Op. 109, to the Preludes known as 'Raindrop' by Chopin, Liszt's Chasse Neige, Ravel's Ondine, of all the obsessive intervals, as in the Mirrors... The examples are endless. Op. 25 No. 7 is another, with its succession of chords.

The *tempo*, in these cases, is absolutely fundamental: there is a need here for hypnosis. If something moves, the work collapses. So above all, this sinuous movement in its immobility must be studied.

This is the case for three Etudes.

For these works, and we now assimilate the Etudes Op. 10 No. 3, Op. 10 No. 6 and Op. 25 No. 7, the best working method is that used by Bach: *the separation of voices, as if it were a Fugue, and the division of the hand into expressive and secondary zones.* They must be studied in this way for each voice, combining them in all their mathematical possibilities: bass-soprano, bass-alto, alto-soprano, and learning them by heart separately.

Let us examine Etude Op. 10 No. 3, for example.

This separation of voices means that each one of them and the clarity of the construction can be heard. Each voice as a line in itself, completed by itself, can be heard.

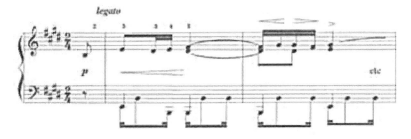

These major lines, the spiritual, vocal respirations must be found, as if they were instrumental lines accompanying an invisible singer.

Chopin excels in handling polyphony in a sublime way. He does this from within and without any heaviness.

147

Therefore, playing should not be too languished. In his initial intention, Chopin wrote in his manuscript: *Vivace ma non troppo.*

The *Lento ma non troppo* was corrected later.

The benefits of this work are felt clearly when we complete it with other major polyphonic works: The Prelude, Choral and Fugue by Franck, for example, Mendelssohn's Preludes and Fugues or those of Shostakovich.

The discourse of the Etude is noble, without being overly *rubato*. It is emotive and reserved. In all of this there is a similarity with the central part of Beethoven's *Pathetique Sonata*. Or better still, in Chopin there is almost a synthesis between Bach and Beethoven. He also/besides develops a more dramatic and more animated central part. But despite all, this remains pure Chopin.

The interpretation of the upper melodic lines is supple and should be played with the whole phalange, without trying to fix the fingers but rather making them flexible; their vibration must be ensured. The central part of the intervals, which is harder and more virtuosistic, should be treated like the Etude for the Sixths: *with the reduction of the intervals to simple fingers* so as to obtain the necessary speed for its definitive execution. The principles applied to the inverted notes help make considerable progress.

The sparkle of the sonorities should be sculpted brilliantly and with courage.

This Etude has become one of the favourite melodies of light music thanks to the cinema, the theatre, musicals and public or personal imagination. Clearly, we should return to Chopin what is rightfully his and not continue to change such masterpieces into mood music, or worse, into background music. Dignity is the first ethical approach to executing this well-known and magnificent piece of work.

And now a few words on Etude Op. 10 No. 6.

The dark tonality of the E-flat minor, dear to Scriabin, gives intensity and drama to the work, without the suspension of the A major, in the *Coda*, being able to contribute some change there. An undulation, an implacable contour, passes right through it.

First let us look at the movement demanded by Chopin.

Above all, there is no Adagio. It is Andante, con molta espressione. This movement is indispensable for translating the feverish and anxious state of the whole work. I feel it as almost *agitato* and passionate, lugubrious and painful, on the whole upsetting. Strange above all, *because it sets a movement against a non-movement*: you might say, in fact, that on the one hand the Etude advances, while on the other, it remains motionless. Clearly the first thing to do is to work separately the *legatissimo* of the semiquavers.

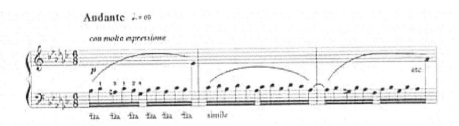

It would be ridiculous not to give them their musical character: the more mechanically one works, the more insipid is the final result. *The pedal should be planned not to disturb;* it is not harmonic but should help the measure 6/8. It must be used per quaver, except in some rare exceptions.

The voices must be combined:

a – Study the bass with the soprano without the semiquavers, and the bass with the semiquavers without the soprano.

b – Study the semiquavers with the soprano.

The soprano should be different than in Op. 10 No. 3: here it is more tense, less serene. But the plenitude of the sonority, particularly its expansion, should follow a path that is not too distant from the other.

What is important in the two Etudes is that the merging of the voices is one of the fundamental differences between the polyphony of Chopin and that of Bach on the harpsichord.

That of Chopin merges more than that of Bach, which is more transparent.

That of Chopin resembles that of the organ of Bach. The octaves in the left hand in Op. 10 No. 6 do no more than recall this.

It is clear that in the Etudes Op. 25 No. 1 and Op. 25 No. 2, other problems arise, particularly those of the sonorities in *the less mechanical speeds.*

Even in the Etude for Thirds and that for Sixths, pure speed serves no purpose if the beauty of the passage is not produced by the beauty of the sonority.

This is what is at stake and what is the fundamental problem. I do not mean that the Etudes Op. 10 are less sophisticated than those of Op. 25 with regard to *toucher,* far from that, but it is clear that these two Etudes Op. 25 No. 1 and No. 2, resemble more gems of sonorities rather than true *etudes* in the mechanical sense of the word. The work on sonority is essential from the very first moment when these works are put into practice. Chopin loved them in a particular way, and they had a place of honour on his concert programmes, which were rare.

Every pianist knows Schumann's appreciation of Etude Op. 25 N°1: an *Aeolian harp*. This after an execution by its author. Clearly the suppleness demanded by this work is particularly severe. In fact, the least contraction of the wrist or the elbow makes the execution violent, taut and ugly. Any additional force by the forearm must also be eliminated. Studying the arpeggios in *PP* is very beneficial, as is a total contact with the keys.

This image of floating, of the arms in water, so dear to Chopin, is not just by chance in this Etude, which is more of a harmonic halo than an articulation. Its beauty does not depend only on the quality of the touch on the upper notes, but also to a great extent *on those making up the arpeggios*, which determine the final result.

It is important to study the arrival of the melodic notes, their boomerang effects and their projection towards the successive arpeggios. This Etude must be worked *without the melody* in order to concentrate on the beauty of the separated arpeggios, *making the hands fly without holding on to anything* when arriving at the thematic note. The articulation of the fingers must then be reduced to a minimum to find the birth of the sound on and from the key. In order to give each finger more independence, the thumbs should be studied in the octave position in order to avoid an excess of elbow movement and unwelcome lateral displacements.

These exercises are a vital in the major leaps, particularly those of the development. In this way, *you will not have the idea of leaping, but of combining the third finger with the thumb.*

The central part, full of modulations, takes off into a more dramatic lyricism, without achieving pathetic nuances, though. The expression must be more pressing and desperate. However, grandiloquence must be avoided, and excesses restrained. This is poetic despair or contained lament. The fact of interchanging the notes between the two hands, by passing one thumb of one hand towards the other, does not achieve a great deal but, on the other hand, it does restrain the flexibility that one might require with Chopin's arrangement. In other words, this Etude comes from the great and complete Chopin. It is worthwhile if only

151

for the aesthetic satisfaction of studying it *according to him.*

The *Coda* is a wonder of lightness, of delicate virtuosity and candour. Do not over-exaggerate the final *soufflé* but rather remain there discreet, reserved and contained. The final chord is dropped in lightly, without effort. It produces *a resonance rather than a sound.*

It is perhaps a glimpse into the inner self. The final little trill is serene and without *crescendo,* as if it were trembling in fear at being the last item of evidence of such beauty.

The brother Etude, Op. 25 No. 2 in F minor is not only a gently brilliant and expressive Etude, but also *a true, very fast, melody* in the sense of Impromptus.

One cannot talk of *jeu perlé*, despite the clarity required from the right-hand. *It is the curve that is most important, and far more important than its angles.* You must know how to model its development.

The first problem, which too often remains without a solution, is the rhythm of the work: it is in fact not written in 6/4, but in 2/2. So, we have four triplets in the right-hand against two triplets in the left hand. What we hear is always in 6/4 *because the rhythm only coincides in half measures*

Clearly to obtain this rhythmic demand Chopin suggests the fingering 1, 3, 2 - 1, 3, 2 - 1, 3, 2 - 1, 4, 5 rather than the traditional 2, 3, 1 - 2, 4, 3 in many editions.

His fingering gives another natural accentuation, better suited to the music then *the apparent convenience* of the other fingering producing the wrong rhythm in 6/4.

Transpose the study into F-sharp minor for practice.

The work in *PP* should be followed strictly and its expression is discreet, delicate, refined and charming.

It is a moment of spiritual refinement and not one of demonstration. It wafts through a suspended cadence like a sad regret without a solution.

We must also observe the "repetitions". It is, perhaps, a good idea not to repeat them exactly, although do not dismiss the *surprise* of the dynamics the third time, after the development, where the discourse becomes animated through the *very* refined modulations and this little *portamento,* in measure 57.

This is preferable as an interpretation, and one doesn't need to change too much the second time. However, if changes are preferred, *they should be resigned, reserved* and scarcely audible. Here fleeting, whispered secrets are transmitted and not baroque effects and displaced echoes. The beauty of its sound emission   is like the queen of the night: the more hidden she is, the more beautiful she seems.

I am particularly fond of Etude Op. 25 No. 7.

Its polyphony is *harmonical*, if you can excuse such an offensive comment.

In these melodic Etudes, *we note an obsession that follows us like a fatal hypnosis.* The somber nature brought by the tonality of the C-sharp minor, sometimes reflects an exasperated state of mind, sometimes tense, as in the development, sometimes tempestuous, as in the great scales and in the great dramatic movements in the left hand, sometimes serene, as in the passages in E major and, above all, in B major. A duet is established from the start, after   a short *recitativo* in the register of the cello. This introduces the atmosphere of the work.

Chopin succeeds in combining an incredible duet: *the pathetique with the* élégie. Each melody could exist on its own; they would still be rich if they were separated. The serenity of the soprano contrasts with the emphasis of the bass in a climate generated by the severity of chords without respite.

The bass covers several registers, but the soprano remains more serene alone.

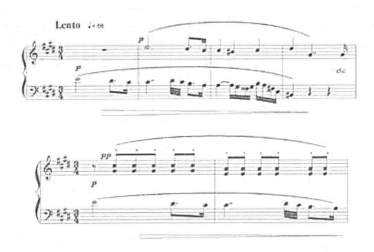

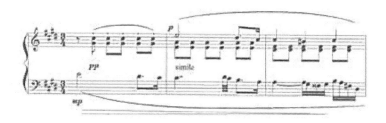

After a moment of peace found again in the bass, the right becomes painfully inflamed. The bass then begins dizzying runs until it reaches a terrible scale in E-flat, terribly difficult to achieve *in tempo*, despite the *ritardando* that helps a little. An oasis of tranquillity then sets in, in the tonality of B major. Once again the music seems immobile; only until this terrible cord F-sharp - B - D-sharp - A, in *ppp*.

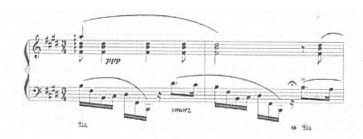

The first atmosphere is so taken up again, but in a more resigned way and more submissive. Only one violent scale is imposed towards the tenor, which despite its movements, melts into terrible, dissonant chords, without hope and in silences more expressive than any music.

A solid technique is required for such a work. Daring to confront it without the expressive, developed means of the left-hand, assumes musical temerity. It is difficult to understand why such an Etude is considered by some to be less difficult than others…

Five Etudes for the extensions and for the more fixed positions: Op. 10 No. 4, Op. 10 No. 9,

Op. 10 No. 11, Op. 25 No. 3 and Op. 25 No. 9

To conclude this "little review" of the Etudes, let us look at the five works with more fixed positions: Op. 10 No. 9 and No. 11, Op. 25 No. 3 and No. 9, and lastly Op. 10 No. 4, one of the favourites with young pianists for international competitions, for brilliant *encores* or simply to demonstrate a healthy, clear and direct virtuosity.

Op. 10 N° 9, in F minor, is a troubled Etude, *molto agitato*, intense and full of exacerbated poesy.
Its respiration is unstable and anguished. It disappears without leaving a trace, gently and almost repentant. In an uneasy left hand, extended and open, it demands a musical diction that sometimes rises to a heated declamation in repeated octaves, *apassionato*, and in the rises in *accelerando*.
The theme is rarely stable: Chopin demands *portato* touches, *crescendi* and *con forza*, in the same phrase and in the same line. The discourse is *stretto* and moves from *FF* to *PP* or vice versa, brusquely.
Before studying this, we should understand that the upper extremes of the left-hand do no more than provide a melodic counterpoint for the thematic quavers of the right hand. Their varying distances are expressive. They do not belong to only one technical formula. We find here that the left thumbs play more melodically, the fifths the harmonic basses and the three central fingers play the axes, and this in an ensemble of six notes *per beat*. As already said, it must be worked together with Etude Op. 25 No. 4, because this joint work helps plunge the left-hand into a thorough form of gymnastics and hygiene. It is also very beneficial transposing the work into F-sharp minor.

The differences between the touch of the right-hand and the fixed touch of the left demand total flexibility of the wrist, which seems to float over the keyboard rather than to penetrate it. It is important to maintain its height to maintain this idea of floating over the instrument. Avoid stiffening it at the moment of attacking the keys. The opposite work - by intervals - for the left-hand is important for becoming familiar with the extensions and distances as well as for the repetition of the same.

For the hand openings of the re-exposition, I recommend the following fingerings, to avoid tension in the hand in the extensions: *play twice with the left thumb for the F - G-flat distances, as in measure 50, for example.* This adds greater stability to the hand during these openings. What makes one prefer this Etude for students first facing the style of Chopin are its dramatic accents. It is also said that it is a little less difficult than others... However, do not put too much trust in appearances because it demands some serious work and analysis. The application of time is therefore important in all cases: but time is required when having to resolve the second Etude Op. 10 or the easiest of the Mazurkas. Each item has its own difficulties.

Some sacrifice is always required to achieve an artistic result worthy of the work, whatever it is, and of ourselves. This Etude suggests above all a vision *molto agitato* of a repeated, insistent declamation. A study of *this diversity* is essential to avoid any parrot talk. The *conception of expressive convulsions*, chained or not, reveals a *changing* Chopin amidst restless sonorities; with the same technical formula and in stability of tempo, but with richer dynamics that are open and ill at ease.

This is already quite a programme.

Etude Op. 10 No. 11 belongs among the marvels of the collection, as an invention and inspiration, as an Etude or quite simply as a *morceau*.

It is incredible to imagine an Etude as brilliant from the point of view of the conception of the technical formula which, at the same time, graces us with such beauty. With Chopin we are used to miracles of inspiration but such imagination for formula is not common, even in him.

It does have a vague resemblance to the great Prelude in E-flat, the No. 19, although the latter is *pure movement*. The two works sing miraculously.

Problems of extension on fixed positions turn into a veritable poem of moving lyricism.

Any resemblance to the harp is entirely false.

There is nothing more pianistic than this Etude. Chopin is not concerned about other instruments, *apart from the human voice*. The piano is his whole world.

Here Chopin explores the secrets and pleasures of the soul in places that are remote, but close in sentiment and harmony.

The delights brought by the little appoggiaturas of the re-exposition are extraordinary. There is no point in hurrying them. Quite the contrary, they must be *fully* incorporated into the melodic system. The basic element for executing this marvel is flexibility in the wrists. The slightest stiffness or tension of the wrist will make everything sound false and harsh. It is like handling crystal: if you know how to handle it, it vibrates; otherwise it breaks.
Distances often exceed an octave and a half, stretching the hand quite remarkably. The utility of the Etude is visible, tangible and indispensable. However, its traps have discouraged many a pianist. In the central part, the melodic lines complete one another and are not entrusted only to the soprano.

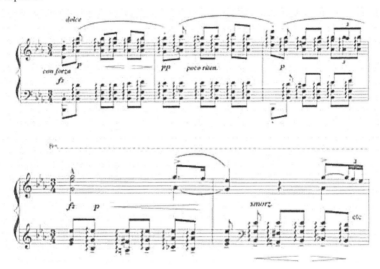

Also, at the end, even the bass has melodic roles.

The end is like a flash of light. It should not be rushed, *but savoured*. The work is above all about relaxation.
It has been said that at all costs you should avoid imitating the harp.

So, the recommendation is to work as follows: *first of all, starting with the relationship of fifth fingers left and thumbs right,* carefully guarding the *coincidences in arpeggios,* in the very   regular semiquavers. *These two starting fingers should be together, like the two arrival fingers: this means that the chords should be parallel and not continuous.*
This is the best way of avoiding the harp effect. All you have to do is follow what Chopin has written!

It is very useful to invert the working formula, beginning with the upper extremities, always very regularly.

It is clear that when there are more notes, the extremes should continue to be together. These formulae should be doubled or tripled to make them more efficient and supple, breaking the chords down into simple notes. The fact of achieving a maximum number of notes by these duplications will strengthen the relaxation.

The distances must also be studied as soon as the suppleness of the wrists is developed. Fixing the axes fingers and making the extremities flexible as in example No. 144 is very beneficial work. Also beneficial is to divide the distances by note, combined with the two or three remaining notes, as in example No. 146. The two last notes on the right must always be more expressive than the rest.

The general atmosphere is not tense, but melancholic, without the tempo of 76 per crotchet being reduced. The central part is more obscure, but not slower. Try to give it a more melancholic image without torturing the Etude with an exaggerated pathos.

Chopin indicates *Allegretto* and not *Adagio élégiaque* or A*ndante mesto*. A fluid movement is welcome; it will accentuate the incredible charms of this marvellous page.

We will now take a look at Op. 25 No. 3, another marvel of fixed lightness, winged like a butterfly.

Good humour, daring conception, casualness, almost nonchalance, make this Etude an excellent companion for occasions of conviviality and joy.

Its figures are spins on the axes towards the outer extremes. Sometimes, these are achieved brilliantly, sometimes gently and sometimes drily. Less often, they form melodies with no tomorrow. They always show different facets, little humorous *masques* that never cease to leap about.

Chopin moves the F major to B major, affirmatively, without concern for the tritones so dear to his friend Liszt: there is no Mephistopheles here, but rather signs of constant mockery.

Clearer accents establish the melodies, but they are not designed as unforgettable lines, but rather as a different *toucher* each time. We could compare *these fifth fingers* with the Etude

with different phrasings, such as Op. 10 No. 10 or Op. 25 No. 4 and 5.
Clearly here it is a question of *searching for mobility in a fixed position.*

The extremities of the octaves must be fixed when this is possible considering the distances, and then work the mobility of the axes.

The work of two intervals is good.

The left hand must turn on the third finger to reach the bass without a leap. If necessary, an octave can be added as a reference.

The passage doubled by demisemiquavers, at measure 9, puts an end to the vague desires to play just any tempo at the start.
This passage *is* precisely *the tempo of the whole Etude.*
This formula is not repeated, except in the *Coda.* It is not to be forgotten. It is a call to order, discouraging ideas of displaced speeds.

The breakdown into simple notes is a very good thing to accommodate the hand and to fix it in real positions. It can make the axes even more independent.

Allegro

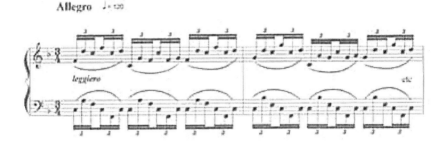

Octaves must be added to the little jumps in the left hand, towards the end, from measure 56, as in exercise No. 150.
The *Coda* brings us a contrary calm to the development of the Etude: the design of the axes becomes a trill and dilutes into a poetic *smorzando* and with practically no weight at all. The chords add a tranquillity that sets a suspension point to this humming top.

To continue, let us look now at Etude Op. 25 No. 9 in G-flat major, referred to as *butterfly* by some charming ladies.
Chopin's theme seems to be a parody of the last movement of Beethoven's Sonata alla Tedesca Op. 78, composed a semi-tone higher in G major.

161

Without its texture of octaves and chords, *you might say the pleasantry of a drop of Schubert in a theme by Beethoven*, but transformed by another genius, a pianistic one, in a trilogy of good humour and *savoir-faire*.

It is a farce, in the like of which Chopin shone.

Neither Beethoven nor Schubert would have achieved Chopin's *appassionato* impulses, nor written such marvels for the piano as in the *Coda* of this Etude, which is full of smiles and mischief.

I do not entirely agree with those who say it is one of Chopin's less brilliant Etudes. Of course, it is not up to the level of the next one, Op. 25 No. 10, but it breathes fresh air and it distinguishes itself from its contemporaries (only Liszt could sit alongside Chopin). Op. 25 No. 9 has some stealthy moments, like its homonym in Op. 10 on the black keys. It is also elegant and unpretentious. You cannot ask the geniuses to write a Funeral Sonata or a Fourth Ballad each time because they also have the right to relax.

Like its brother Op. 10, the black keys (considering it also is in G-flat, and sometimes, as *black* as its brother), should also *be transposed into G major* to understand the difficulties of the *white keyboard*.

The words best suited to this page are perhaps: carefree, relaxed, nonchalant, agreeable to the ear and comprehensible from the start. Despite this, in only a few modulations, Chopin is able to remind us that he is not our cousin.

The words of Rubinstein come to mind when he put a stop to the pretentious comments of someone who came up to him after one of his not so successful recitals (I repeat here *his* own words, because I would never criticize Rubinstein!): *"You might indeed say that today I did not play very well. It was a bit like the way you play. But when I play well, then the comparison between you and me is not quite the same."*

We must remember that a genius may sometimes write more conventional things without losing anything of their grandeur.

The work of our Etude is first of all to understand *that we are dealing with three octaves and not two.*

The exercise in triplets increases our understanding of these things.

The following work is to be played in quintuplets in order to render everything more *supple* and to give the broken octaves the speed of simple notes.

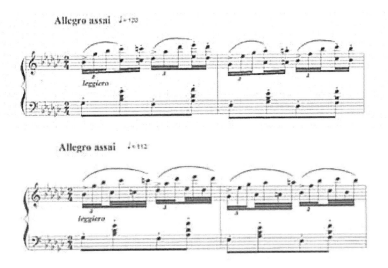

We must fix the axes of the second finger to relax the muscles required for the octaves and to help the antennae of the axes of the central fingers to find and consolidate their new positions.

In the *Coda*, when the axes are more open, in the intervals of fourths and fifths, the work is, of course, the same.

For the left hand, simply apply in the wider distances the principles of the octaves, just as Chopin did in his score. It has been indicated for other jumps, in the analysis of other Etudes. *Everything must be played with a higher wrist, floating and avoiding too great an accumulation of sound*, with absolute lightness, essential even in *FF appassionato*. The mass production of sonorities would compromise the unbuttoned character of this special page that vanishes in a charm and in a unique gesture.
Its disappearance is a masterpiece of surprise.

Last but not least, Etude Op. 10 No. 4, in C-sharp minor, is perhaps the favourite of every young pianist, because of its intrinsic traits of clear, effective, total and vigorous virtuosity, bringing together in two minutes a whole life of work and remarkable aesthetics. You can prove a great deal in two minutes: particularly that you are not a good pianist!

The *nervous tension* of the work is phenomenal, as is its *rigor*, while the *energy* it unleashes is exemplary.

Bach's model is obvious, but not his speed. The cadence of 176 for the crotchet (or 88 for the minim), indicated by Chopin, is   a barrier not often crossed without turpitude: the imitation of motifs is severe and not even the slightest concession is permitted. It is almost a synthesis between the past and future, between genius and the conventional, between *dizzying movements and immobile movements*: the return to the principal theme, after a diabolical climate, is a fantastic *suspension* and causes a moment of impressive feverishness, after a total silence on the left hand, broken by raw chords that are almost violent.

The *Coda* is a sublime moment, *con più fuoco possibile*. It is   the use of *extreme* and imprudent possibilities. It is the *heads or tails* of the pianist. Musically, this *Coda* rises to the heights of expression, *because musical tension is at a maximum*.

It also demands maximum delivery of technique. The *rigor* of conception, logic, rhetoric and eloquence is all found in the spaces reduced to nothing, *four notes*, but of an exemplary quality and presence.

It is said that this Etude followed Op. 10 No. 3, because the word *attacca* was found at the end of the latter. Chopin would murmur "Ma Patrie!" each time that he heard it.

All this is possible and worth savouring. These are fine tales, but none of this helps in the execution of the piece.

The Etude uses one of the most fortunate formulae for the harmonious development of all ten fingers. It is a fixed position for successions of four fingers, on each hand and alternating: 1, 2, 3, 4 on the right and 4, 3, 2, 1 on the left. There is, therefore, the constant development of four successive fingers. This is the case until the centre of the Etude, or the succession, complicated by a note sustained by the thumb, *becoming* the formula 2, 3, 4, 5, in all the modulating passages.

Simplifying this passage by transferring notes from the right thumb to the left hand, at measures 24 and 25, *is quite simply inadmissible and intolerable.*

This is recognition of incapability and laziness. You lose all the benefit of this much sought-after difficulty: *the development of the upper fingers at great speed without the help of the thumb, as in Etude Op. 10 No. 2.*

I find this behaviour *not only unworthy but also idiotic.* We undermine our own development in this way. It is one way of denial in teaching and recognition *of a dual failure*: that of the pupil, who loses out, and that of the teacher, who agrees. *It is disloyal and distressing.* It even went as far as correcting Chopin's score: in fact, the right thumbs should *be crotchets and not quavers!* The adoption of these, in bad editions, is presented shamelessly, so that they can be released more easily, together with the intervals in the left-hand. The crotchets in measures 29 to 32, played by the thumb and after by the fifth fingers in *melodic function*, speak for themselves!

What should be done is to exercise these groups 2, 3, 4, 5 - *the major problem in this Etude* - in the positions determined by Chopin and of course for longer than the normal groups.

In order to play them faster, with greater suppleness and flexibility, they should be exercised in *PPP*, almost without sonority, which will help to eliminate all tension.

The economy of means applied clarifies the idea of the work and the methods to be used. The cadence is a succession of four fingers on the right and four on the left.

On the right, the axis will be the 3 and on the left it will be the 2. The axes, and therefore the groups, alternate their paths between black and white keys, being the tonality of C-sharp minor not at all innocent.

The best way to study it is *to eliminate provisionally any chord or interval of accompaniment concentrating exclusively on the execution of the semiquavers as if the Etude had been written without harmonies.*

It is better to exercise the speed in each group in both directions. The articulation should be glued here to the keyboard: *there should be no space between the fingers and the keys.*

The speed is born out of the key and you can feel how the key pushes the finger upwards in return and propels it towards the next key.

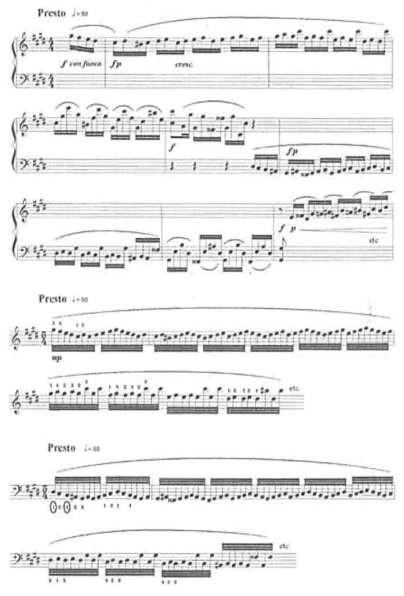

This system should be applied throughout the Etude in order to find the *pure* speed of the fingers without any help or support.

Of course, when you have *two lines* of semiquavers, for example in measures 39, 40, 41, 42, 43 and 44, or in the *Coda*, in measures

75, 76, 77 and 78, you play both hands together.

You have to be able to play it in its entirety, in tempo, with only this material.

In the grand descent in scales in measures 31 and 32, it is better not to change the fingerings when you pass the thumbs over the black keys, following the progression.

It is advisable to study the voices separately.

In the following measures, the displacements of the left are less problematic than *the fingerings of the mordents* in the right-hand. They should be carefully played with very sharp articulation.

When both hands play almost symmetrically, in measures 39, 40, 41 and following, you must consider the extremes as *returning to the centre* in order to give the thumbs dazzling impulses. Greater articulation is desirable here.

Of course, the same commentary goes for the right-hand in the *Coda*.

The little leaps made by the left-hand, in measures 71, 72, 73 and 74, as in measures 77 and 78, must be exercised by adding octaves to the second quaver, on the C-sharp or on the G-sharp.

This exercise will help with the dangerous final arpeggio.

For me, practicing using rhythmic formulae is highly contestable, *because the interruption of inertia is a very bad thing.*

When you stop a natural movement, you risk far greater accidents. The continuity of this movement, dominated by reasoned work is, on the other side, wiser as an intellectual conception.
Hiding behind a mechanical barrier promotes *an accumulation of endless distractions*, whether you like this or not. Soulless mechanics are the main cause of accidents. The lack of reasoning, analysis and spiritual development in the pupil reflect this mind- destroying practice that has no real future.

On the contrary, the development of maximal control brings, over time, the most extraordinary benefits. It is best to obtain this using intelligent, logical and acceptable means, and without any cheating that changes the rules of the game.

Severity does not prevent the music from emerging, but rather helps it. The hope of one day being able to coordinate a muscle with the mind, with brilliance, can only ennoble our daily task.

Studying these 24 marvels enriches us each session, and as we develop, we become better. This growing familiarity is like making contact with the gospel: *nothing that Chopin ever said was wrong.* Nothing that Chopin ever said was equaled.

Did he know that he was creating a Creed for all the generations of pianists who were to follow in his footsteps?

But I would say that he did know! We can only *thank him*, very kindly.

BOOK IV

Part one

The great "enemies" of our work:
Tendinitis
Memory
Stage fright

1 - Judas Iscariot, the traitor, or tendinitis

No relaxation is effective if it is not *the result of an order from the brain*. Exterior, pompous and grandiose movements will serve for nothing if they have not been determined by specific orders aiming for a studied result. Obviously, a tendon is not designed to practise ten hours of octaves without a break. Nor are the legs of a footballer or a cyclist initially destined to do the work that athletes force upon them. After strenuous training, a hard game or an exhausting race, those who practice a sport will suffer from fatigue and even muscle pain. Why should it be different for a pianist, who is after all an athlete, but a musical athlete?

The accumulation of work and effort gives rise to growing fatigue that may end in a total breakdown. Clearly there is *a risk*, and we know that there is no such thing as zero risk. What is required is to reduce the percentage of this risk to acceptable levels. If we cannot achieve zero risk, we should at least aim *to minimize it to the maximum*, to use a play on words.

2 - The Perpetual motions of François Poulenc or « L'Entassement réglé » by Vassily Kandinsky

All work strives towards the final goal: the performance. As mentioned above, the aim is to achieve maximum output with the minimum effort. This is the wisest rule.

An initial observation must be considered: *a repeated movement causes fatigue in the muscles and tendons more than a varied movement. A change in activity, requiring different movements, is more relaxing to the mind than constant repetition of the same movement.*

Clearly *uncontrolled* muscular over-drive will have only one outcome: pain and inflammation of the tendon. We know that if a muscle executes its normal movement, nothing abnormal should happen, in principle. For this, the muscle must do its work freely with flexibility, and without accumulating effort. Above all it must receive oxygen constantly.

A weightlifter who spends his day lifting weights risks suffering more pain in the muscles of his back, arms and shoulders than a swimmer, for example. In each job or profession, we know there are *occupational health* hazards: the static position imposed by office life, the eyes of those working with computers, lung problems caused by working in mines, contact with harmful substances, etc. All of this is known, and our social system seeks to find a lasting solution to combat these problems.

The slightest strain on the muscle produces tension, rigidity and restricts movement. The muscle remains *without any vibration*. As a result, *oxygen* does not reach it. Therefore, it does not receive the blood supply required to survive, it hardens and is *half dead*. This lack of vibration leads to tendinitis setting in. The fundamental cause of muscle rigidity and the ensuing pain is this lack of vibration. This contraction takes place if there is a *lack of coordination* between the muscles. Movements become un- coordinated and there is more uncontrolled movement. In short, this is *muscular anarchy*. This happens:

1 - **Before producing the note**: the muscles exert a disproportionate amount of tension that spoils the sound and prevents the movements of the fingers, the hands or the arm, particularly at speed.

2 - **While producing the note**: the muscles are under abnormal tension, either because they are in a difficult position or they are stretched too far, or they are over-strained, etc.

3 - **After producing the note**: this assumes the incapacity to relax and to eliminate all stress once the sonority has been produced.

The most logical conclusion is no doubt the incapacity to coordinate the three fundamental stages: *conception – execution -relaxation*. Added to this is the excess of weight behind the touch on the keys and excessive pressure at the moment of work when *practicing* as if being in a *performance*.

Chopin comes to mind here. He taught us *facility* in all movements, in all musical production and in all attempts to find technical solutions. Even with the slightest tension, he considered that the pupil had gone into a state of *brutishness*. Sclerosis at the piano made him feel disgusted!

Liszt's teaching also tended to agree with this *facility*. We know that with the great pianists there is one constant factor in their teaching: everything should flow and become easy and as light as air. We should be fully aware of the amount of work this could take.

3 - « Brouillards » by Claude Debussy

We should do everything to detect the origins of these muscular problems so as to neutralize their effects. To this end we should admit that the best solution is to understand the cause of a problem, so that we can avoid it and find remedies, because *"ignorance is the cause of our blindness"*.

The very first cause is without doubt nervousness: this is what will produce the false, fatal movement, the absurd, forced repetition of a passage, due to the absence of strict control, a failure to listen keenly and a lack of concentration.

The second is poor teaching by a teacher who demands without warning us: non-control of the repertoire, non-control of defects in execution, non-control of emotional tension, a failure to treat pupils as intelligent beings but rather as products likely to win an international competition or get stunning exam results.

The third, a consequence of the second, is the *state of stress* to which pupils are submitted when their exams or competitions approach.

The fourth is the political demands made by institutions and conservatories: there should be a formula somewhere that allows pupils *to develop at a normal rate and not at the rate of political subsidies*. We do no more than create nervous individuals, or worse, disillusioned individuals.

The fifth is that the provocation of stress by the music market, this music business that *distributes* concerts and *classifies* artists.

The sixth is the lack of a major desire by the institutions to give pupils the necessary oxygen to make them feel more than just numbers on a class list, but rather true human beings.

False movements in execution apart, much of the problem actually comes from the teaching, the institutional hierarchy, politics and a failure on the part of the market to understand the musical business.

4 - Feet firmly on the ground, if you please!

We have just said that in routine work a difficult passage should become accessible without any major problems, but to this end   it must be approached with intelligence, method and analysis. Agitation, bad form, exacerbated pretensions, unreasonable desires, an unhealthy imagination, nervousness or exaltation impede the serene use of possible solutions. *Without even thinking about it*, we are *forcing* the muscle because we are submitting it to superfluous, unproductive pressures. Disorder, anarchy and clearly a lack of coordination of movement prove to be extremely destructive.

Training is no longer rational but becomes stupid and we resemble the dammed. The fingers, the hands and the muscles, as well as the whole body, work *without the brain*. We end up *hitting our head* against a wall in an attempt to bring it down, without thought and reflection. Of course, it will be our head and not the wall that is demolished. At such times, we are no more intelligent than a bull charging towards the bullfighter *with its horns lowered.*

An unhealthy imagination is equally harmful. I *imagine* that I *am* playing Rachmaninov's Third Concerto at La Scala in Milan and that the concert hall is full. But, in fact, *I am at home* within my own four walls. Or I *imagine* that I must redouble my efforts to win the next competition on *my* agenda and that *my* muscles are *capable of doing far more*. In both cases, *the lack of serenity and analysis* takes us along the wrong road. It would be better for us to observe that *we are at home*, in *our* laboratory, working on *our* sonorities and solving *our* problems, and not let *our imagination stray* perniciously, which at this precise moment is *more destructive than constructive.*

Such working methods, tainted with a lack of intelligence, do no more than bring on tendinitis. Until we spare ourselves wasted effort the risk will go on increasing. It goes without saying that we are not talking about *saving on working time.* On the contrary, the suggestion is that *if we work correctly nothing will go wrong.* I will never tire of repeating again and again that the main cause is this *anxiety in the work, this lack of intelligence in analysing problems, this absence of any method, this lack of a view of the objectives to be achieved mixed with an imagination that plays every kind of trick and that is without doubt the fundamental cause of these uncontrolled efforts.*

When working, we must make harmonious movements, coordinated displacements and play relaxed chords; we must ration our efforts, spare ourselves tense leaps and respect less tiring dynamics (often those in *pp!*). When all is said and done, we must work with tremendous mental and muscular variety *to be able to avoid over-strenuous effort* in our work.

The fact of alternating problems, avoiding harsh repetitions that only go to strain a muscle - because we begin the work at "5" and, without being aware of it, we end up at "double" because we are not applying our intelligence -, is the best guarantee of maintaining suppleness, relieving tension and avoiding fatigue, which although the latter is unavoidable, should be held off for as long as possible.

5 - *Sutor, ne supra crepidam* ("Cobbler, stick to thy last", or in other words, 'mind your own business')

For us pianists, tendinitis is a true scourge. It can cause incredible misfortune, ruin concerts, exams, competitions and even a whole professional career.

It strikes at the worst possible times, and at the most unexpected moment. It can destroy a career because its harmful effects are not exclusively muscular and often have psychological repercussions that bring on destruction on an unimaginable scale.

The weaker a person is mentally, the more vulnerable that person is to the risks of tendinitis and its devastating effects. *This is why total control must be exerted on the nervous system during routine work.* We must teach that without this control we are seriously at risk and we must help the pupil to eliminate the serious causes of these deplorable states of mind: ignorance and exaggerated, forced repetition. We must recall at all times *that our muscles have a memory. Everything is recorded.* Pain comes *through accumulation* or by the memory of *something badly done or badly studied.*

Tendinitis nearly always manifests itself when we are working. Suddenly we feel a burning sensation, a small pain or warm current that rises up to the head. It rarely comes at any other time, although sometimes it appears after several hours of work. The start of tension turns into a muscular contraction, a fixation of weight and a blockage that brings with it the complete or partial loss of freedom of movement.

6 - Little glimmers of hope

Even in the case of a tendinitis already installed, *an absolute lack of movement is not necessarily the best thing.* Of course, I do not wish to play the role of the doctor here, but I think that the lack of movement deprives the muscle of its vital functions and therefore of its oxygen and flexibility. Furthermore, after a period of inactivity, re-education is necessary. While waiting....

The elimination of all dynamics from *a reduced work* does, however, produce astonishing results. As I said about the work of the Finale of Chopin's Sonata in B-flat, studying a *voiceless piano* gives spectacular results. This work without sound, without tension and without force, *almost without moving*, but still with real movements, can in no way upset the cure. It means wasting far less time during *the inevitable rest period, because the studying continues*. The movements have *to be reduced more to vibrations*, with absolutely no force and no resistance. I can bet that *any symptom of pain will be reduced by 95%.*

Above all, psychologically, we feel better because despite all the misfortune we do manage to do something. *This is a positive feeling that must be cultivated, because this will be our greatest aid.*

At this point, the teacher plays *a major role in inspiring the pupil*. It is a well-known fact that in cases of arthritis or joint pain, lack *of movement only goes to aggravate* the disorder and that circulation of the blood produces beneficial effects. On the whole, medication is debatable. We are not talking about *chronic cases* where the diagnosis is made by a doctor, but of *common* cases. Anti-inflammatories are dangerous because they have secondary effects. They should be avoided wherever possible, remembering that they also upset concentration. As always, warm water, *home* gymnastics, very small, gentle flexing movements, walking and relaxation are recommended.

It is at such times that we can assess the level of morale of an artist. Everyone has gone through this. Sometimes we want to hide it, but truths should not be hidden but rather used to help the young not to succumb and not to repeat the mistakes of their elders.

We have to accept, as a rule of life and musical conduct, that all hands are not those of Richter. We have to understand, and it is better to be reasonable, that there are limits to our hands and there is no need to do as Schumann did to change Nature. One cannot borrow what Nature has denied.

Render unto Caesar that which is Caesar's, and in God, that which is God's.

You can NEVER go against it nor beyond the fatigue of a muscle. You have to allow time for recovery, relaxation and a return to normal.

But when the ill is there, the role of the teacher and the institution responsible for the pupil is fundamental, because the misfortune is tremendous for the young pianist, and even more so when, often, *we have contributed to the problem*. We must support the pupil effectively and give hope during this difficult period: knowing how to give advice at this difficult time will be proof that the teacher and the institution merit the teaching role entrusted to them.

7 - Memory, or in "search" of lost Time, by Marcel Proust

Man *is* a living, walking, memory.

Everything, but absolutely everything, is recorded in a corner of our brain. Each act, gesture, word and experience that we produce in our lifetime remains with us. Sooner or later, we can find it again as in *an old film* and note that all of this can *resurface*, with or without our consent, whether we want it or not.

Clearly, as a result, *the mistakes of our daily practice are also strongly and equally recorded*, at least as well as the *correct movements*. These mistakes may *surface* at any time in an execution, particularly when the circumstances of an emotional or nervous atmosphere change, for example, at the time of recital. This is a whole programme for examination.

Let me say, then, a couple of words on this *famous* problem of memory, the true *bête noire* in our concert life. The *fault* goes back to Franz Liszt, god among pianists, who invented playing from memory in recital. We have all accepted this *imposition* of Liszt, becoming not only a *habit*, but *"second nature"*. We accept this imposition in recital as one of its fundamental component parts. Many people admire this *technical feat of memory that has nothing to do with the artistic skills* of the artist. *Memory is one more technical element* that, in many cases, allows the pianist to be freer to play, without having to depend on the score. It allows *for another type of concentration.*

Many artists, and not the lesser ones, have contested this rightly, Richter for one. No one would doubt the incredible skills of this historical pianist. Of course, we are not going to discuss whether he was ill or not to take his decision never to play by memory again. That is not what we are discussing here.

The memory is, then, a *liberator* because it allows the pianist effectively to concentrate more deeply on the core of an interpretation. However, it is *restrictive*, because it does prevent the pianist from playing, conventionally, in concert something that he does not know *by heart*. It may then cause considerable anguish to the interpreter!

This was Richter's main argument, claiming that one could change concert programmes as one changes a shirt, without worrying about whether he was going to remember his programme or not. But we are not going to waste words on this because if anyone proved that he had a gigantic memory, it was certainly Richter.

One can only compare his memory to that of Arrau, able to perform *the whole* of Bach in twelve recitals in Berlin; *the whole* of Beethoven or the 32 Sonatas in the space of a week, as he did in New York; *the whole* of Mozart, *the whole* of Chopin; *the whole* of Schubert, *the whole* of Schumann, *the whole* of Brahms and *the whole* of Debussy. He presented his manager in Buenos Aires with 70 recital programmes without replaying a single work! The repertoire played by Richter was *equally* phenomenal. We find the same thing, this type of gigantic memory, in Gieseking, Ashkenazi, Pollini and Daniel Barenboim, to speak of *only* pianists.

But gigantic *does not mean infallible…*

We have seen many great pianists at some time or another, place a score before them and that, *in no case whatsoever*, has affected their exceptional performance.

For example, I attended a concert by one of Bartok's pupils with the National Orchestra of Argentina, the Hungarian pianist Andor Földes, who was playing the First Concerto of his Master with the score, because he felt, as he said after the performance, that on that particular day the Muses were not with him. Nevertheless, it was a fantastic concert.

We could speak of Arthur Toscanini, Von Karajan or Klemperer, to give other examples. You may prefer one to the other, but all three belonged to *the great*. One, Von Karajan, or the other, Toscanini, conducted *everything* by heart. The third, Klemperer, thought that you could know *nothing* completely by heart!

Who is right? *All three were right*, of course, because the problem is only relative and not fundamental. As Claude Debussy said, you have on your right a whole library that says you are right, and on your left another that says you are wrong. *The fundamental mistake comes from the fact that we are comparing the memory with an artistic element while it is no more than a technical element,* as said earlier.

Whatever the case, this memory plays quite a lot of tricks on us in concert. It, or rather the accidents, make us realize that it is better to study its nature to the fullest extent possible rather than risk continual hitches, omissions and gaps and all that goes with them. A career can be destroyed if the artist's nerves are not sufficiently strong. In unhinges the whole nervous system and contributes to ruining a concert completely. In this specific case, stage fright is a far more determining factor than memory for a successful recital. We know that any artistic act should rest on emotional balance. What artist has not suffered, at some time or another, from this lack of stability and balance in a concert? If we decide to make a career and proceed to do this, careful thought must go into this one day.

It is a well-known fact that there are four types of memory: *digital or muscular, visual, hearing and analytical.*

The last two types of memory are more professional than the first two, but none should be overlooked. *In fact, nothing should be overlooked in such an imprecise profession.*

The first thing to be noted, as said above, is that our brain works like an ultra-sensitive recording machine. And this means that anything understood or not by the senses, whether consciously or in unconscious repetition, any motor phenomena and any gesture or word, absolutely anything that we do, *is recorded in the memory and is ready to appear in any circumstances,* which means that the least distraction in control risks *the repetition* of a wrong gesture. Or, on the contrary, gestures may be ordered, more exact and less anarchic.

A musical work, particularly if counterpoint is a feature, suffers tremendously if it is learnt only by the muscular memory (speaking here mainly of amateurs). A single finger applied wrongly will surely and certainly bring with it a fault.

This is why the best solution is always to record as many "precise" gestures as possible, produced through ordered work, so as to increase a base of *tranquillity* in case of error. In this way we increase our chances of success.

7.1 - Digital or muscular memory

We will examine the first two types of memory that are common to all beings on earth.

We repeat the same movement hundreds of times. The muscles are therefore able to record these movements and *to recall them unconsciously.* Trained, animals can climb on to a ball under the crack of a whip. The pianist repeats the same passage a hundred times and this passage is inscribed on his muscles and is recorded. However, at the least sign of nervousness, at the least change to the keyboard, the atmosphere or the room, *the error appears because nothing is controlled any longer.*

This may be primary memory, but it is not at all negligible.

It serves those *in practice and in panic*: it is used for a few seconds until the moment when a superior control takes over.

7.2 - Visual memory

This is a little more professional because it can *photograph* the score. Despite that, this memory is still *common*. Everyone has it: you can remember the colour of your car, your room and your pictures, and the colour of your favourite shirts, etc.

This is no solution to the Fugues of Op. 110, nor to understanding them, nor their coherence or conception. You can see these Fugues *with your eyes closed, write them*, but it is a bit like reciting the Bible without understanding the words and the symbols.

However, this is a very important, *very practical*, memory.

7.3 - Hearing memory

This is an entirely professional memory.

It allows you *to anticipate at least one note* after the one that follows, like the conductor of an orchestra who marks his *tempo* and is *ahead* of the orchestra. This means that *in advance he can hear* what is going to happen. Above all it helps *recognize* the harmony without ambiguities, the form, the repetitions, etc.

This is a *fundamental memory* for a professional pianist.

7.4 - Analytical memory

This is the true memory of the artist and it helps him to understand, to live and to love Music. There is no repetition here; each note is created. *Everything is analysed*: form, harmony, exceptions, differences, message, colours, timing, climax, psychology and the characteristics of the work, style, atmosphere, and so on. You could add whatever you want.

One example is given here of a working method and the gradual application of these principles for the beginning of Beethoven's Sonata Op. 31 No. 2, in D Minor.

1 - After deciding on the fingerings and playing, reading the passage in question with considerable concentration, *the first stage of the process* is assured, that is, *the digital or muscular memory:* the controlled repetition of the same passage - five or six times -, in this way recording *the preliminary stage of the work*. It goes without saying that for the first three memories

- digital, visual and hearing - *this work will be done with the hands separate: clearly memorizing each part.* For the analytical memory, the most definitive for the work and the last stage of the process, the exercise *as a whole is desirable, because after analysis synthesis is necessary.* The *complete work* is therefore essential.

2 - You begin immediately after *forming the musical image*, that is exercising *the visual memory:*

a) The eyes and the brain indicate the G-clef to the right and the F-clef to the left for the first bar.

b) Tonality of D minor. Bar 2/2.

c) Inverted position of the Dominant chord, on the leading- note C-sharp in the bass: two *arpeggiated* chords, the same, on the right and the left. But the left occupies the whole of the bar and three quarters of the second. It closes in a *fermata*. The right, a minim and two crotchets in *portamento*, the notes C-sharp and E, develops with the same notes and finishes with an A, also in *fermata*, in the following measure. They are *PP* and linked by a pedal. The general movement is *Largo*.

d) A new motif appears on the right, in *legato* quavers (slurred by two) descending from the same key A to D, forming four groups. On the left, on a pedal note A, the Dominant, the intervals ascend from C sharp, D, E and F, twice. The whole is *Piano*.

e) The same motif then descends from D to G and G-flat, only once. There is a *crescendo* here. On the left, ascension begins from F-sharp to B-flat (this repeated twice). Everything is in the pedal in D. The general movement for this episode is *Allegro*.

f) We then fall on two major chords, the first *sforzando*, the second in *fermata*. The first is a six-four chord in D minor, with a retard on the G-sharp that proceeds in a *grupetto* and finishes in a B-natural - A resolution into the Dominant, in the inverted position, in *diminuendo*. The last chord is *piano* and on the Dominant. The general movement for this two-chord bar is *Adagio*.

All of this should be clear to the eyes and the brain. It is *an image* that one should be able to *describe*, reproducing *in writing*, and/or be able *to see* as if looking at a photo.

3 - You then exercise *without the piano and you listen in advance*, like the conductor of an orchestra, *anticipating the whole of a note.* For example: the first chord is: C-sharp, E, A, on the left, and C-sharp on the right, E ... G, D, F ...? This is impossible, because it is the Dominant and the same chord as the left. The note is, therefore, A. You make the effort to listen in advance to a slow chord on the Dominant, in the first inversion. Then the first note of the following motif is B-flat, F or D? ... You know that you begin again on the same note, so it is A, and it forms the chord of the Dominant still.

All this becomes the basis for *hearing memory*, through deduction and intelligence and not by repetition. It is clear for the inner ear and using this exercise, with reasoning, we develop this *hearing memory*.

4 - We then apply *all that we know* about the Sonata and *build* from the conception we have of the work. We examine all the similar passages, particularly their changes and their modulations. The dynamic and phrasing differences are fundamental. We study the style, the history of the work, the reason for its creation, its aesthetic background and its relationships. Above all, we imagine *the ideal version without ourselves* and its spatial result. We imagine it *as a human organ, as a continuity and as a proportioned relationship*. We should read Shakespeare and his Tempest!

g) The first chord is interrogative and almost loaded with threats. It will be the basis for the *recitativo* later on, where a voice is heart rending in this terrible pedal. It is obvious that it cannot be played too constrictively; this is deduced, because it must *speak*.

h) The new despairing, anxious motif, like a cavalcade of the mind in ruins, expresses itself through the tragic phrasing of the German music, slurred *by two*: consider the *Finale* of Mozart's Sonata in A minor and the beginning for the piano in Brahms Concerto in D Minor, one written after the death of his mother, and the other written after Schumann's attempted suicide.
Two opposing forces: the motif of the cavalcade descends, and the bass ascends. Beethoven lays himself bare to us. We believe we can glimpse the Appassionata and Op. 111 in a vision of youth.

i) On the *crescendo* of the second part of the same motifs the traces will be the same, but far more anguished because they end by being crushed in the chord played *sforzando*.

j) the *Adagio* movement for the *grupetto* indicates a declamation that fades away in the acceptance, also expressed by *three tempi* in a single line.

However, we could and we should know more. What is being described here is *no more than an indication* of what should be done without fail.

Perhaps only then will we be able to say that the six bars have been *studied* but, *for better or worse*, each day we discover that something escaped us the day before and that once again we must correct it.

Therefore, *an examination of each memory each day remains to be done*. And our despair also grows because despite all our efforts the error will perhaps still be there.

We could also mention the *collective memory* as the fifth type of memory, according to the archetypes of Jung. But because of its complication of transfers, we would fall into the terrain of mental shadows, the explanations for which would lead us into less specific spheres for us pianists. Moreover, this interpretation of the *mysterium tremendum* would have no place amidst the modest observations on the inconveniences confronting a musician.

Some musicians neglect one memory for another. *This is no more than snobbishness*.
In fact, *none of the memories mentioned can be neglected*. At any time, should one memory

fail, another must be ready to replace it, if only provisionally, and particularly the muscular memory.

To imagine that *only* one of the memories can prevail during a recital is as lacking in intelligence as imagining you can separate the action of one human organ from another.

External disturbance signifies risk. Our margin of *security* is, as a result, very slim. We cannot, then, understand a work *in detail* in a relatively short space of time, or certainly not know it in depth. Think only of the works learned for exams, those works *imposed* on us. Once played, they are forgotten immediately. Anything learnt in haste is quickly forgotten.

The rhythm of Nature imposes the cadence on us: our deepest, strongest memories are the most vivid and the ones that come to mind.

Neither should we confuse what is learnt rapidly for a specific reason - this belongs to what I call an initial labour of memory -, *with what one learns for concert life or to be used throughout a career.*

A well-trained memory can learn a work in several hours or several days. The final stage of the Queen Elizabeth Competition, in Brussels, demonstrates this clearly. Talents that are not always exceptional learn the Concert imposed on them in the space of a week and they play it with the National Orchestra (even if they can play with the score, many play by heart). This is more a question of *job* than talent.

In the case of failure, the big problem is the imbalance that can occur between reason and emotionality, emotionality and technique and the technique of interpretation in public. The pianist should have this balance between the following elements because otherwise there is the risk of endless accidents:

1 - Hands, fingerings and technical faculties.
2 - Sensibility and emotion.
3 - Reasoning, and analysis and synthesis.

Should there be disharmony, each of these elements could upset memory and the normal development of the whole composition: the wrong fingering, a confused pedal, a poorly introduced dynamic, a poorly adapted *tempo*, a weight badly placed, poor coordination, and so on.

At times like these, *the fact of not knowing* is the worst possible danger for a slip of the memory. Imagine a great orator stumbling over a word and not knowing how to continue his speech: we would immediately deduce that *he did not know what he wanted to say.*

The memory works naturally by stages of impregnation. The clearer the image - the form, harmony, psychology, style - the clearer the mind and the more chance we have of succeeding. Notes should never be learnt *like an isolated language because like this the relationships between them would become invisible.* The phrases, structures and ensembles must be learnt, *just as we learn to construct phrases in a specific language.* It is not with separate words that we are going to compose one of Petrarch's sonnets. This language would become the ghost of a soldier, but not of a soldier belonging to an army. You do not win a war with *isolated* individuals. You need a well-trained army that is well *disposed* and ready to fight. So, *every possible reference* to the work and its text must be learnt.

We have already spoken of external disturbances such as a keyboard that we do not like, lighting that upsets us, an audience with which we are not comfortable, a person that we do not want to meet at our concert, unsympathetic acoustics, etc. *These can all compromise the reproduction of mnemonic devices.*

This leads us to see that we should know a work far more deeply than what we believed possible. *Commanding* the work 100% is not sufficient. We need more and more to refresh the images and *the four memories each day.* We must develop our balances and control our imbalances. In other words, study the work more. Georges Cziffra commented on memory: "*provoke the fault so that you have the possibility of analysing once again*". This is quite a brilliant piece of advice.

The reasons for memory failure are not entirely known, not even medically. We can only detect *its functions* and understand them partially, but never with any proof as to how it fails. There is perhaps only some advice on how to neutralize memory failure, *but nothing is guaranteed.* We should attribute much of the problem to the risks of our profession and just accept them.

8 - Stage fright, our enemy … or our friend?

Who has not, on some occasion or another, been the victim of stage fright?

Who has not, on some occasion or another, felt this anguish or fear, sometimes unjustified, before an important concert, the finals of a competition or an essential examination?

No matter how much we say that everything is under control, that this is *not reasonable*, that one is *well-prepared, that everything will go well* and all these other platitudes that we invent to calm the anguish, this is but slim consolation and of help little.

Very often the truth is that a person is paralyzed by fear, but you must learn to master it, or at least reduce it.

Alfred Cortot used to say: *"fear? You have to be able to sleep with it!"*

That is an *amorous* and clear way of saying that you cannot *avoid it.* The knees begin to tremble, breathing is poor and irregular, the heart beats too fast, you smoke one cigarette after another, while some drink tea and others coffee. There are artists who take tranquillizers, alcohol or drugs, all sorts of things providing t h e y neutralize this feeling of unrest.

A pain in **the** stomach causes disorders and acidity *that have everything to do* with the Pictures at an Exhibition that you must play on this day. There are also cold sweats and you feel electric shocks in your backbone. Nothing calms us down.

You try to smile, sure of yourself, full of experience, joking, but nothing helps when you have the sword of Damocles over your head and the best thing to do is perhaps to keep quiet, to concentrate and to deal with your ill-ease patiently.

There are no remedies for this. Siesta, rest or extra work will not help. No more will a change of activity. We must each find our own *recipe* and own balance without drawing inspiration from the self or others.

9 - The rules of the game and "me"

The most difficult thing is probably *accepting stage fright*.

We try to get round it, to reinvent the experience of the concert or to find miracle solutions although we are fully aware that it can ruin us and that everything can collapse in just a second like a house of cards, and that we are playing for all or nothing, as in poker.

We have analysed our nervous system; we have spoken to our doctor and we feel that somewhere there may be a small glimmer of hope of doing well. Everything is in place and our readiness to succeed is at the zenith.

We have also passed all the exams although *the fear levels are not comparable*; we cannot *exchange* them or compare them to the fear felt at previous concerts or to situations that do not create the same stress levels.

We should know all of this: *there are no two types of fear that are the same*. It may attack the memory, control of the fingers, the force of playing, the pedal, the breathing, in fact anything. And then it strikes! We are overcome by fear just as we are about to set foot on stage.

I once heard Stefan Ashkenazi say that he thought he was *human* and that he had the right to make a mistake. That helped him tremendously in moments of fear.

The main cause comes from how we value the *self: I, me, I cannot make a mistake*.

The face of egoism is installed in us and all reasoning is forgotten because of the "*me*", and hence *the ego*.

It is a great moment of *vacuum* in our reflective state. We have no comparative parameters at all, but we overload ourselves with our own unique states of mind without the slightest regard for others. The reference is *I, my state of mind, my concert, my nerves and my terrible anguish*. Modesty as well is seen *in regard to the self*. It is my shame as well: *I am* terribly afraid of what people will say about *me*. We forget what to do and concentrate on our nervous state *forgetting to think any more about our real difficulties*. We lose our bearings and fall back on very limited ideas.

Now we have not covered so much ground, done so much work and studied, to reach *this maturity*! It is precisely at this moment that we forget everything - the work, the composer, the music, the communion - to (re)locate the problem purely and simply in our personal egoism!

In reality, we are regressing. *Therefore, it is not surprising that we are afraid: we are looking for this fear and preparing the terrain for it.* We give it the green light to unleash a whole process of nervous tension and dysfunction. We give in completely because nothing comes forward by way of resistance. We set off down the opposite road to the one we should take.

Every artist goes through this. There is no human being in the world who is perfect and who has not felt the same.

I read somewhere about someone who said that "*fear is in inverse proportion to the level of preparation*". Of course, that did not come from a pianist. Clearly this is not a serious suggestion: if we do not know our programme and we go ahead with a recital, this is not to be considered here. That would reveal not only arrogance or stupidity but would also mean embarking on an *impossible* mission.

I speak only of *pure and problematic* artists and not of those playing to the gallery or at charity soirées. The *fear felt by the artist* is something that is known and something that is serious; I think it would be ridiculous to hide it. The greater the event, the greater the fear for *my reputation*, and as a result the chances of stumbling into the trap of fear increases.

10 - Grandma's remedies

The only solid advice to help gather our wits together is *to control our breathing*. We know that calm can come through deep meditation, through equally deep concentration and tranquillity that comes *from reflection and not from instinct*. Once again redefining the essential role of the artist should include something to offset the turmoil of the mind and the rebellious anguish of our fear.

Are we *only* there for our *brilliance*? Are we there to be *greater than the greatest*? Are we there to take credit for all the success, without sharing it with the composer and without thanking the work itself for allowing us to be there? Are we there to be the centre of the world? Are we there to serve only *ourselves*?

Should the answer to these questions be *yes*, we can be sure that we will never escape the nature and the harmful consequences of stage fright.

You cannot *just let it go*. We know that the "*I cannot control myself*" is the road to nervous disorders and depression. We also know that we need to understand it, be aware of it, get help and find a solution to the problem.

Breath control is fundamental because this is directly related to muscular tension. Incorrect breathing reduces oxygen supply and increases tension not only in the muscles but also in the nerves. Breathing should therefore be practiced accompanied by deep reflection, involving the spirit, magnanimously. The abdomen should feel this renewal of air from above. It should feel it as if receiving manna from heaven.

We should slow this breathing, calm it and reduce its frenetic rhythm *consciously*. We should nourish ourselves on this magnificent air *that will be our salvation*.

This is the moment to read about and reflect on the sublime feats of great artists, on the generous works. of the composers, the great moments in Art and above all the privilege of *being there*. Ourselves.

You cannot become distracted with frivolities and nonsense. You must have regard to the gravity of the moment before you and confront it with dignity, confronting your responsibility and not avoiding it. *It has to be faced.*

Should we then adopt a *musical* breathing pattern, that is one adapted to the character of the work that we are playing at the moment, or should we make it *completely independent* so that the muscles receive oxygen despite any eventual passion or relaxation in the music? *It must be independent*, of course.

Clearly if the breathing is regulated independently, the muscular and psychological results will be greater because calm will preside over our artistic act. As Busoni used to say, "*an ardent heart in a cool mind is necessary*".

In this way, the spiritual and nervous state before the concert performance will be more controlled, more tamed and more professional. No emotion can be controlled if not dealt with like this.

A Formula One driver, whose mind, self-control and heartbeat must be as solid as steel, cannot allow his breathing to get out of control at each corner and risk a total loss of control. Should that happen, he will become part of the debris along the way and will not reach the finishing line.

Of course, losing control or not does not determine *the degree of implication* in the Music. This has nothing to do with being colder or more emotive or being more of an artist or less committed. But the more *you let go*, in the amateur meaning of the word, the more mistakes are made. This "non-control", this *inferior feeling*, will then triumph. You are in fear's debt and this means that the superior faculties of our being come less into play.

At all costs, this disorder and chaos must be avoided.

11 - « Me » and « Him»… as well as « Her »

You teach a person nothing by saying that they must eliminate all amateur behaviour from their conduct and aspire to moments worthy of the *great artists* and an approach guided by the mind and reason.

We must interpret, suffer with the Music, take joy in the work and feel the composer. We should create the illusion of being *him* while at the same time *being me* in every nerve ending. Our whole body, each part of our being, should not die in the literal sense simply because we are interpreting something that is tragic or funereal. We must keep a *cool head* to be able to strike the *right strings* of the piano as well as to pierce the nerve centres of our listeners.

To travel a great voyage of a thousand kilometres you must know first of all *where* you are going, according to the wisdom of the Chinese.

I believe that this is fundamental in dealing with stage fright. We approach it with our feelings and *not with my programme*. I mean to say that if during the minutes of nervous tension *before* the concert we were to be *already* emerged in the message *to be transmitted*, our egoism would be less and our attention more focussed on the composer and the work, and not on our own *personal brilliance*.

12 - The fine machine: breathing

In short, we should examine breathing as a major technical problem and something that could impede our motor apparatus. What we must do is to guide the ship to a safe haven, that is, *guide our muscles and our mind to their natural states*. In other words, they must receive oxygen constantly. I advise exercising the breathing during working hours, by interrupting pianistic and musical exercises in any period predisposed to change the pace of breathing. You need *points of reference* for breathing as for the memory. You need to know where to go, where to get *extra* relaxation, where to catch the momentum for a more extreme passage, hold back in others, etc. None of this can be improvised without the risk of falling into intellectual disorder.

Plans must be built up in the same way as an engineer or an architect would proceed. It is also important to listen to the sonority of what we produce because, at the end of the day, poor breathing ruins the supreme result of the concert, which is the sound.

Reasonable exercises of any type are of course welcome. Yoga, relaxation, transcendental meditation, swimming, walking or gymnastics will no doubt help us.

However, the discharge of adrenalin may upset everything in our job, positively or negatively. So, you should plan something other than a good walk or good siesta. I think that the most intelligent thing to do *is to take responsibility and be aware* of the concert. There is no need to look for odd ways to explain the obvious. The situation is *exceptional*. This you need to accept and not put off until later.

The fact of understanding, being aware and feeling responsible for taking part in something important, seeing everything as a privilege in being able to face such a programme, this noble and grandiose sentiment that speaks to us just a few seconds before beginning Beethoven's Fourth, in short, this supreme truth helps far more than any medication.

We should convince ourselves that if we can help ourselves, God, Beethoven and Mozart *will also be on our side.*

13 - The courage to accept

Running away is not pretty.

It does not matter whether this is done using drugs, alcohol, medication or whatever else. We must know that *that* which we *fabricate in this way* is not exactly *us*.

We are witnessing something almost done by *someone else*, because we are in an *abnormal* state. Even if it is done out of egoism it is absurd because we can only satisfy *some other being*. We should look this anguish in the face, man-to-man, and tell it that we are going *to fight it*. We must accept our being as *a whole* and not as a separate body. Our whole musculature and our whole motor apparatus depend on our psyche and on our nervous and emotional system.

The only thing that exists in us is *unity* in the face of good or evil. We must have the courage to face these things *not with tranquillity*, because that would not be possible, *but with dignity*. Almost solemnly, like ancient gladiators. Lastly, we are a bit like gladiators because we have to go on stage and fight for life, the difference being that this life is not only ours, but also that of the musical work.

14 - An odd kind of friend, when all is said and done

And what do we do when this stage fright, this odd friend, is not there? Could we play? Would everything be easier? Could we really gain an Olympian tranquillity that would allow us to perform *to perfection all* that we have studied and planned? Would we be *liberated* from this odious sensation of fear? Indeed, would we be able to play *better*?

We can't be entirely sure. In fact, I am even convinced of the opposite. Excuse me for giving a personal example, but when I play a programme five times in the same week, during a tour, the first concerts are always the best because the tension and the attention are right there. Afterwards, relaxation sets in as experience is gained, and accidents happen more easily when the control is not redoubled.

The fact of playing more calmly does not necessarily mean playing better, because if there is no tension *the music is more reluctant to come* to us.

This means that Nature must be accomplished. Pain, suffering, nervousness, sacrifice, acceptance, renunciation and joy are all part of the job, just like the scales and the arpeggios.

Any responsible human being who must produce important tasks feels this responsibility, this anxiety, this anguish and this fear of doing things badly. I do not believe that the pilot of a 747 taking off from Buenos Aires for Europe with 500 passengers on board is not secretly worried by the fear of an accident. We could give endless examples, but it would be useless. Everyone should understand that *there is no magic formula*. This fact must be accepted with humility and generosity, but also with hope.

The error is there. It lives with us and *in us*. It is our virus and it keeps a close eye on us like sin in religion. So: *"you will just have to take things as they come"*!

Let us be a little more humble, a little more generous, a little less of a prima donna and a bit more intelligent because, in fact, we are the only replaceable beings.

Like this the feeling of fear will be less aggressive and less powerful. We will then feel a serene peace, resignation to the will of God that we cannot change.

After all, *if all is not in writing*, then it is for us to prove it.

BOOK IV

Part two

International Competitions: the neutrality or the stalemate or
« The last Judgement » by Luca Signorelli… or rather
« The card players», by Paul Cézanne.

Every Artist is unique, and it is impossible to compare one with another. This is what is most sacred about Art. It is its very essence, its nobility and its superiority. It is, when all is said and done, *this symbiosis between the work of art and its being that makes it immortal.*
Hence the paradox and the debatable principle, as an underlying idea, raised by an artistic competition.
The three fundamental aspects of the idea must be distinguished.

1 - It is impossible to compare artists.
2 - Despite all, the competition must exist, *as a social necessity.*
3 - The competition should signify a pedagogic aim for the participating pianists, the opportunity to play before a large audience, the fact of learning another repertoire or of playing with an orchestra, the chance to test their nerves and to play without stress.

You can time athletes in a race and deduce that the fastest runner is the winner, but you cannot say that about two pianists who play the same Etude or the same work in a competition and declare the one who has played the fastest or loudest to be *the winner.*
If, tactlessly, you were to hold an 'Historical International Competition', I would award places of honour to Frans Liszt, Frédéric Chopin, Sergei Rachmaninov, Sviatoslav Richter, Claudio Arrau, Dinu Lipatti and Martha Argerich.
This would be the same as saying that Vladimir Horowitz, Rudolf Serkin, Maurizio Pollini, Benedetti Michelangeli and Walter Gieseking would get to the semi-final! And Vladimir Ashkenazy might well be eliminated in the first round!
You might also ask why there is a need to classify artists *into categories*, like the products in a supermarket? I think it is reasonable to *classify* bottles of wine and cleaning products. But musicians?!

The idea of holding a *competition* developed because of the disproportionate increase in the number of students of music and *facilities* granted in policies, no doubt with good intentions, to gain access to more advanced levels of study. As education became more widespread, and became *free* in many countries, the arrival of students from every corner of the globe, particularly from Asia, overloaded the market to such an extent that it became necessary to control, classify and select out of all these young people.

The production of pianists then turned into a worrying *over- production*, like the production of cars, television programmes or computers. We are no longer capable of *consuming all that we produce*. This is proof of our social sickness. So, we rush, without any courageous reaction on our part, towards *the destruction of the market*, which is being crushed by its own products.

After all, how could Music expect to escape these social ills?

As a result, the problem is the need to give proof of considerable professional responsibility and to assume the preparation of our own descent. It is not *to organize a collective death* or a musical cannibalism that would cast the profession of pianist into the realm of memory and things forgotten.

You can read in the book by Norman Lebrecht "The Myth of the Maestro" a definition of 'conductor of an orchestra': "*a breed on the way to extinction*". In fact, one could certainly *die musically* in the general indifference without getting any pity from anyone. After all, this only represents the description always claimed for the human race, that of *our superiority* over other living species that authorizes us to destroy ourselves, to kill one another in uncontrolled sentiments, for pleasure or money, jealousy or vengeance, and not just for survival.

We also have our *ego*. We need to live *parallel lives* and to see our photo in the newspapers, on posters, on television and the Internet. We swim in waters that are dangerous and likely to lead to de- multiplication and the reproduction of *policeman* who control these ambitious needs that devour artists. We ourselves created the monsters that now think to reduce us to nothing. *It is we ourselves who open the doors to corruption, to commercialism*, to no consideration for others and to exploitation. There is no point complaining by crying out about "*lost paradise and illusions*"!

And so, Music enters the world of commerce. That is, it enters this world thanks to the artists. The words "*artistic value*" are replaced by the 'art of business' or "*commercial value*".

"*Egoism inspires such horror that we have invented the politeness to cover it up, but it pierces through all veils and betrays itself at every encounter*", are the words we find in The Morality by Schopenhauer. This has always existed.

Organizing a concert, involving an orchestra, renting concert halls, the publicity, the instruments, the artists, the taxes imposed by the government and the insurances are all becoming more and more expensive, *bearing in mind the mechanics of those who are parasites, each time more inflated, all hovering around the artistic act*. So, for this kind of mechanics there has to be a rational *commercial policy*.

However, let us hear from Hector Berlioz, always so very... kind on this subject: "*The composer depends on a crowd of intermediaries placed between the public and himself; these intermediaries may be intelligent or stupid, devoted or hostile, active or inert, and they may from the very first day to the last contribute to the marvel of the composer's work or they may deface it, malign it or even destroy it completely*".

We are instrumental musicians, products to be sold, marketed, distributed and, as a result, to be classified somewhere. Within this context, the idea of a competition or awards for the piano, violin or any other instrument becomes normal.

The big problem is to harmonize *these products with the ideals of Art*. And it is on this particular point that those involved have difficulty in agreeing.

We began by defending the uniqueness of the Artist. This initial idea must now be balanced with *the social need* of a competition and with the need *to bring order* to our musical life.

The realities are many and painful.

1 - The public's indifference to concerts.

2 - The financial failure of festivals.

3 - The crucial need to merge orchestras.

4 - The financial need to merge conservatories, institutions and the bodies involved in the business of Music.

5 - The bankruptcy of musical associations.

6 - The collapse of recording companies

7 - The ever-growing reduction in subsidies for artistic events.

8 - The lack of private sponsors – by-gone patrons such as the Medici in Florence - because Art has become less popular, despite its massification, then a major tennis or football match, for example. Therefore, that makes it less profitable.

9 - All of this can be added to the more fundamental reason: the number of pianists.

In a non-too brilliant social context, the idea of a competition begins to take shape to try to bring some order to the situation.

This idea will give rise to some magnificent things as well as to some very regrettable things. There will be a tremendous difference between what the competition *should be* and what it *is distorted into*, because of personal ambitions and, above all, because of bad management.

1 - The Games and the Stakes

The competition is, for the young, the same thing as *an unemployment office* where they must go if they are to find a job. It is the same for certain members of the jury also. Let us look only for the moment at the problems facing the young pianists. Let us look first at *what it should be*.

1 - The initial motivation to take part in a competition is to exceed yourself and not the fight against or supremacy over others.

2 - The second motivation is to learn, to study new works, face a new repertoire and to put it all to the test before a large audience.

3 - The third motivation is to test personal resistance, nerves, psychology, muscles and morale.

4 - Another important motivation is for young people to have the opportunity to play

with a large symphony orchestra.

5 - The Competition *should therefore become* a concert. *The idea of competition should be eliminated.*

6 - The candidates who applied for the same competition should aspire to helping one another, listening to one another, criticizing one another without their teacher present, accompanying one another to concerts before the tests with the orchestra, to be happy for whoever makes progress and to make friends.

But all too often the reason for taking part in a competition is the personal need of each artist to be recognized by the masses and by one's peers. This narcissistic personal need then opens the doors to every good and bad fortune.

It is therefore for the teacher, prior to the competition, to clear away *the idea of the competition* as such and to change it into *a performance or a concert.* Without that, the candidate will be completely lacking in inspiration because all he will be doing is making as few errors as possible, at least fewer than those made by his colleagues, without looking to the supreme objective.

2 - Places of luxury

The location of an International Competition has certainly become *a place of luxury.* Any organization, anywhere in the world, tries to make miracles with hotels, restaurants, excursions and unforgettable beauty spots. Exceptional treatment is not limited to only the Jury but often includes the candidates as well. This in itself is a good thing and all very nice.

But the prestige of an International Competition lies with the reputation of its Jury. Clearly if this Jury is formed by organizers alone in their circle, the results can only be relative and without great value. Jean Cocteau used to say: "*Every now and again you have to rest of doing nothing*".

In selecting the members of a jury, the content should not only be fair but above all intelligent. The ideal would be to have, firstly, as Artistic Director, a famous pianist for the piano competitions and a famous violinist for the violin competitions. It is also important to ascertain that the jury selected knows the repertoire, which is not always the case!

The absence of great instrumentalists from a Jury is felt painfully. How can anyone judge the *technical* aspects of a competition, or, to explain quickly, the Etudes, and the polyphonic works, etc. if the members of the Jury themselves are not specialists? It would be a good idea to avoid having members of the jury who have never touched the piano for 30 years, because if the candidates play better than the jury members, *the roles in the whole business would be reversed.*

Let us recall Shakespeare when he said in The Merchant of Venice: "*If to do were as easy as to know what were good to do, chapels had been churches and poor men's cottages princes' palaces!*" We know perfectly well that if we were to change the Jury, the names of the laureates would probably be different. All of these risks exist. They are inherent in the life of competitions.

It would seem important, then, that the teacher help choose the competitions for which his pupils will apply and *advise against those in which the criteria of the jury do not respond seriously to what is indispensable* for events to run smoothly.

Also, to be avoided are *teachers' competitions*. Certain competitions even grant an award to the teacher who brings the largest number of participants. This has nothing to do with Music, and such manoeuvres offend it. *There is no reason to support them.*

(NB: a small comment on restaurants: it would be better to avoid table wine for certain juries before afternoon events. The armchairs provided at the competition are far less comfortable than a hotel bed for a siesta....).

3 - Voting: how can one get it so wrong?

I had the good fortune to study Composition with a great musician, awarded the Premier Prix de Rome and a Professor of the Brussels Royal Conservatory, Professor of the Queen Elizabeth Music Chapel, Director of Belgian Flemish Radio and, to conclude, Chairman of SABAM, Master Victor Legley, a very great musician and a very great man, who dedicated his Second Piano to me. He was also the President of the First Bösendorfer-Empire Awards in Brussels. He was one of the most brilliant minds that I have ever met.

I can remember his comments when he was setting up the jury for a competition with my brother Nelson and me: "*Usually a jury loses half of its intelligence whenever it sits behind a green carpet*", he said.

I was never able to forget his words later when I had to play the role of jury myself.

Importantly, I learned from him a taste for the *non-secret* ballot. In fact, every possible type of ballot for competitions has been tried: "*this system is better than the other*", "*it does not penalize*", it is "*fairer*": the marks "*are unfair*", and the "*yes*", the "*no*" and the "*perhaps*". Each competition thinks it has a better system than that of its neighbour. In fact, *only the honesty of the jury is valid*. If people have integrity all *open* systems are good.

What is important is that these systems should be known to the candidates and to the public *in their application*. The vote should also be public. Lord Yehudi Menuhin thought the same thing and applied it in London in the violin competition. The candidates would learn a great deal knowing *who* has eliminated them. In discussing matters with these great musicians, they can learn a lot to help them in the future.

Generalization should be avoided, and responsibilities assumed: it is not the judgment of the jury, but only *of some juries* who eliminate in most cases. The fact of exposing intentions is the best way of neutralizing them.

Perhaps, one day, costly juries may be replaced at competitions by computers, going by the current economic context. These machines would also be able to record the number of *wrong notes* (the exact number, of course) played by candidates. The candidate with the lowest number would win the Premier Prix, of course. In that way we would save on the flights, the luxury hotels, the five- star restaurants, the receptions and the arguments.

Perhaps the result of the competition would be the same…

4 – The audience at Competitions and "the love of Music" …. and that other audience

There is nothing more spectacular than the final stage of the Competition. The whole town is there!

The whole population is in love with the fine Music and with the discovery of new talents. The best of intentions are expressed among the chic guests at the sumptuous receptions, the fantastic banquets and the superb concerts! Comparisons are the order of the day, and a very "good lad": everyone is very gifted, but…. The favourites are the new Ashkenazys and Argerischs! There are even those who surpass them…

Let us remember Voltaire when he said: "*At all times and in all places the public is unfair. Horace was already complaining about this under the empire of Augustus*".

The spectacle of the Competition ends, as in the Coliseum in Rome, when the gladiator-pianists have left. The public also leaves with the promise of returning the next day to the concert of the laureates to listen to their wonderful talents again and their promise of an assured future.

What a disappointment it will be to listen to them the next day. They are far less good than they were the evening before. It is perhaps because "*we are more tired today*", but it seems to me also "*less of a genius than yesterday*". Obviously, the competition is over. The world has returned to normal.

On the whole, the audience at the competition and that at a concert is not the same, although there is a need to "educate" *every* type of audience.

This must begin in childhood. This is possible thanks to all the investment we make through our taxes and as good taxpayers. We do not create Schools of Music for nothing, but for the love of fine things, and also to develop an extreme sensitivity and to provide balance for all human personality that has respect for itself.

But, thank God, there is another type of audience.

What can we say about this admirable example of Queen Elizabeth of Belgium in person, who never missed a single stage of *her* Competition, in the dignity of her loge, sometimes alone and without her court, but who was there for the love of Music and the candidates? In turn, Queen, chamber musician with Ysaye, nurse during the war, she always acted with the same class.

Such cases are rare, but how fine and edifying they are.

5 - And "afterwards"?

The fact of winning or losing a competition is only of relevant significance. It is a momentary experience, fortunate or unfortunate, just like a tennis match. *It is only one moment out of our life and not our whole life.*

The influence and the scope of a Competition is highly debatable, because the real impact on the later development of the participants is quite a different thing: the true Artist evolves. The artist never stops, neither at success nor failure.

We return readily to what Wilhelm Kempff said one day after a magnificent concert:

"You can measure an artist by his capacity to pick himself up after failure".

Of course, the meaning of failure is relative: *why and from whom? And before whom?* We are referring to juries, of course.

"What I want to know, above all, is not whether you have failed but whether you have accepted your failure", Abraham Lincoln would affirm.

Removing the mystery from competition should be a law, or a golden rule.

Each Artist has his own, unique, approach. You can like it or not, it doesn't really matter. It can be measured in neither mathematical terms, money, nor in anything else. Life undertakes, no doubt, to return each and every thing to its place.

The artist must know that he will always be able to shine in a circle round him, even if has not reached the height of a star, or whether he won the competition or not. The whole thing depends on his health, nerves and education beforehand. It is one of the fundamental messages that the teacher should *transmit* to the mind of his pupil instead of insisting on creating muddle and confusion in that mind.

6 – True or False?

Another thing (the first or the last) to ask yourself is: *can competition be truly and completely honest?* Can we be free of complex in saying that there are no hidden interests, interests that go beyond the Jury?

This jury is always made up of human beings, capable of being misled or of misleading others. For this reason, the competition must always be placed within precise context and social fabric. The candidates come from Conservatories where professors teach. These teachers are also part of juries and know the participating pianists fairly well. The organizers themselves take pleasure in inviting *this one* and not *that one* to be part of the jury. We will not even mention the time of harmful political influences concerning the composition of international juries!

And so the circle is closed.

All of us, teachers, candidates, audience, organizers, juries and the media, know all of this by heart. But *we only protest when we are the victims*. Not one of us is innocent in all of this. The teachers themselves bear a large share of this disgrace, which is that of *fabricating* national and international awards instead of *training, first and foremost*, musicians and artists according to the great convictions of Art. We know all of this, but we continue to do it. As Rachmaninov said, *"Bad business, bad business"*!

I had already proposed to the major world schools of music the idea of creating a parallel and complementary course to the course for instruments, so that young people could be informed of the *misfortunes* of the career and made aware of the musical parasites surrounding it. The idea was to teach how to deal with an excessively greedy manager, with the media, the Mafia and the orchestras, and how to react when faced by certain costs to be paid to take *a few more steps* in this musical life. Clearly this would be teaching about the *humiliations* that might be suffered in this career.

A silent and educated response, but with no true comments: *"We cannot restrict the enrolments because of the school lives from mediocre pupils are not from those who have talent*". You might be talking about cattle and not about human beings.

This explains the malaise of a 35-year-old pianist who has *not been informed*, misled by the system, by his teacher, by his school and by society, who still insists unrealistically in accomplishing a dream, in which he hopes to gain a position in a world where no one wants him. Resentment sets in and if he becomes a teacher there may be the risk of destroying those who *follow him.*

The circle can only lead to a disaster in which anarchic production and industrial quantities of musicians lead to no work. Such a state of affairs can only grow worse.

BOOK V

Part one

Liszt's Sonata in B minor
Years of career

1 - « Faust » by Goethe, or « Years of Pilgrimage of Faust and Mephistopheles » and on to ... Franz Liszt

The worlds of Music, Aesthetics and Beauty would be much the poorer without Liszt's Sonata.

It emerges like the Lighthouse of Alexandria in proud and illuminated solitude. For us pianists it is one of life's major references. To embark on an analysis of such a vast subject is no mean matter. And in dealing with this subject inevitably it will *exceed* all expectations. Ernesto Sabato, the great Argentinian poet, claimed that one reason for artistic creation was that *"If the artist did not create, he would explode"*. Not every artist is driven by the same needs when creating, *but all the great masterpieces are born out of love.* They blossom out of transcendental vision. The critics, possible publication or financial considerations simply do not come to mind. There is, however, a deep need for spirituality.

The Sonata in B minor is just that.

The first thing that comes to mind is that the piano, as an instrument, *is only the point of departure for Liszt and his Sonata.* It is through this instrument, his and ours, *that he will make his epic in Music, laying bare his problem* and travel into unknown regions, never before explored by the musical mind, not even by Beethoven in his Op. 106 or Wagner's Tristan that was a result of it.

Liszt will find in them unimagined solutions, and the most important will be *the meeting of all the Arts*, surpassing the bounds of a sonata for piano, even if entirely new. We confront here one of the most brilliant works of music and one of the most representative of Art as a whole. This is a work that marks a break in the musical landscape: you might say that part of the universal repertoire for the piano was written *before* Liszt's Sonata and the rest *afterwards*.

We have already mentioned that Bach had organized Music for two centuries, and then Liszt, in his *disorder*, opened the way to modern music that was impressionist, expressionist, atonal, contemporary, minimalist, and so on.

Liszt's vision is grandiose: like Ulysses, he embarks on a fantastic journey knowing nothing about where it will lead.

Even if Liszt had composed no other works, the Sonata would ensure him his place of glory alongside Beethoven and Bach, because rarely has a composer ever achieved such mastery in his art.

However, few composers have been as ill served as Liszt, even, and above all, *by the great pianists*. The decadent period in which he lived used his music like a circus performance, *out of ignorance*, placing him on a level with Thalberg. The name of Liszt did not go beyond the limits of Purgatory, and, still today, it does not stray far beyond.

Pianists have used, and still use today, these sublime pages to exhibit their muscular baggage. Also today, the ignorance surrounding the work of Liszt *is incredible*. Certainly more is known about it than before, but a great part of the symphonic work, the chamber music and the religious music, for example, remain almost unknown: the St Elizabeth, the Graner Mass, his Mélodies, the Dante and the Faust Symphonies, his Sonata for violin and piano on Chopin's Mazurka in C-sharp minor, just to quote a few, are less popular than, for example, the Campanella (although this is indeed a marvel).

Tremendous *historical* differences separate the work of Liszt from that of his contemporaries. Look no further than what was written in the same period (and brilliantly), by Chopin, Schumann, Brahms, and a few years before by Schubert, to get an idea. Perhaps it was due to his conception of even the role of artist, his desire to unify all the Arts in a superior manifestation that made Liszt different from his contemporaries. He was not just content to be a pianist, composer or musician. He was also religious, a patron of the arts, a Don Giovanni and a great humanist.

His day has not yet come. The History of Art has still much ground to cover before understanding what *the art of Liszt represents.*

Of course, Liszt also wrote some bad pieces, but who could boast of the opposite? Schubert? Beethoven? Wagner? Debussy? Mozart? We remember the great composers thanks to their masterpieces and not thanks to their minor compositions. Beethoven has passed through the centuries because he wrote the Ninth Symphony and not because he wrote the Preludes for piano, quite rightly forgotten.

The first difficulty that the interpreter faces is that of knowing what he is going to do with a fairly complex score that will last for more than half an hour without the slightest break and that is written in such a *condensed* way. The aesthetic idea of "*without form*" for the Sonata has fortunately ceased to be. What to do with all these long parts with no interruption, in other Sonatas known as *movements*, to give them some apparent unity, a logic to their construction, a structure or a skeleton?

We must think of its colossal form before dreaming of its cosmetics and external beauty, although these are not negligible.

Of course, and it is neither too soon nor too late to recall this, the fact that playing the octaves of the Sonata faster than your neighbour resolves very little. Any technical demonstration in such a work is superfluous, because the demands of the *performance imposed by Liszt* are already impressive in themselves, and their *barriers* highly selective. We often exceed the limits that are easy to *cross*, but the major barriers are far less *surmountable*. Similarly, singing a particular passage well will not be the solution for the work as a whole. Memorizing the work and resisting the nervous tension it imposes is no minor matter but is only one aspect of all that has to be resolved, among a thousand other things.

Most pianists are led to making concessions in many of the passages, to finding *intellectual solutions* or *compromising* between certain technical difficulties and nervous resistance. Despite its *apparent accessibility, the Sonata in B minor is not within reach of every pianist, neither technically, nervously, psychologically and, far less, intellectually.* This must be established, then, as a universally accepted principle before beginning a brief analysis of the Sonata. We should first recall the words of Wilhelm Furtwangler, the mythical leader of the famous Berlin Philharmonic Orchestra, in his Talks on Music. They are very pertinent for our subject: *"What music demands today of our interpreters is precisely the opposite of the logic applied before. Everything happens as if there were no need to be concerned about the whole, to refuse to understand it, in the literal meaning of the word, but always with recourse to what I call the "bouquet of flowers" style - the empirical juxtaposition of details dictated by good taste, or a taste for sensation, for whatever you want apart from the authentic meaning of the form. It goes without saying that music composed in this fashion is more difficult to interpret than the classics. A certain technique is enough - because it is never difficult to play a series of musical impressions and images well: the actual job of interpretation, and the difficulty in interpretation, only begin once you have found, to the extent it exists, the form that underpins isolated impressions and images into an organic style"*.

All forms of interpretation, despite *the name Sonata*, are present here and underscored by Liszt's *unity of thought*: the relationship between themes, their conflicts and their dramas, the relationship between *tempi*, unchanged or proportional, the passionate development of personalities, their mutation and their emotional transformations. *The theatricality of the work*, obviously, *provides the listener with a true stage just like watching an opera.*

This is far more difficult to produce then trying to hide or camouflage intellectual incompetence of the interpreter with extravagant distortions, particularly with *rubatos* and out of date dynamic effects, and his failure to understand the work. This is no more than a rather sad confession of the interpreter's incapacity to resolve the fundamental problems raised by his interpretation. Certainly, there are *longer* works but they are *divided*, if only because of this principle of respecting a psychologically acceptable timing, which refers to the concentration span of both the audience and the pianist. Pauses, if not *movements*, allow both the interpreter and the audience to breathe, cough, to relax for a moment and to raise their eyebrows to their neighbour.

Schumann's episodes, for example, are of a shorter inspiration, despite the length of his works. He *'aggregates' more than he actually develops*. There are always new themes, as in the *Carnival,* the *Humoresque* or the *Kreisleriana.* Even in the *Fantasy*, paradoxically *his best Sonata.*

In his great Sonatas, Schubert respects a *form*, even when he ventures into all its repetitions rather than in its developments. On this, Stravinsky said once to the Paris École Normale de Musique: "In certain of his Sonatas I risk dropping off to sleep …. but I always wake up for the Paradise" (sic). This is an *elegant* way of admiring Schubert's repetitions…

Brahms divides his Sonatas like Beethoven, which makes them *healthier* but perhaps less clear in their length.

And lastly, Chopin, has an absolutely perfect sense of timing. Nothing is ever too much or too little with him. He is the model of perfection. He administers all his magnificent inspiration and creation with the precision of an engineer.

Liszt's Sonata, on the other hand, is a challenge *throughout*: it requires timing, concentration, intelligence, nervous resilience, psychological, moral and aesthetical integrity, technical and musical training and background. Here we may note mistakes in our counterpoint, our touch, our timbre, our octaves and our consistency on the recitatives. Here you can detect weaknesses for the leaps, for the emphasis, for our eroticism and hedonism and our grandiloquence. We detect here failure in our interiority, our religiosity and our mystery, although we cannot disguise this in any way at all.

Of course, this happens to us in other works as well, particularly in Chopin's Sonatas, but it is difficult to find similar problems in other romantic sonatas that could only be *resolved together*: this concentration of time, the construction, the technical and aesthetic demands undermine the psychological resistance of the pianist who must confront the problems in the Sonata in B minor.

Liszt's Sonata left its mark on the History of Art not only for its *form* or its *harmony*, but above all for its profound motivations, for its mystery and for the secrets that surround its creation and aesthetic motivations. Artistic courage and titanic brilliance are required to dare to compose such a work after Beethoven's later Sonatas.

Being an artist means having chosen one extreme and having assumed a decision; not to align with the majority in showing false respect for one's cultural and social environment. Our role is not to be in agreement with everyone. Quite the contrary, one must be up *to choose* and as a result *to refuse*. To a certain extent, choosing signifies dying a little. This is, without doubt, the curse we face. And of course it was that of Liszt. But it is also our redemption. Courage is required when an artist perpetrates a choice that goes against the majority. The musician cannot go against his deep convictions because *his destiny is his solitude*. He is alone before his destiny, just as in the concert when *no one can help him*.

The creation, the true moment of communion with immortality, assumes the choice of path where *the birth of his idea will take place in a sentiment mixed with joy and pain that will determine whether his contact with immortality was lasting or fleeting.*

Liszt fully assumed this duty personality and uniqueness. He confronted his own solitude.

2 - « Les Demoiselles d'Avignon » by Pablo Picasso

Who could argue against the incredible beauty of Chopin's Sonatas or those of Schubert, particularly the last three? On the other hand, the Sonatas of Schumann and Brahms, although at all times *beautiful*, are less convincing, with the exception, perhaps, of the Sonata in G minor Op. 22, sublimely *condensed*, or the Sonata in F minor Op. 5, sublimely *extended*. Schumann's Op. 11 and Op. 14, "Concert without Orchestra", are weaker from the point of view of *form* because of their endless *ritornelli* as well as their true lack of development.

Those of Op. 1 and Op. 2 of Brahms are sometimes naive, although one should excuse the youth of the composer in this specific case. However, we should not forget that Op. 5 is from the same period. But one work is not the same as another. The Sonata of Op. 5 is *brilliant*. The others are *very good... magnificent...* It is undeniable that the second theme of the First, Op. 1, or the first movement of Op. 2, are marvels, but the *whole* does not come close to the Fantasy Op. 17 or the Paganini Variations.

The Sonata in G. Minor, despite all its tremendous qualities, can only seem like the *little provincial cousin* of Liszt's Sonata in B minor, and not like its *sister*. Brahms' Sonata in F minor, as we have already said, is far more *classical* than Beethoven's Op. 111... At the same time, it is *less visionary and less committed* than that of Liszt. Throughout its development, Beethoven's themes - in the two first Sonatas as well - are omnipresent. The Scherzo of the Fifth Symphony, the percussion in the second movement of "The Tempest", the four notes off the "Destiny" of Bonn's genius interrupt the thoughts of Brahms relentlessly and without pity.

Lastly, the historical coincidence of composition between Liszt's Sonata in B minor and Brahms' Sonata in F minor (in reality they are contemporaries because they date from 1853-54) only go to accentuate the *aesthetic light years* that separate them.

Chopin's Sonatas are much closer to those of Liszt not because of their *form*, because Chopin remains a classic, but certainly because of their *vision* and their *transcendental message*. The extraordinary Finale in Op. 35 is without doubt a moment of *unique inspiration* and one of the *most brilliant* moments in the whole of piano literature. The atmosphere reflected by Chopin is absolutely apocalyptic. What is there after *Death*, that is *after* the Funeral March? Such is the problem raised.

I do not believe at all in the Russian conception of "*a procession that draws near and then moves away*" defended by Anton Rubinstein and Rachmaninov (with its terrible dynamic changes), for the March, nor do I believe in "*a wind blowing over the tombs*" during the Finale. For a mind as sophisticated as that of Chopin this conception seems to be too... *innocent*. Besides, Chopin was a French Pole and not a Cossack Russian, neither by birth nor by aesthetic taste.

The lack of dynamics, the *sottovoce*, the fact of "*murmuring in two hands*", *the absence, this non-existence* – the "Being and Nothingness" of Sartre, suggest more a metaphysical conception of the problem of Death on the part of Chopin rather than the *Hollywood portraits* of Russian artists.

As to the Sonata Op. 58, in B minor, what else can be said other than that it is pure beauty? Very clearly, the first at the fourth movements are among the finest moments for the piano, as is the *Largo*. But the Finale of Op. 58, to conclude the *non-Russian* idea, is no more a Cossack cavalry charge, as the Russian artists would have it, *but a catastrophic vision of the* world, with the horses of the Apocalypse descending on the Earth, in a movement of *punishment and Death*. Flashes of fury are felt as they strike the piano in headiness and turmoil. It is the greatest *piano march* that I know.

In this Third Sonata, through this triumphant modulation into B major at the end, Chopin draws closer to an almost philosophically positive Beethoven, while in Op. 35, where the downfall *is* absolute, he is closer to the *Appassionata*.

And this is the essential difference between him and Brahms. Chopin is, like Brahms, a classic. *Spiritually* and with conviction *he follows* the pure lines of Mozart, Scarlatti, Bellini and Bach! Brahms, on the other hand, in his Sonatas, *evokes Beethoven's themes* to the edge of nightmare, in the manner of Schumann, and they become *"his second nature"*. But Chopin works with *his own material*.

Obviously, I will not risk making any laconic criticism of the brilliance of Brahms or Schumann, whom I love almost as much a Chopin... I am just making a personal comment on works I admire differently, but which I play with the same love. This is not at all a value judgement on the intrinsic nature of these works, but rather a view of their major characteristics, and that from a personal point of view.

3 - The problem with Death or « Extinction of Useless Lights »
   by Ives Tanguy

Chopin, Beethoven, Liszt and Ravel, later, all seem to have reacted differently to the question of Death.

Beethoven›s response, and we shall look at this later, after the terrible struggle in the first movement of Op. 111, the Nirvana, Heaven, Paradise, Nobility, Goodness and *the eternal trills of the inner peace*, as essential values, set in like forever in the *Arietta*, as a symbol and in the mind. *The reaction is therefore positive.*

According to Chopin, after Death comes Nothingness, an idea that comes from the reflections of Sartre and his negative philosophical sentiments. The Finale of Sonata Op. 35 is, for me, the symbol of this desperate Nothingness. This is what always makes us '*subtract*' in the execution and never 'add'. *The reaction is therefore negative.*

Despite his Catholic faith, Liszt, *with the signature of the Devil* as well as his *confusion with God* in his Sonata, replies that it is perhaps Mephistopheles who will win the final battle. He w i l l never decide and will always remain the *servant* of both. *His reaction is more nuanced* than that of Beethoven and Chopin. It is perhaps less asserted and less clear. Liszt was faithful to his ontological duality until his death.

A little later, Maurice Ravel would react differently to the same problem. If we consider his *Gaspard de la Nuit*, after the lone corpse of a hanged man, Scarbo blends into the atmosphere without leaving a trace. "*He could not understand how he got in, or how he escaped*", according to The Tales of Hoffmann. As is often the case with Ravel, the reaction is *more enigmatic and evasive.*

4 - But... immortality

Despite being such tremendous and incomparable geniuses, neither Chopin, Brahms, Schumann nor, above all, Schubert would have undertaken an aesthetic venture such as Liszt's Sonata. Once again, we are talking of neither the *capacity* nor the *genius of either*. Their Sonatas exist to our great good fortunate. And each one exists with its own dignity.

Nevertheless, they follow the main lines of masters such as Beethoven, Mozart or Haydn, at least in form. You can also feel this *distant* relationship between them, even if only in their sound continuities and their formal developments, although from the emotional point of view they belong to different worlds and spheres.

Liszt's B minor Sonata does, however, remain unique. It has no family. *Its grandeur is its solitude, its drama* and its uniqueness. Its major dimension is that no one could follow it, neither Brahms, Prokofiev, Scriabin, Bartok, Debussy nor Ravel (in their chamber music Sonatas). Nor have Ginastera, Barber or Rachmaninov been able to cast even the slightest shadow over it.

There are, of course, brilliant portraits by Rembrandt, Murillo, Vermeer and Titian, but there is *only one* Mona Lisa. And similarly, there is only one Liszt Sonata.

"*Unfinished*", as Leonardo said of his work. "*Unfinished*", as Liszt said of his.
The same enigmatic smile infuses the two creations.

5 - The birth of the Prophet at the Topkapi Museum in Istanbul

The Sonata in B minor achieves, by its synthesis, *a principle of superior unity*.

Its elements are presented in stages, but with continuity, as in Beethoven's Sonatas Op. 109 and Op. 110, at least for the first three themes: The Scale, Faust and Mephistopheles. Their contrasts, their struggles, their violent disputes and their transformations lead to this impression of grandeur and epic proportions to the conception of synthesis, the superiority of the straight line, purification, at least apparent, in all its elements.

And so we will find here, after half an hour of musical epic at its maximum paroxysm, *the same scale as at the beginning*, a third higher, the B, or a sixth lower, the B again, perhaps as a symbol of the nobility of these two intervals, the finest of any scale, *in their birth and their return to the Principle and the Silence.*

It is just like Liszt to surprise us until the end: on the pedal note of C natural, strongly accentuated, the major chords then close the Sonata *in Olympian serenity, in the triumph of God*, apparently, because in effect, these chords bear the signature of the Devil. After the chord in A minor, and that of F major, without any movement at all, Liszt hides the Triton with a chord in B major by *a little chromatic movement.*

Mephistopheles is there!

The idea of God and the Devil are thus confused, merged and disguised. The characters, God and the Devil, are amalgamated, locked in struggle to grasp the soul of Faust. This makes me think of the dialogue in the work of Goethe, and on reflections on the subject of God and Mephistopheles mutually calling one another *"good people with praiseworthy intentions"* …

6 - The « history » of the Sonata…and our imagination

We know from pupils, contemporaries and friends of Franz Liszt, that when someone asked him if he wanted to illustrate Faust with his Sonata in B minor, as he had done *more clearly* in *"Après une lecture de Dante: Fantasia quasi Sonata "*, an enigmatic smile was his only response.

However, he revealed more in his abundant correspondence. As in all sources of aesthetic inspiration, in the absence of confirmation from the creator we can only but let our imagination run free. As the Italians say: *"se non è vero è ben trovato"* (Even if it is not true, it is well conceived).

So, I start with this idea through imagination and love of tradition. Love of Altenburg as well. Nearly everyone knows the alternatives: the Sonata may reflect the life of the composer, follow passages of the Bible, tell tales of adventures in paradise or even, *without a programme, simply develop a splendid piece of music*.

In the absence of a response from Liszt, I will opt for *the interpretation* of Faust.

Clearly with his hypersensitivity Liszt would have been incapable of not absorbing German genius, particularly that of Schiller and Goethe. *"Should we then deduce that the Sonata is more Germanic than Italian or French"*? Alain Walker raises this question in his magnificent book on Liszt. The answer is probably yes, given the sparse decoration in such a work and the severity of the form, even if Lisztian.

However, within the work there are *small forms within the major forms.* These are impenetrable pathways, disconcerting intentions that hide the gems of conception and hold mysteries and secrets. Faithful to his style, Liszt is the uncontested and undeniable master of *emotional variations*, without formal development in the sense of a Beethoven. Here there are no models for Liszt. Neither Bach, Beethoven, Chopin nor Wagner could have served as models. Certainly, he would deny it. In his modesty he would say that of course *there had been* models. But then, only from the spiritual point of view, and in a fairly general and wide-reaching artistic sense, because Franz Liszt, *"the King of de Minims"*, in his own words, thought of himself as *"the least important of all"*.

Is he perhaps the outcast of the group?

We have just named four of his gods, all true masters of development. Bach was his dream. Beethoven had recognized him as a genius at the age of 12 and kissed him on the forehead in public. He was to remember that throughout his life: to be kissed by the greatest living composer! Chopin, his favourite friend, was the one he admired most in the whole world. Later, he greatly admired and particularly loved Richard Wagner, who, however, exploited him and squeezed him like a lemon, although Liszt had given him so much musical inspiration.

The Sonata is the *opposing model to development* in the *classical* meaning of the word. It is the most polished proof of what one calls *conflicting variations* of the brilliant improviser, in which the developments represent changes to preceding themes without any interruption, the *leitmotif* of different and mingled essences. The most seductive is without doubt that of Mephistopheles and Marguerite.

And why? Was it because the eternal feminine fascinated Liszt? Why always associate the Devil with a woman?

7 - *Divide ut regnes…*

Of course, each pianist can divide the Sonata as suits him, play it in *rhapsody*, capriciously and placing it at a lower level, or in *Sonata form*, trying to reflect its whole structure.

Clearly for the *rhapsodies* the problems are less difficult to overcome, because they adapt the speeds and the sparkle according to what they are capable of doing, as second-class artists. They interpret pictures *without connecting them*. They use a work of demonstration to amaze the public for half an hour in *"all their adorable emptiness"*, the opinion of the disciples and followers of Johann Brahms, who fell asleep during the playing of the Sonata by Liszt! But let us not be unfair …no one is perfect…. not even Brahms.

8 - The first strives between four, or the "First Movement"

On the whole, we can agree on four major themes that are very visible and very different. To this must be added the fifth protagonist, the scale:

This scale is the Joan of Arc of the work and endures the Way of the Cross. It goes right through the Sonata at war, runs through all the themes, preparing them in their turbulence and calm.

The first battle, or *the first part of the first movement*, is characterized by the struggle between Faust and Mephistopheles, between measures 32 and 55.
All this in a continuous exposition, as I have already said, as in Op. 109 and Op. 110.

A small anguished and agitated bridge, *with vital dynamics* (because this is *crescendo* and not *diminuendo* between the chords, despite the phrasing), prepares their first battle:

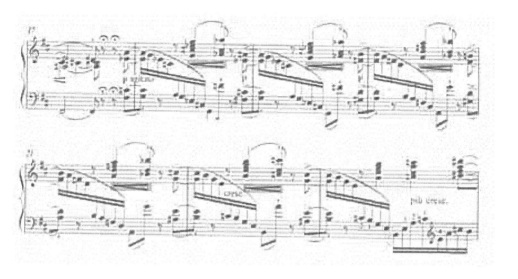

This tension, created by this bridge, leads Faust to win the first round; *his triumph is grandiose* in the double octaves, from measure 55 to measure 72, a hymn *to the glory of human strength*. From measure 72 in E-flat major, the scale is at first *ascending and inverted*, and, after a terrible fall, reaches the last note of the piano, the A, in measures 81 and 82.
It goes on to develop *descending* in *ascending* registers, by sixths, and imposing chords and octaves in the bass, before leading us on to the theme of God, the third, in D major, in measure 105, *Grandioso* until measure 119.

These extremely difficult double octaves *must be played absolutely in the same tempo* as the start of the Faust theme in measure 8. Otherwise you would fall into the first major trap of the work and its unity would be compromised, *because we would be playing the same theme, in the same movement, at different tempi.*
The octaves require specific technical work because the *grandeur* of the passage, as well as its speed, or rather its *tempo*, demands this.

1 - One must practice *the octaves between the thumbs*, what I call *the third octave of the passage*, without the fifth fingers, to ensure their highly risky displacements.
2 - The fifth fingers must play the octaves *without* the thumbs.
3 - Practice in broken octaves, starting with the thumbs, starting with the fifths and combining all parallel and symmetric possibilities.

4 - A path must be created between the thumbs of the two hands avoiding any leaps where possible. This is possible using a wise combination, for example in measure 59: the right thumb, D, should be followed in the same line by the three left thumbs, C, B-flat, F, and so on in each group: that is, you must create *a central line to follow* formed by the two thumbs. *One right thumb followed by three left.*

5 - The wrist must be made flexible by repeating, *without a pause*, in *PPP* and with very tiny movements, at least four times each octave. This goes for the whole passage, from measure 55 to measure 81.

This brings us to the *Grandioso* with the exact *tempo*, that is,
keeping the relation between the minims: 2/2 and 3/2.
This theme, *Grandioso*, has all the catholic colours and pomp of the Vatican.
The arms must be loose from the body and the three major articulations, the wrists, elbows and shoulders must be completely relaxed, to draw circular movements in the air, as if you were swimming.
The rebounds must be developed *without the fingertips leaving the keyboard*. Contact with the keyboard is, therefore, continuous.

Bells announce the suspension of the Word of God, from measure 114 to measure 119, where one of the first difficulties in *tempo* relationship becomes apparent: we move from a 2/2 to a 4/4. This is mainly a question of writing, because the crotchet must remain the same, but *calmer* in nature, of course.
This theme of Faust, in measure 120, then takes on the air of a young lover full of class and dignity and not a degenerate, with *caprices* and extravagant *rubati*.
His small intervention over, his *friend* Mephistopheles appears once again just before the appearance of Marguerite. This moment is one of the finest transformations of the Sonata. The inverted scale brings them together, in the lower notes of the chords in the right hand. Marguerite's theme is *one of the most beautiful cantabiles* that I know. It is difficult to imagine a piano singing *better* or in a *purer* way.
The best technical advice to give here is supple contact with the key, an up-down movement with the very last articulation of the finger, with the full phalange. *The descent on the key is as slow as possible.* The pedal is also very slow in order to let the hammers and the chords *breathe*.
This woman must be given all her beauty and innocence, almost her virginity.

Shortly after these two incredible episodes, in D major and in E minor, both modest and full of charm, so appropriate for a young flower such as Marguerite, temptation returns, suggested by the tritone of *friend* Mephistopheles.

It is absolutely essential *to change the colours* of the personages to be able to distinguish them. Here you can achieve this, for example, with the intelligent use of the pedal: *tre corde* for the E minor (Marguerite) and *una corda* starting from B-natural and the following passage in B-flat (Mephistopheles).

The cantabile rises in irritation to become more *tense*, changing into a *duetto*, in the form of an unbalanced conversation between the protagonists. The major sevenths A-sharp/A-natural, and B-sharp/F-sharp/B-natural are agonizing and anguished. They instil in us the imminent drama.

Marguerite's next intervention, in measures 171 to 179, *is more impatient*. Her variation, surrounded by arpeggios, turns her into a wonder.

From measure 179, Faust arrives and soul-searches again. He agonizes within over the terrible choices to be made. The scale follows him, very discreetly, in the upper notes of the right hand. Take care not to change the *tempo* in this passage too much because it is dealing with the same personages.

The struggle will be *agitato* between Marguerite (soprano) and the scale (bass), between measures 191 and 195. It is as though a force - the scale - *will bring her down*.

Both our personalities fall into a Faustian *dolce*, in superb, *bellissimi* trills and cadences: the first entirely *en dolcissimo*, the other much more virile. Superb forces are picked up again in the latter and they are rushed forward in *accelerando molto*: Faust is once again ready to resist.

Allegro energico sets the theme in measure 205. This indication is not found in all editions. The theme is certainly that of measure 8, in 2/2. But here it is in 4/4. I think that this variation in the score will show how Faust's theme and the ascending scale in the chords of measures 209 to 213 merge. *It is a moving osmosis.*

Support is necessary for this scale and Liszt marks it at each note: it would be unthinkable *to do it in cut time, in 2/2.*

The extension of Faust's theme in the left-hand in measures 221 to 232 and the precipitation that follows it is one of the key points in the work:

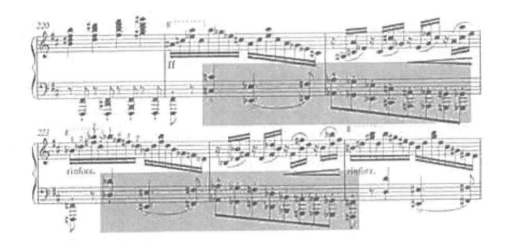

The work to be done in the octaves in the left-hand is the same, separately, as the work indicated for the preceding double octaves.

A more lively melody appears: Faust sings, very optimistically, scarcely interrupted by a whirlwind of notes, to break into joy once again. The exaltation is complete and radiant, the surge of sound sublime and the whole a jingling of gems.

But Mephistopheles returns in measure 255 and drives Faust into an infernal disequilibrium, *incalzando, sempre con strepito, stringendo*. The vertigo is tremendous and the articulations of the left-hand become increasingly virulent.

Fortunately the scale, this time *grandioso* in measure 277, splendidly imposes itself.

9 - The strife between three, or the "Second Movement"

We fall here into another battle.

This time it is the *second* movement: the great recitatives, or the *dispute* between God and Faust, His choral, and the *new dispute*, more violent this time, between God and Faust with the *unexpected interruptions* of Mephistopheles.

God speaks gently, *pesante*, but calmly.

Faust, on the other hand, has reached the peak of his rebellion and by inverting his theme he rebels twice consecutively.

The left hand of the recitatives suggests sustained notes, forming a choral. The last cry, accentuated on the chord A-sharp, E-natural, G-sharp, sustained on the following A- natural throughout the whole recitative, *and even during its fermata*, resolves itself on the last chords just before the last *fermata*. In fact, there is no break between the chords.

The same goes for the second time.

Note the third chord: *a faster arpeggiato*, in the form of a chord and not in the form of an extended arpeggio like the others.

The recitatives must be played *forte et appassionato, in crescendo* and not with the fragile *diminuendo* to which we have become accustomed. A virile, desperate execution is desirable, free of any feminine sensitivity: *this is Faust who is enjoying himself and not Marguerite.*

The choral disappears in the last chords of measures 306, 307 and 308 and dissolves into the ascending scale of fifths that leads us to a tremendous *agitato*, with imposing basses (one part of the scale). It reflects a further struggle between Faust and Mephistopheles, very clear this time, between measures 319 and 330. This is a *Coda* that will turn into a *beatific theme* in F-sharp major, something of a fetish tonality for Liszt (that of his "Bénédiction de Dieu dans la solitude"), but only in measure 334, *and not before.*

Faust and Mephistopheles *are going to pause to listen to the echoes of Paradise.* I think that measures 331, 332, 333 and 334 represent *this entrance to Paradise* where all behaviour is calmed. Our friend Mephistopheles in person *is calmed* in a *dolcissimo con intimo sentimento*, in measures 348, 349, 350 and 351.

The fourth theme is there.

It is exposed in *Andante sostenuto*, in choral form and with a fine polyphonic richness. Soprano and tenor argue for these beauties. You are carried to regions similar to those of Bach. A feeling of peace and noble quietude give the impression that the music is *suspended in time*, in complete immobility.

The transformation of Mephistopheles makes you think that he too was an angel, in a different age, barer of light but degraded by God, despite all. It is because of this *old angel* that I think of him in this case and not of Marguerite, in this way avoiding the *feminine rubato.*

The greatest spiritual and muscular decompression is demanded here. It is absolutely indispensable. We must feel that we are expelling all exteriority and that we are returning to the essential. This polyphony and its development are absolutely magic because they make us dream or perceive the themes of the Sonata as if we were in a state of lethargy.

There is a synthesis here that places Liszt alongside the greatest of all time.

The sonorities achieved make you think that he must have found an instrument that had no hammers. To achieve this *dolcissimo sentimento*, he demands that we rise to the occasion, to leave our woes and human sentiments behind on earth to be able to rise with him heavenward. *A touch from hardly farther than the escapement is required* because the sonority *is floating* and not a *reality.* The fingers press the keys down no more than four or five millimetres. They should not leave the keys for a fraction of a second. They must also be applied on the most sensitive part of the fingertip. *Finger and key* form a whole element.

In the last apparition of Mephistopheles, *his return to reality*, in measures 360, 361 and 362, laments rise to the tenor in the left hand. They must be emphasized until the seven last notes of the cadence: A-sharp, G-sharp, E-sharp, B, B-sharp, D-sharp and its *fermata*, C-sharp, and in this way fall into the theme of God.

We then find developments of preceding recitatives wondering among themselves why Liszt did not divide the Sonata *psychologically. We can do nothing else but bow to this.*

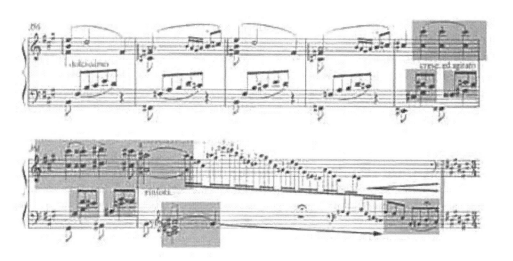

The transformation is then produced in God in person.

You might believe in the reincarnation of God made Man and think of Christ's suffering on Earth. *The Catholic references are clearly present*: God become Man (from measure 367 to 375) as in the Scriptures. With His impassioned cries and His imprecations, He sends furious flashes of lightning to Earth, on two occasions (in measure 380 to 395). This exasperation is unleashed against Faust, represented by the extension of his theme in flames.

The great basses and Dantesque explosions lead to one of the culminating points of the Sonata, in the *FFF* of measure 395: *it is then that the most impressive transubstantiation takes place,* and the fourth theme, the choral, polyphonic the first time, *is filled here with all its harmonic beauty* (measures 397 to 433).

They no longer resemble either the piano or the harp. They are rare beatific sonorities. They do not belong to us, *but to another world.*

Those who think that a piano, by nature, *cannot sing* and that it has only a very (too) short sonority, have only to listen to these measures played by Arrau, by Richter or by Argerich.

The choral established by the chords in the left-hand that follow before this *first finale* is more Wagnerian than Wagner himself, in measures 419 to 430.

The last *sustained left thumb continues* on the right for the last two quavers, B and A- sharp, and develops on the right in measures 431 and 432, to have us once again fall to an anxious Marguerite rather than to Mephistopheles. This is a Marguerite full of nostalgia, sadness and introversion.

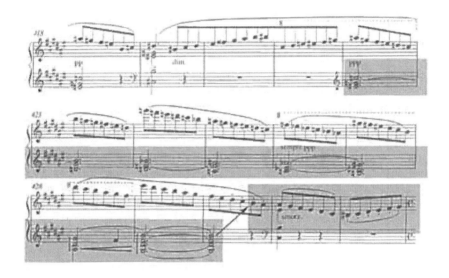

A *dolcissimo* execution is demanded, without exaggeration, but with an agonizing lyricism, full of desolation and resignation, as if truly reaching the end.
Muscles suspension is absolute. The arms should be weightless.

We should feel as if the last drops of blood are flowing out of us. *We are no longer playing. We are listening to someone else. It is someone beyond; the Nothingness of Chopin. Everything is extinguished. The music seems to have returned to its dwelling place. In the Silence...*

10 - The strife between two, or the "Third Movement"

But....
After the *PPP* in measure 452, the muffled blows on F-sharp bring the scale back on stage. It is going to recreate all the expectation and all the mystery. It will lead us up to the activity. *This is the "resurrection".* This is the enharmony, the Eureka: Mephistopheles and Faust have returned!
We are plunged again, this time into the third movement, this one very short, like a diabolic scherzo. What good fortune to be able to talk of Scherzo for such music!

215

This scherzo might be considered to continue until the recapitulation, at bar 533, like a *third movement*. It might also be considered to continue until bar 523, where Faust regains control. Lastly, it could also be thought to continue to measure 555, just before the left-hand chords that plunge the Sonata towards the Finale.

Our characters are in any case so merged that the three possibilities seem plausible. The fact is that he, Mephistopheles, goes into

serious battle with Faust, who fights him with dignity.

It is a *fierce*, brilliant, amazing dual. Claudio Arrau thought that this *Fugato* was like an *apparent triumph* of Mephistopheles. Whatever the case, this dual is a great moment of pianistic virtuosity: a diabolic pizzicato for the left-hand (Mephistopheles) opposes Faust's unruffled theme on the right. Everything takes place with *sordino*, without witnesses. Evil spirits seem to leap and bound on the keyboard; they are not exactly nice little gnomes. They are almost like Scarbo: sharp, unwholesome, odious and curious. Tonalities follow one another madly and illuminate the music with mysterious and fascinating images. Departing on G-flat major, you cross the first time with B-flat minor, then move to F minor, on to E- flat minor and return on B-flat. It is a devilish dance between two skilled fencers. The continuity is magnificent. Nothing holds back this fatal dance. You might say nothing holds back a single note. *It is a phantasmagorical vision of the piano and of music.*

The touch, or rather the attack on the keys, should be designed upwards. We should leave the keyboard because the least fraction of a second resting on the key will be fatal. *Hence the need for this attack on the keys at lightning speed:* the music here requires this as expression. It must interpret the hypocritical, masked smile of Mephistopheles, and particularly his pitiless laughing and infernal re-apparitions. The devastation of the fire, as in hell, follows. *It is a piano catastrophe, an apocalyptic vision, but brilliantly refined,* and almost all in *PP*.

When has there ever been such a moment in the whole of preceding musical literature? I cannot remember nothing like it.

Only Faust rebels. Make the wrist tremble ever so slightly to   be able to execute the passage because Faust does not perform pirouettes all the time.

The work of the *fingertips* is advisable here, *applying a certain dryness of touch*. Resonances should be avoided because *the whole should regenerate*. I speak here, of course, of the left hand on the first page, but also of the right when the theme modulates to B-flat minor and does the same thing as the other hand. The speed of the hammer should be insane, and articulation of the wrist reduced *to almost nothing* in order to protect the speed of the movements. What counts is repressed nervous impulse, not amplitude. A springing movement of the fingertips should facilitate the task.

Reversing Faust's theme in measure 509 *is unique and symbolic*, as if Faust were finally admitting defeat and allowing Mephistopheles to triumph, *in his emotional reversal*. But in measure 519 he manages to escape again and reassert himself on reaching E-flat major, in measure 523, just before the recapitulation. Here he predominates with solemnity and some uneasiness, because, after all, the battle has not yet been won entirely.

Far from it.

The *tempo* of this *Fugato* is not a problem in itself. It *has* become a problem due to intellectual dishonesty. Clearly, from the indication *Allegro energico* in 2/2 (measure 460, the start of the *Fugato*) and the recapitulation that follows, *it cannot* be played at a different *tempo* from that of the first theme, on the first page, bar 8. Liszt expresses this clamorously: there is not the least indication of any change.

Let us show our respect to Liszt for having the courage to introduce such a striking *Fugato* into a Sonata, and in such a place! Here I find him, spiritually, to be the successor to Beethoven. Not that of the Fugues of Op. 110, reflexive as they are, but that of Op. 109 (also almost *double*), or the *Eroica Variations* Op. 35, considering the contrast in touch and their brevity. Above all, because of his desire not to finish the work with the Fugue, as the final synthesis, but rather falling back into different waters.

The problem for Liszt, as for Beethoven, was to coordinate the severe spirit of a Fugue with the formal spirit of a Sonata, because they are opposing elements. Liszt, like Beethoven, uses *artistic license*.

We know that it is hazardous to pour an excellent beer into a great wine, and it is the same with fugues *in* sonatas. But… both Liszt and Beethoven succeeded.

11 - Weary heroes, or the "Fourth Movement"

A different ambience suffuses the *Piu mosso*, in bar 555.

Of course, I know that the recapitulation begins at bar 533, or at bar 523, but what do you expect, no one is perfect. I get the impression that the blows of the scale, in the bass notes, the initial G, here   in E-flat and there in E minor, but surely I am wrong, and I beg young pianists not to follow my opinion, but what a temptation it is to believe that the recapitulation begins there!

In "my error", I defend myself with the words of Alberto Ginastera who said *"Certainly witches are just imaginary, but .... they do exist, of that I'm sure!"*

It is absolutely amazing how Liszt managed to transform Faust's theme in the bass by the arrival of a pedal in F-sharp, the last note of the bass (bars 569, 573 and 577).

Perhaps it was to introduce the idea of the *dominant* in the Finale of the work. Whatever the case, this F-sharp carries the whole tension of the passage. It is absolutely fantastic! You have to juggle with the pedal so that this note does not get lost, stupidly, in the second thematic note. Perhaps you could only half change the pedal? I don't know, but that is what I do in any case. I also hold it with my finger to be sure of its resonance during the undulations of the pedal.

It is from this dominant of B that the whole finale begins.

A phenomenal ascension begins on his F-sharp with the same formula of octaves as for the *Prestissimo* in bar 682. It is Faust's theme compressed, accelerated and agitated. It seems to be definitive.

Nevertheless, a veritable cascade of octaves precipitates it to earth in terrible doubts. Faust struggles, bends, despite the fact that Mephistopheles shrieks weaker each time to address himself to God.

But these octaves have to be dealt with.

They are, as in the *Prestissimo* later on, true barriers for whoever dares to face such a work with muscles that are too tender or inexperienced. Liszt warns us that whoever challenges him must know who he is dealing with.

The work of the thumbs as was done for the first octaves in bar 55 is indispensable. The major problem is *combining strength and speed*, which is a true nightmare. These three passages of wide octaves (the doubles first, those that we are addressing and those of the *Prestissimo*) are *culminating points of the work. These are summits and not moments of expressive or grandiose deceleration.* It is also clear here *what you can do and what you cannot do.*

The first, before the *Grandioso*, are in exactly the same *tempo* as the exposition of Faust's theme.

A culminating point of the *stringendo* and not the deceleration, these *are faster, to the metronome,* than the start of the *Piu mosso* and the start of the *stringendo*!

The final octaves of the *Prestissimo* are *the summit of the whole work.* They are faster than the *Presto* and the *Stretta quasi presto* that precedes them. *Not in the mind, but to the metronome.* This is difficult to accomplish, but this work was not destined to be played by everyone, although every pianist wants to play it. Any concession granted on these points would be like agreeing to break the Sonata without remedy.

Here are the three hurdles to jump!

Studying the *Eroica*, in the Transcendental Etudes, is very beneficial, as is the *Second Etude* and the *Mazeppa*. The *Sixth of Paganini* is also good, and of course the *Sixth Rhapsody*. The breaking of octaves also, as already explained for the firsts. And do not forget the repetitions of the wrist to make them flexible and more effective.

I recommend working the preceding two passages with the metronome in reverse, once the maximum speed has been obtained for the octaves. So, having completed the work and done all the recommended exercises:

1 - Note, first of all, what the final speed is that can be achieved in the octaves, and descend (step-by-step of the infernal machine), to understand the best tempo to engage the *Piu mosso*, and to avoid putting yourself, by being silly, into ridiculous situations that lead to nothing.

2 - This way you will understand what the mathematical speed at the start should be.

The final speed, as in the octaves of the *Prestissimo, should be obtained as a result.* This speed is the result of the components intelligently added by a musical impulse *en accelerando,* by an enthusiastic *crescendo*, by the force of musical conviction, by a perfectly healthy assimilation, without additives or colouring materials. It should become natural, without effort, because it is impossible to hide yourself here. We would be entirely bare, and we would blush with shame if our means were not honest.

The recapitulation of God's theme in B major, in bar 600, now gives the impression of the Creator being discouraged, perhaps because he has become tired at not being heard.

The bells, each time clearer, become calm and then silent to allow Marguerite to return much richer in experience. At the end of her *cantabile*, she attempts a distressing ascension: the chord unfolds a major seventh.

The passage gives this woman an air of beauty that is more wrinkled, more disappointed and sadder. This is *her dissonance* alone. The re of her song, extending in long arpeggios and in double quavers this time, is celestial. To accelerate here would be as stupid as the first time. From measures 642, Faust is once again troubled. He leaps on the keyboard just as Mephistopheles did on him in the great battle of the *Fugato*. Liszt accomplishes admirable unity in the phrasing with the two principal themes.

Mephistopheles, during and after his dialogue with Marguerite, prepares a noisy return in the *Stretta quasi Presto*. Laughing ironically, he rushes around terribly to stop, desperate, in measure 673.

The scale, once again, divides the territories between him and Faust. The latter then sinks into total despair in the *Prestissimo* octaves of a difficulty never before encountered in the history of the piano.

Just a few words on these octaves as well, because they are terrifying.

The first thing to overcome is *the different speed* developed in the two hands. The octaves in the left-hand have one octave more, that of the bass, that does not belong to the theme. This extra octave does not quite help solving things.

Several different types of work must be done here.

> 1 - They must *be studied together, in parallel octaves in unison* (despite the very slight difference in notes), *by adding one octave* to the right-hand, that is, that of the bass in the left.
>
> 2 - You must study *the right-hand once and the left-hand twice*, proportionately, in order to develop the resistance of the left-hand with *the extra octave, until you achieve the real speed with separate hands.*
>
> 3 - *The wrist must rebound at least four times on each octave and without the slightest pause between them,* to ensure the suppleness indispensable in the speed and to *quadruple* the resistance of the left-hand.
>
> 4 - One must also *develop the dynamics starting Piano, in crescendo towards the third tempo, increasing the tension towards it* and not putting it on the inconvenient extra octave, in the left-hand.

After this terrifying passage, the explosion of God's theme is impressive in measure 700. It is like a cataclysm and seems to announce His triumph and the Final Judgement.

12 – The end … or eternity found?

You might believe we have arrived at the end of the Sonata, also knowing that Liszt had written another ending for this work, but his genius told him to do the opposite of what would be *expected*: and here we have the artist's choice!

On this pedal in E, in the bass, in measure 708, seventh of the chord of the principal dominant, the tradition and custom recommend two solutions: gradually cutting the resonances with a *tremolo* on the right pedal or cutting them by sharply pressing the *una corda* until all sonority disappears.

Neither of these two solutions pleases me very much. I think it would be more significant, more poetic and more profound (the work being in constant mutation) to prolong this immense sonority and to change it in chorus one measure later, or perhaps two, in the chord of B major, on the third, in measure 712.

The chord that reintroduces the chorus in measure 711 is the same as that of the resonance of the dominant chord. Merging that chord with the pedal and its resolution in the inverted tonic chord, in *Piano*, associated with this grandiose sonority, *gives the idea of redemption*. The idea of total transformation *would be accomplished like this*.

I use this solution personally and talk about it with my colleagues and my pupils without imposing it on anyone.

There is also a line at the end of the choral that moves from the tenor to the contralto in measure 728, after the *quintolet,* that goes to the D-sharp and C-sharp. I think it has to be continued on the C-natural of the *Allegro moderato*, within the chord. After, each pianist will find his line. Mine is C-natural, D-Sharp, E-natural, G-natural and, lastly, B major.

In the left-hand, Mephistopheles seems exhausted and bloodless. Faust also seems to render up his soul. This disappearance of all the themes, of all the elements, of all sonority and all reality is accentuated in a *tempo* that defies the eternity.

Let us now look at the last scales.

The very last ends on the C-natural, the terrible second minor of B major. This accent on the C-natural suggests that Liszt wanted this prolonged, disturbed, strange note. It is particularly threatening. To express that, I hold it with the tonal pedal, held by my heel, and I press the *una corda* with my tiptoe.

The chords spread with *maestosità, wavering and hesitant* due to this bass pedal of C which I hold in an imaginary *legato* until the final B, the latter played in an extinct, mute and short way. I hold the right chord a little longer.

At this moment you are not sure whether you have risen to the heavens or descended into hell because the chords, in their last relationship, sign - with the smile of the Devil - the triton between the F major and the B major, scarcely hidden by their closeness. *The serenity and immensity* of God are there also… together…

It is impossible to respond to the doubts that assail us given that the Silence devours us immediately.

BOOK V

Part two

The Career, the random, the ephemeral... and the market

Why go on to talk of the career of a pianist after analysing Liszt's Sonata? What could that Sonata possibly have in common with a social career?

Perhaps they are not comparable, but I think precisely that this Sonata *is* the representation of a pianist and of *the life of an artist*. The dramas, the brilliance, the fervour, the virtuosity, the conflicts, the doubts and the constant discouragement facing a full-time working artist, all *his superficialities and profoundness* are all there. It is the symbol of an activity that is at the same time religious, social, amorous and artistic.

It *represents* a whole. It is *una commedia del arte*. It reveals the doubts that assail the mind and spirit of an artist, the crises and the triumphs. In all of this, I feel that there are passages in the Sonata that serve as a backdrop, as a fatal warning.

It is a premonition.

Building up a career, however, is not a simple matter and cannot be predicted. It does not respond to precise rules: it would be difficult to say *who or what* determines whether an artist will be successful or not. Certainly not competitions, no matter how important they are, nor talent in isolation. It would be preferable to speak of *multiple talents* for a pianist wishing to commit to the career of soloist.

These talents would most certainly place *artistic talent* at the head of the list (little could be done without it), followed by *social relations*. Then *intelligence*; *financial and social power* (indispensable); *charisma* (the power to convince); and *personal leverage* or knowing what *he* represents and for *whom*. These talents also include *belonging* or not to groups or mafias of every type, racial, sexist or political; *support* of every kind, *the capacity to organize* for *others*, *the capacity to socially act* with hypocritical individuals and *the capacity to juggle* with circumstances of every kind.

The relationships the pianist will establish with concert managers and others should be added to this list, because for those people we are marketable *goods*. There are no sentiments in all of this or any underlying dishonesty. You can seldom come across a *humane* manager, but he will probably be outside the commercial circuit or, certainly, he will not be given access to *the important circuits*. You have to juggle with all of this, while maintaining your integrity, which is not at all easy. You have to face the corrupt aspects of the job, and those who are corrupt, with a smile and an unfailing strength of conviction.

I would like to quote here the words of Daniel Barenboim who, in terms of careers knows a thing or two: *"Directing an orchestra as a unique activity is a 'sociological' and not an artistic invention of the twentieth century",* the words he wrote on the sleeve of one of his own CDs.

Think carefully on these very wise words.

1 - Clean accounts make for good friends

As for all careers, the route taken by a musician is peopled with the incapable.

Very often someone gains a place without deserving it, either due to money or for reasons that lie beyond music. Currently, *being sponsored* opens the doors to everything. It doesn't matter very much how you play; the important thing is to know *who* is backing you or how much money you represent.

So, money plays a major role in a career. This is also fairly normal if you look at it from the side of the organization. Concert halls have to be hired, publicity organized, printed and distributed. CDs have to be recorded, and sound technicians and engineers must be paid. As a result, productions are fabricated and then marketed. This means paying the people that do this work. Who will pay the producers if the CDs are not sold?

This requires a *financial* trilogy to organize the musical and social act: *the manager, the artist and the sponsor*, whether private or with state involvement. It is not a question here of musical *talent* but rather more the power to cover the tremendous underlying costs.

How many managers do not ask their potential artists, sarcastically, for money upfront as a guarantee of payment for office, telephone and travel expenses? How many people agree to this? Of course, such attitudes on the part of those artists who consent to this treatment *prejudice* those artists who do not have the means to do the same. We know that money is necessary, and it should fulfil its essential mission. One has to bear in mind how much it costs for a symphony orchestra to perform at a concert where one wants to play as soloist.

The problem is, therefore, human and social, because it does affect the labour market. Money attracts money. Whoever has it, therefore, whether it is your own or belonging to someone else, may aspire, despite being the lesser performer, to do more than the better performer is able to.

1 - As a student, the one with money can pay for the masterclasses that are more costly.

2 - As a student, he can travel to any country he fancies.

3 - He can pay for the production of CDs himself, hire the better concert halls and have more sophisticated advertising.

4 - He can even pay for his own orchestra. 5 - Later on, he can do his own promotion.

6 - He can organize things, events that will focus entirely on him.

7 - He can acquire the finest instruments on which to work.

All of this is possible and has nothing to do with the true musical talent of the person.
Carl Flesch, the great violinist, wrote in his Memoirs *"There is no other profession as contaminated by imposters as ours"*.
So, you can see that unfortunately this is a regular feature, whatever the instrument.

2 - Dignus est intrare

Critics such as Norman Lebrecht of the London Daily Telegraph, think that we are completely lacking in true talent. However, we have never had as many musicians, and not only pianists. Access to the study of music has never been easier.

We are in a period of over-production in the industrial, cultural and political sectors. The selection of people or products is therefore increasingly more difficult; selection has become almost impossible. The overall quality of pianists has improved, but not individual quality. We have far more people who play *better*, because the technical level *collectively* is far higher today than it was a hundred years ago, but we struggle to reap the dividends and we find that *individual* artists are *less good* than before.

Just like today's cars: they are more comfortable, technically more sophisticated and they perform better but they do not last for as long as before because they are not as good. They are manufactured, in fact just like artists, *to be replaced more quickly*. We are living in the age of *"use and discard"*, and all done as quickly as possible. Therefore, it is not difficult to understand that we have a tremendous need for managers able to *manage* this crisis. They do not need coaxing, far from it. Veritable gurus in the job, they are to be found in all the strategic cities, in the key orchestras, in distinguished Festivals and in the important cycles of concerts. They discuss and decide the future of this one and that. The most important are those one sees least. They are very discreet, sometimes anonymous, and they lurk behind the figures of stars without even these stars being able to take a decision on anything. They may even *recommend* programmes to artists, turn them into personalities ready to play to society, and hire them for *this particular concert* but not for *that one*.

3 – "The Limoges market" by Mussorgsky

This leads us to speak about *the market*.
Pianists considered as *artistic merchandise*, have to be marketed on *the market where someone wants to buy them*. This in itself   is neither good nor bad, neither honest nor dishonest, because it is a question of *supply and demand*. When one artist is in more demand more than another one, his wages become much more important, and as a result, his concert agenda as well.
You can have an extraordinary *market* in a particular country and be unknown in the neighbouring country. There are very few artists who have achieved the universal fame of Rubinstein or Menuhin, for example. These two names are synonymous with magic. Even in towns such as Ushuaia, Batoumi or Tulsa these artists are always associated and *identified*

with the piano or the violin.

They are phenomena from an era different to ours. They became known to people and remembered in a remarkable way thanks to a wise *market* that managed their careers. We can only but admit that all this was due to the rare talent of these artists as well as to correct planning by their managers.

The role of the latter, then, is to *classify* artists once they know what their main qualities are and knowing how to present them to a public likely to buy them.

In a contest, for example, the demand is for *competition* above all. People are interested in this specific phenomenon and not in the intrinsic qualities of each participant. The jury chooses the first three laureates, but they may not correspond to what the *market* demands at that particular time. So, they will not be the favourite artists of this particular public, because they were *imposed* according to the taste of others.

So, we must understand the role of the manager: whether he is intelligent, and whether he will help the winning candidates to find other audiences, that is, *a different market*. This has absolutely nothing to do with the skills of any of them, I repeat, but more to do with the versatility of the public. We have thousands of similar cases in the past: why did Leonardo leave Italy and go to work and die in France? Why must certain artists emigrate in the search *for better publics*? Obviously, we are not talking here of the essential role of the artist: what I mean is that it would be better *to help the public to forge a taste and a culture that respect the laws of Art*. We can and we should help that public, of course.

What we need to know is whether this public wants to follow or whether it would prefer to turn its back.

Recordings assume the same thing. The CD cover, with its visual impact, knows what *it is dealing with*, and is often more important than the musical version of the artist performing on this CD.

The same goes for the posters, the publicity and the concert programmes. Clearly the artist does not *enter* only *by the ear*, but also *by the eye*.

The similarities with politics are astounding. All too often the charisma of a politician is more important than his message. You just have to turn the television on to know this.

The consequences are inevitable.

An artist who represents *a gilded market* is more important than another who does not have the same charismatic qualities. Once the artist represents *power*, for example, directing an important festival that gives him influence over orchestras, recording companies and associations, *he becomes adored and celebrated regardless* of his musical qualities.

It is a well-known fact that in the great world orchestras *the choice for the position of conductor takes place depending on   the contracts* the candidate *may represent for the orchestra*. The *existential* questions put by the steering committee of the orchestra are similar to these:

Which prestigious festivals is he proposing? What recording contracts could we benefit from?

What tours could we accomplish under his direction?

Clearly this work is done by a manager who handles the money and not by one who must tax his mind deciding on how to interpret the "Resurrection" Symphony, although some of them can often handle the two things!

4 – Father Christmas

It is therefore not surprising that we want to prepare young, inexperienced musicians for this terrible war with people who have nothing to do with Music, other than its *management*.

These discussions stray away from the problems raised by the interpretation of Liszt's Sonata, even of knowing whether it was indeed Liszt who invented the formula for the recital. It was he who gave ideas to Wagner to influence Ludwig II and to create his Theatre. It was he who organized the first Festivals: who does not recall the Berlioz and Wagner Weeks, and concerts for Schumann, Beethoven, Chopin and so many others. It was he who organized the first masterclasses demonstrative and public. It was he who invented the concert tour. It was he who had the role of *Kapellmeister* changed into a diva as conductor of an orchestra.

It was he, with his multiple activities, who combined the jobs of composer, pianist, conductor, organizer, sponsor, critic, teacher, guide, abbot, politician, and we so on…, out of respect for the ladies. It was he who, with his unrivalled generosity, but also with his vision, *designed and organized our life today*. It was he, after all, who guided the rays of modern music and not only from the aesthetic point of view.

In fact, this current idea of being *no more than a pianist* is not such a good one. We should not believe blindly, for lack of information, in a possible life without playing the cards right, as this leads to wrong judgements and false appraisals, on both sides.

Education should play a major role here.

The basic idea should be the following: we cannot demand of life rewards for the time, enthusiasm, confidence, dreams, illusions and money that we have invested somewhere, but mainly in our career. We should be happy with our choice of life without expecting anything else. *The privilege of being a musician is our biggest reward.*

I can understand that some will not agree with this, but they should not want to be called *musicians* in the true meaning of the word. We have *duties* towards Music before granting ourselves *rights*. No one forces us to serve music. This choice, to be justified, must come from love, like that which inspires monks in their oath to serve God.

For us musicians to be happy is to be able to enjoy music, not as a *job*, but more as a *vocation*, full of love and pride at belonging to a category of individuals who have not chosen the common road from among those suggested by the labour market. Consequently, it is not because we have studied a Rachmaninov Concerto that we *should* play it at all costs.

It is important to return to the values that Liszt represented. These values are not at all those of Wagner. Liszt did not ask for a fee to give a lesson. He felt obliged to share what he knew.

Today, organizing a concert means discussing money above all. We must find the means for *being able* to play first of all and only *after* to think about the programme. Clearly *current day motivation is nothing like it was in the days of Liszt*. (So we cannot imagine that we are going *to arrive at the same results*).

There is sometimes a need to isolate yourself and to store vital energy to be able to continue along the right path. We have otherwise, set out for the business world, and that is a world that has ever less to do with Music.

BOOK VI

Part one

Sonata Op. 111 by Beethoven or the return to Silence
« Moses » by Michael Angelo
« Le Prieur » by Brancusi

What remains to the said on the subject of Beethoven's last Sonata, the struggle between Good and Evil, the Testament, the transcendental Sonata, at once Angel and Devil, Heaven and Earth, Hell and Paradise?

The finest thing to be read on this work by Ludwig van Beethoven was written by Bettina von Arnhin: *"One day Beethoven will write a work that is to be the key to an initiated language. This key shall open the doors of a beatific world, full of purity and with nothing in common with the world we know".*

It is a definition fairly close to what the work arouses in me: *this Sonata is the ultimate one.*

It is enough to feel the vibrations of the final trills, the descending scale - as in Liszt's Sonata -, the movements towards the perfect chords in C major, in their more tranquil and more divine position, without looking for anything else.

There is in fact nothing else to find. The only thing to do is, perhaps, to listen to the Silence that follows it.

It holds the mystery of God, the mystery of the unknown, the mystery of Life and Death, which almost makes us shut our eyes and look within ourselves. There is nothing more on the exterior, nothing more to listen to or to hope for. After this tour in space and in life, we return to the Lord spent, without protest or reproach, at peace.

We are before the Truth, quite naked. Our career begins to be extinguished, we are in the decline and we no longer feel the warrior in us. The Appassionata is already far behind us and we find only its debris there.

In the Arietta everything seems spirited, vaporous. The matter has disappeared. We almost forget the first movement of the work. The strength of this Arietta is no doubt *its absence.* Its tranquillity is such that no power in the world could make it turn a hair. It is like watching your own life pass before your eyes.

The sense of smallness before such a supreme creation almost makes the applause that follows detestable. How can anyone dare to make any noise after such sonorities? Any disturbance of this Silence should be *prohibited*, after these beatific, *initiation* revelations, just like prohibiting any one from splashing ink over a magnificent painting.

Beethoven always considered Music to be a revelation, the consent of God, Who used it to address a few words to us. The problem is finding this immateriality in God's words, re-entering the cosmic spheres without impediment, flying free of the weight of the body, and so feeling *incorporeal*.

The words of Stravinsky suddenly come to mind: *"Music is incapable of expressing the human soul"*.

With all due respect to such a great musician, I think that no one gains anything from trying to "destroy" others. Stravinsky tried this with Beethoven, in his *Poetique Musicale* at the École Normale de Paris.

As if that were possible!... It is a shame that genii, even at a different level, fail to get on. Music has everything to lose with such comments. Business, on the other hand, gets richer. But let us return to Beethoven…

There is a major difference between Opus 111 and Liszt's Sonata. After the latter you feel ready to confront anything: it stirs the blood, the mind and puts fire in us, and with its very panache it turns us to steel. This is why I have compared it to the life of a pianist: we *need* it as a vital force for the soul.

After Op. 111 *one needs to be alone*, not receiving compliments and not giving account to *humans* on what you have just done. This would be as absurd as giving yourself up to God for the Final Judgment and then leaving Him all alone and returning to Earth to deal with those like us and to give them explanations and advice. It would be too late.

Different to Liszt's Sonata, Op. 111 *drains us*. It takes the little force that we have and replaces it with *another that is more serene*, and less of this world: *the force of the soul*. It is almost like taking a step into the beyond.

There is no Mephistopheles here, and no Faust or Marguerite claiming the territory. We are the protagonists in the struggle and, alone, we are ready to overcome this odious life and this human struggle of the first movement, with *the second as a supreme weapon*.

The *Arietta* will see to putting everything in its place, without any battles, cries or violence: with the sole conviction of the Truth, *with the serenity of a non-human language*, without the common shadows of life. It addresses sonorities that do not belong to us, but which make us feel privileged, as I said earlier, to be a musician and to be able to play it, if only to take part in *this Last Supper*.

Perhaps only then we find the meaning of the words:

'Muss es sein?' 'Es muss sein!'

What is incredible is that Beethoven, deaf and unwell, in a dirty room, with spaghetti broken-down like the chords of the piano, could even have imagined such sonorities, felt this state of grace that carried him to the most unfathomable regions of the mind. Imagine the fourth variation of the *Arietta* on *his own* piano of 1820 assumes he had not only transcendental vision, but also a vision of the future and of what a piano *would be* capable of producing in future ages. And all that despite his hearing preventing him from fully grasping what he had written. I have already mentioned *this visionary side* when commenting on the pedal in the *Waldstein* and in *The Tempest*: he *forced it* as he wanted to force destiny.

Clearly for a mind of this scope the *material* quality of the instrument that was not that of the current day Steinway, added to the drama of his hearing, must have caused him extreme nervous tension. What would he have said had he been able, as a hidden listener with his hearing intact, to listen to Arrau, Serkin or Kempff playing Opus 111 in a current day concert hall, with devotion and artistic respect united with the miracle of sound produced by an instrument of quality? What would he have thought of the Berlin Philharmonic Orchestra conducted by Herbert Von Karajan or an Arthur Toscanini interpreting his *Seventh*?

Not to bear this in mind in an interpretation played today *is a major crime*, because playing as if using the instruments of another age seems to me as silly as wanting to play the *Ninth Symphony* with an orchestra of his time, which would have been *out of tune, forged and ineffective*. And that is how musicians in those days heard things!

Why would you want to repeat sonorities that today offend us? What is the real reason for this desire? Is it to serve Music?

The Music business knows absolutely no limits. *Anything is justifiable to produce money*: provocations, false and ambiguous situations, and performances that have nothing to do with the intrinsic intentions of the author. All of this is very much in vogue. However, it would be good to suggest to the same people, so anxious to protect *the original message*, to go from Paris to New York to play their concerts without flying in the aircraft airlines use today, but in a dugout canoe, and so *perform their historically informed performances*.

The role of an interpreter today, who is well-informed and has access to a plentiful supply of musical material and excellent instruments (orchestras and pianos), is to continue understanding the essence of the intention of a composer and not to take Music *backwards* into ages in which the means of making music were different or lacking.

Wanting to play Scarlatti today on a modern Steinway applying *a sonority that would have been heard by the composer* in his day and age, suggests incompetence, bad faith or ignorance, because *this sonority is pure imagination*, because our instrument, from its very *nature, does not sound* to us like one of Scarlatti's instruments, with its very particular tone. You listen to *La Campanella*, in Liszt's piano version, without *physically being able to* hear Paganini's violin. *You imagine it*. We *savour* the spirit of Paganini, mixed with that of Liszt of course, but not *the reality* of Paganini's violin. If that is what you want, it would be wiser to listen to the versions by Ruggiero Ricci or Itzhak Perlman on the violin. We would then be far closer to Paganini's *sonority*!

1 - The hecatomb, or the First Movement

But let us return to Opus 111.

Anyone knows that we divide the work of Beethoven into three periods. Franz Liszt, who was *not just anyone*, did it better than *everyone* else. His division was *"adolescent, man and God"*. Opus 111 was to be his *final word* on the piano. Even if he wrote other works later, he never surpassed it.

Beethoven had had heated discussions with his editor on *the missing third movement*. He would have said quite simply that *he had not had time* to do it! It would have been good to see the expression on Beethoven's face at that moment. It would not have been recognizable although his response was fully comprehensible... Another comment I would like to refer to was made by Lenz, author of an extensive work on Beethoven: *"These variations (referring to the Arietta) might one day be understood, but I doubt they could ever become beautiful and that his rhythmic innovations will be called upon to play a very important role. What does a rough scene by Shakespeare matter before such lasting beauty (sic)"?!* I think that if a man could be resurrected, Lenz would choose to remove these words!

Wagner on the other hand, after hearing Liszt play the work, said of the Introduction: "*That is how Beethoven was able to take Destiny by the throat*".

In fact, these notes cause an explosion, a dazzling, atomic, disintegration of matter. They also create a dangerous risk for the pianist nervous about getting the octaves wrong. According to Schnabel, Arrau or Serkin, the changing of hands and the *easing* of problems manage to remove from the Music *the essential sacrifice* it assumes: *the expressivity and tension in the effort and risk.*

You may agree or not, it doesn't really matter. This is a *moral problem*, because you cannot economize on effort when it is supposed to lead to the solution. No one is obliged to play Opus 111 if the basic means to do this do not exist. The risk is feeling this *difficulty* as a *component* part of the Music, where everything often involves pain.

Changing the disposition of the passage to make it more *brilliant* if the music demands this, as in one of Liszt's *Paraphrases*, for example, is legitimate because, at this precise moment, the music has *other aims*. Here the brilliance and *the effect* are integral parts of another musical discourse, producing an *equally visual impression*.

But putting Opus 111 at a similar level suggests a rather low intelligence, because it addresses the *mind*. You must listen to it with your eyes closed. Like this it provides no visual effects. It would be better to find the means not to get the octaves wrong by using a more conceptual approach. For example, by thinking of the relationship, the approach, *between the fourth finger on the E-flat and the thumb on the following F-sharp* (studying them separately, without the octaves, and *the relationship 4-1*) and by *holding them for a little longer* in the final execution. Like this we are halfway there and have made *far more progress as a pianist.*

Op. 111

The ascending arpeggio is the symbol of *the elevation of the human being* observing this Destiny and challenging it. We feel an extraordinary force here in that the courage of the man is proved *by his resistance and not by his acceptance.*

Beethoven is the example we must follow. He helps us to become better. He has proved to us that the world will be saved by Ideas and not by armies. Even Hitler, a somewhat inglorious but explicit example, used the music of the *Fifth Symphony* to raise and lower the morale of his troops in order to galvanize them in unfavourable circumstances.

On two occasions this arpeggio shows itself ready for combat. All the energies of the human being are committed here. The power of the *double-dotted* chords is also proof of this relentless drive, of this force that comes from moral certitude, the steel-like character of Beethoven that would bend before nothing in the world.

These diminished sevenths are also a base in the harmony deployed later by his greatest spiritual disciple, Franz Liszt, who loved them so much. In the History of Art, nothing is written, and nothing is done by chance when you are one of the *greats*. Nothing falls into oblivion. Sooner or later it is found again. Let us recall a *certain* Felix Mendelssohn who found *certain* scores by a *certain* Johannes Sebastian Bach! Without ceasing, another of the *greats* takes up the torch. Beethoven knew something when he embraced a *certain* 12-year-old lad called Franz Liszt!

Terrible chords then spread out in a voluntary succession. Strict, sharp, threatening and concentrated. When they stop, *we find Destiny in these four fetish notes*, at the end of bar 10. Muted dissonances settle in bar 11.

The two forces oppose one another, and one melody rises and the other descends, the two having the rhythm of hard and implacable double dots:

An octave lower down Beethoven insists. What is its meaning? Is it duality? Is it Good and Evil? Is it man facing his Destiny? Is it his need for peace despite the fatality? Is it acceptance of fatality? We can go on questioning, but it is more difficult to find answers. The tone hardens and sinks into an incredible trill, measured and muted, and doubled. This can only explode into a furious, desperate, tragic and powerful theme:

Beethoven does not seek out the *unexpected*. He *is* logic itself. He has nothing to hide, but everything to show in order to illustrate his own suffering, and ours. The choice of only three notes for his major theme recalls that of the *Appassionata*, its no less tragic younger sister, also based on three fatal notes:

Op. 111

Op. 57

These two themes are not parallel but complimentary, one based on the chord in F minor, and the other on the tonic chord of C minor and its leading-note B- natural. Here, in Opus 111, an *awaiting fermata* creates all the desired anguish. In the *Appassionata*, the *waiting* on the first F becomes fatal. *But the waiting remains the same.*

The interrogation recalls a distant sensation, that of the exposition of *The Tempest*, providing equal premonition. The ascension that follows is similar to the last movement of the *Appassionata*. It is a fully active volcano. *Sforzandi* make it more aggressive and less *virtuoso*, opposing brakes and blows as if *Beethoven were striking this Destiny in the face*. The fall of this ascension will *calm* the theme and will dominate this accursed Destiny, in bars 29, 30 and 31:

It is no more than a lull, mainly in measures 34 and 35:

However, the terrible battle is going to begin pitilessly. There is no question of putting on a more tender or human face. *Beethoven's power of synthesis is supreme*: he manages to reconcile the three notes of the theme with its ascension. They alternate in a powerful dialogue until, once again, they reach the upper extremes of the instrument as, again, in the *Appassionata* or the *Hammerklavier*. This is the story of his life, the summary of his work, the perfection of expression and the result of his faultless trajectory.

He does this *in two* voices (the octave does no more than *doubling* one for auditory reasons), such as suggesting there is *no third to blame: he is alone with his destiny.*

Opposing the acute notes with the more bass notes, the imposition of the bass over the cries of the acutest, determines the difference between the two worlds that confront one another:

A voice is isolated, wounded, in the top of the piano. A desolate lament is heard in bars 50, 51, 52, 53, 54 and 55, until an *adagio* where our eyes rise Heavenwards:

His spiritual disciple, Franz Liszt, perhaps recalls it in the Recitatives of his Sonata...
In the following bars Beethoven leaves no hope, and the fall is implacable. It falls furious, broken into pieces, as in Opus 31 No. 2. It is mutilated; it cries out, jostles, argues but then miraculously finds strength again with a short ascending scale, in bar 57, and asserts the fatal theme by plunging into imperious bass notes three times in low notes and three times in the soprano, as in the Introduction.
Beethoven then reverses the descending lament in bar 50 to begin a triumphal ascent where he makes another illusion to the material of the second thematic movement: it explodes into the tonality of A-flat major, both grandiose and monumental.

In bars 67 and 68, continuous *sforzandi* ill-treat this ascension. This is the gesture of an indomitable will, the assertion of a steel- like character. Nothing can contain this invincible man. His heroic side causes damage thanks to a relentless determination. He aspires to the Ideal, to the Ascension, and demonstrates this with aplomb in the triumphal movements in the *tempo primo finale* of the second Fugue of Opus 110, in the last two pages of the work. In bar 71, a thunderous blow of the dominant tells us that the fight goes on and the development begins. A pseudo-fugue that goes nowhere begins. Perhaps Beethoven felt voices rising on all sides, as Schumann did later, *but he has no time now to write a fugue:*

The themes succeed one another by augmentation and inversion. They cross one another. A descending scale in the bass retakes the theme enriched by harmony, which is full and dense, plunged into diminished chords, in bars 86, 87, 88, 89 and 90, until reaching the high notes, where a violent unison separated by three octaves forms a *tutti* in double octaves, in bars 92 and 93 - worthy of inspiring Franz Liszt in his Sonata -, as if the *Appassionata was being developed*, as if it had not *said everything in its time*. I think the two works are *an extension in time of the same tragedy*.

The pain, the rage, the fury, the grandeur and the agitation reach a summit here.
The descent of alternating octaves creates not so much a moment of respite as an uncertainty. Reaching D-flat major, in bar 98, and the provisional solution that follows it, are not in a position to hold back the fiery lava that breaks out in F minor, in bar 100, in the *"a tempo"*:

The instrument is treated with *violence*, without any pity. Terrible syncopations reveal the disarray of the composer. The three-note theme floats on this lava. It has difficulty in making itself heard: the tempest breaks out.
Shoulder to shoulder they reach the high notes in bars 109, 110, 111, 112 and 113.
You wonder how the devil an instrument, even today, can resist this type of treatment: it is worse than Kreutzer's unfortunate violin! How can the force be found to make this passage *sound* without basses?! You need ten pianists! You also need a steel articulation, colossal strength in the fingers as well as a head to think at the same time of the sound waves mixed with the richest pedals. We are far here from the clarity of Mozart. Perhaps a pedal cadenced every four notes is required?...

Let us add here a word on the arguments of the purists on the subject of the four minims that follow in bars 114 and 115.
Great teachers say that the fourth note, C, *could not* be E-flat according to the parallelism of the first time (bars 48 and 49) because Beethoven's piano did not *have* such a high-pitched E-flat. I play the C, of course, but not for that reason. Beethoven *wanted this change*, which is more concentrated than the expansion of the first time, and as proof against the E-flat in question - *"which he did not have"*... - let us look at the second note in the top of the new descent in bar 132. Is it an E-flat derived from a current day piano?

The same lament as before is found in the high notes of the piano. Bar 116 suggests some relief, fatigue or discouragement. It is time for confessions. Beethoven speaks in *meno allegro* with sadness and anguish.

The same theme and the same lament then sink into the low notes in bar 124. Rarely in the literature of the piano *has sadness been expressed in such an eloquent but also raw way*, and particularly with so few notes. The desolation is complete.

The design of the accompaniment of the right-hand is the same as at the start of the passage in the Finale of the *Appassionata*. In the *meno allegro* of bar 126, it seems to dissolve. The expression of *la voce* is troubling. You might say that you can *hear* Beethoven in person *speaking, lamenting* and almost crying.

But this is no hindrance. It only lasts for an instant: *one* bar! Beethoven arises and in a Herculean, colossal effort rises to the summit of the *Tempo Primo*, in bar 132. In this recapitulation in C minor he affirms to the world in this way that he is there, in full combat with his Destiny and having reached the final outcome.

The theme inverted towards the light (in bars 141 and 142) falls back into his last scale. He had, in the four chords that follow, like *a battle axe* in his hand: he gives four blows and immediately all the fatigue that this demand is felt. The other four successive chords express his laboured breathing.

And everything changes.

I do not think that the *Coda*, the most wonderful that I know, *belongs only* to the First movement.

It is the moment when you want to *die* in peace, exhausted and ready to leave this Life for *the far beyond. It is the moment when the pain leaves the body overwhelmed by serenity.* With this spiritual ascension, nothing but good and benevolence, in which the upper C does not extinguish itself, you find the verses by Borges: *"Death lends the face definitive beauty".* In bar 150, the C never again leaves *the divine resonance of transformation of mind over matter* (C, D, E, C; C, F, G, C; C, B-natural, B-natural, C; C... C).

We have attained the vision of the Arietta.

2 - The Arietta, without words

We are no longer in combat. There are no more traces of it, no more disasters and no more chaos. We have caught a glimpse of the *Arietta*.

The effect of this balm is complete. Suffering is no more. Pain only belongs to humans! Now, in exchange, we enter the heavenly world.

This is the arrival in Paradise.

To succeed in this union, Beethoven's *wonderful pedal*, so often *forgotten, must be respected*. In bar 157 of the *Coda*, Beethoven writes the indication *pedal*, but *without a sign to change it in the following final bar*. This must mean that *this pedal is to be kept until the first chord of the Arietta*, as already said, in parallelism, for Liszt's Sonata, before engaging the Choral in B major, on the penultimate page. This analogy strikes me. Perhaps it does not truly exist, but I prefer my doubts to brutally cutting the two movements, stopping to cough and to clear my throat.

Oddly, the same pedal is indicated between the first and the second movements of the *Appassionata*… The resemblance and similarities between these three works are enigmatic, striking and moving. Perhaps *one mind* conceived them together?

I do not know where to begin to speak of this *Arietta*, because if it is not *the finest piece of Music*, it is, at least, *unique*. It would be inconceivable to think of comparing it with anything else.

Is it possible to make harmonies more simple and at the same time more beautiful, more serene, more beatific, more initiated and more transcendental?

Is it possible to find a blend more precious and more precise of God, the Cosmos and the human soul?

Is it possible to find a more perfect Unity between Philosophy, Music, Ethics, Religion and the Aesthetic?

Is it possible to be closer to God?

Is it possible to discover yourself in what is most transcendental? Is it possible, in a few minutes, to do *better* from the point of view of *form*?

Is it really possible for a piano to *sound* better?

These Variations *achieve a state of trance, tranquillity and order, in brief, a state of fecundity of the soul* that suggests they were not written by any human, however much a genius, but by a god, or by God himself.

Did Beethoven reach God or did God find Beethoven once and for all?

This is a rare moment in which we can be thankful, thank Heaven, weep with joy at having been born an Artist and at being able to share, miserably, this bread and wine, the true Body and Blood of Christ.

The theme of the *Arietta* is not to be played, *but to be listened to*. Time has ceased to exist, or perhaps has been suspended, but whatever the case *it does not seem to be there*. You have the same sensation as if looking at Heaven or the Cosmos, and that you could almost touch them with your fingers. *He is there*. Nevertheless, light-years separate us. I do not know whether this is real. I do not think it is in any case: I believe in a prayer *without words*, a glance into the interior, a transmutation of the soul towards another supernatural state and an awareness, at *least*, of what has *been*.

The passage leading to D Minor, in bar 6, is incredibly gentle. It is *full of gratitude*. Avoid *any excesses* in executing this passage: one can give nothing to it; it is the passage that gives us everything. Its serenity is not changed by the modulation, quite the contrary. Any exaggeration in the crescendo, any dynamic movement in the human sense, or simply *musical* sense, would make the expression *false and hollow*.

Listen, listen and listen. That is what one must do!

Feel your arms floating, feel the sound directly, imagine that there are no hammers between the keys and the sonority.
Feel that the piano has a resonance box in space, in the heavens. Avoid articulation. Rest on each note.

Feel the eternity.

And begin to listen again. And go on listening.

Personally, to help the imagination I use *entirely personal names* for each variation, even if at the start you need to know what the variations are *without words and without names*, in which the overriding principle is unity. However, the names I use help me to free myself.

The first Variation is *witnessing the creation of the Movement*. The second Variation is *witnessing the creation of the Thought*. The third Variation is *witnessing the creation of the Activity*.
The fourth variation is *witnessing the creation of the Cosmic Immobility*.
The fifth Variation is *witnessing the creation of Memory or the remembrance of Sadness*.
The sixth Variation is *witnessing the creation of the Gratitude in a Hymn to God*.

Then the trills at the end, the Seventh or the *Coda*, is *witnessing the Suspension of the soul in God*.
I think there are *seven*, as in the Bible, and *not five* as in other analyses. My opinion differs from that of certain colleagues who think that the passage contained between bars 96 and 130 is a *Coda* of the preceding Variation: *recognition of the complete theme in the chords and the minor character proves the opposite*.

I consider it to be an *entirely* different Variation, in view of its different expression and its instrumental construction that is different to the one that precedes it.
I do stress the word *witnessing* because it seems to me, an interpreter, that I have very little to say at that moment. Nothing at all, in fact. I do no more than *assume the Music despite myself: I am witnessing a miracle*. The dispossession is complete. This inescapable march *seems to be accomplished without my participation*.

Creation of the Movement

Creation of the Thought

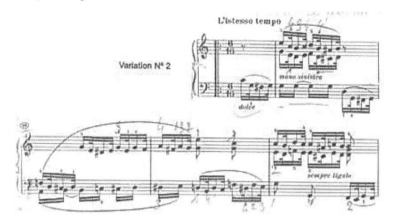

Creation of the Activity

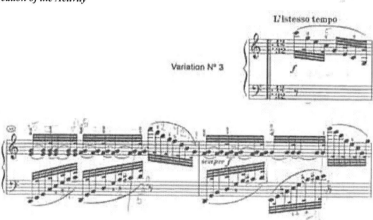

Creation of the Cosmic Immobility

Variation Nº 4

244

Creation of the Memory

Variation Nª 5

Creation of the Gratitude in a Hymn to God

Variation Nª 6

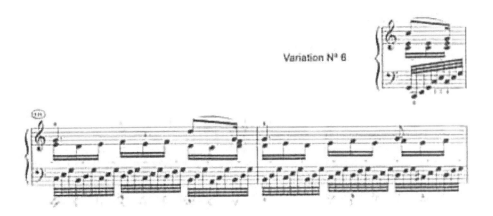

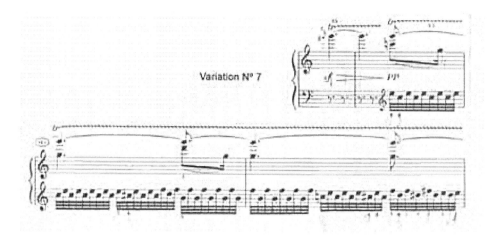

Beethoven arranged these Variations in *two* ways.

The first three are more formal and more organized; they are even separated by double bar-lines. From the fourth, the bars disappear, and *everything is unified*. Is this a symbol? Did he catch a glimpse of and foresee the variations of his great disciple Franz Liszt, with the space of 30 years? It is known that Liszt does not divide his Variations but rather joins them into a whole.

The structure is *more solid, more classical and less free* in the first three variations, and there is a liberation in the other four. Everything joins and merges without thinking any more of the word *variations*.

The first two are *horizontal*. The third is like a balance, a crossing from high to low, and from low to high, as in very ancient music, in which *the descending scales and arpeggios came from Heaven*. Man *would respond to God towards the highest notes*.

In bar 53, crossing ceases and parallelism is formed. Clashes are avoided, but *sforzandi* are placed at unexpected places, causing bursts that are not tragic, but *uneasy*.

The crossed dialogues begin again in A minor, in bar 57. The music achieves sublime expression. It is already perhaps the *memory* of pain, in anticipation, without this being truly agonizing, as in the first movement.

The fourth Variation, the core of the work, it is an absolute masterpiece. In its first part the whole *cosmic organization* is felt. The chords seem to be eternal. The *tremolo* in the left-hand (so dear to Liszt!) suspends all movement: everything floats in the unreal.

Bülow called the following passage *"stardust"*, beginning at bar 72. Nothing can sustain this *immobile movement* in the right hand. Has anyone written demisemiquavers more sublime than these? The very plentiful pedal imagined by Beethoven, haunts *this keyboard that seems not to work*. The action of the instrument remains imperceptible.

The stability found in the chords, that is, the entry to the fifth Variation in bar 96, first in the left (*where all the notes of the theme are recognized*) and then more extended in the right, reflects what can only be tranquillity. The chords in the right-hand, with a left- handed transformed by the technical formula of the penultimate Variation, elevate into a melody in which the pianist can only but raise his eyes to Heaven.

The arpeggios cross the piano on four octaves, towards the upper notes. The shortest passages descend as if the responses were not the same. There is here almost a synthesis of *earlier and later formulae. Everything is condensed* here: the trill, the arpeggios, the theme, the chords, the immobile movements…

This will stretch into the first trills where another dialogue takes place and where the four notes of Destiny are now hidden and ascending, G, G, G, A-flat, in bars 109 and 110.

Lastly, the trill becomes motionless in three, then in four voices: an impressive chain, a superior vibration, rises towards the highest regions of the instrument. The spirit guides it because there are no longer any low notes that can sustain it.

The expression is at its zenith and is completely diaphanous. Arrau used to say that *the trill had philosophical significance* for Beethoven, because it was a question of finding in it *a symbiosis of two sounds*, an alchemy of the mind and not the friction of two keys. This is demonstrated here in a dazzling way: rarely, in all the literature of the piano, can you find a more expressive chain. The theme seems to be an acceptance. A very interrogating resignation floats in the midst of these miraculous trills and the total interruption of *creation* beyond shows a state of limitless vibration.

It is no longer the matter that is being touched. The work seems to disintegrate. You seem to be moving towards a supreme Silence. The dissociation of the voice then takes place and the ascent towards the upper extreme of the piano seems to abandon the left hand forever, in bars 114, 115 and 116.

The vision of the trill, even the dynamic trill, is *metaphysical* with Beethoven. Here he develops his trills of the *Waldstein* and the *Concerto in E-flat*, those of the second movement. Later, no doubt, Ravel would recall them also, in the undulations of the trills of the Cadence of his Concerto in G major.

But a B-flat in the bass, in bar 116, manages to sound like a warning. It is incredible what Beethoven manages to do in dynamic terms with only *two voices*. He manages to reconcile them once again by having a sad memory without new wounds hover in this *sphere*. The anguish belongs to the *past* and this atmosphere of *faded sadness* scarcely ignites: its sound carries, *despite all.*

A strange dialogue takes place between the soprano and the bass, while the contralto with its repeated chords once again outlines an eternity in a distant, but attainable resonance.

One should avoid executing the passage with emphasis: it is beyond pain and all suffering. *This moment is superhuman.* Never a *Minor in Major* (because this is a modulation in E-flat major), in a variation, has reached such an elevation. The microcosm of the minor is in the macrocosm of the major, but without any force being present.

I have never heard such eloquent, expressive, anguished silences *without showing it*, that are so evasive, so notable and so meaningful. *You can almost imagine Beethoven gasping for breath*. Oh! Mozart was right when he said that silence was the finest moment in Music!

The path of this modulating passage will lead us towards the C minor that here is not a dialogue with Destiny, but *with the self* - hence this sadness. It is expressed *in relation to the self*.

The transmutation to C major is therefore the symbol of elevation. The *start of the route towards God* is a symbol in tonalities: the C major and the C minor have never been so eloquent. The aquatic movement of the left-hand seems to depict *a Christ* - perhaps not *the* Christ - walking on water.

The theme is found intact, and the intervals of thirds and sixths of the contralto with the bass express a perfect harmony between the material and the immaterial, the elements, beauty and the tendency towards the *Heights*.

It is the return towards the Beginning.

The music seems to be freed of all weight and the distances between intervals are almost non-existent, the muscles of the left hand having to obey a spiritual ballet.

We are beyond all technical problems.

The ecstasy, the stasis, the immobile, the minimal oscillations and the undulations and vibrations that are scarcely perceived, stroll through in infinite, serene gratitude. You might say you are living in a galaxy where only the spirit rules and considers God to be right: *man, on his return, is not as bad as that*.

Beethoven has even more reason to prove to us that he was not only great, *but unique*: he develops his theme *by creating another variation*. A certain excitement is felt because the modulations become impatient in a succession of sevenths, reaching a piercing ninth in bar 158, in the high notes of the keyboard, passing through dialogues without interruption.

But it must also be said that there is no *Appassionata* here! Everything takes place within limits unlikely to be achieved by common mortals: aspiration towards the transcendental is such that you feel that the spirit has *evangelized* all suffering and pain. Contrariwise, the trill reappears, and is once again in celestial realms. The theme is compressed between it, the light and the water of the left-hand: *it is a deliverance*. Perhaps it is the response that he gives to himself, deaf, deprived of the good fortune of listening to the marvel he conceived: *the imagination of the goodness of God*.

When the theme rises to the higher notes, the trill in the centre unfolds with the same vibration, without distinguishing itself from its more acute brother. You might say that the distances shorten but the tranquillity, peace and serenity remain the same.

The soul has found its rest.

The addition of a lower voice, a C, in the last bars of the trill shows that all dimensions are respected, without violence or trouble. No accent announces the end, or *the beginning* to something else. Everything dilutes in the *pure spirit*, to move towards the High and low. It is like a *carefree wander* through Paradise.

Imperceptible movements of sublime chords in the last three bars plunge us into a kind of anguish: *not knowing whether what we have experienced was true, or whether it was no more than our imagination*.

Beethoven leaves us with this doubt and gives no response. The mystery is always there, and the enigma remains. The sphinx is before us. Something superior to all awareness, to all knowledge, to all intuition, to all creative power has been accomplished: *we were with God, but He has made us return to Earth.*

BOOK VI

Part two

1 - Götterdämmerung

As the lights of the concert hall or the theatre, and particularly those of the public start to dim so too do our lights, our own, fade away slowly, surely and inevitably.

We feel very gradually that the driving forces that have helped us make it are leaving our body. These forces seem to move to a new house and move in with the young artists following on our heels.

A new *relay* is forming; we must pass on the torch to someone else, as in the Olympic Games. *We must pass it on to a generation that, in principle, should be better equipped than we are*, as well as being more assured and better disciplined, in other words, stronger. They are making themselves heard and say they are ready to face the challenge, as we did in the past. It is the hour of our decline.

We have no right to hold back this generation, or to hinder their accomplishment. We cannot refuse them access to this world of Art. Quite the contrary, we must help them settle into it, as we help our children until that time in life when they are capable, like Icarus, to realize their dreams for themselves.

Above all we must avoid this wish *to go on indefinitely and become eternal*, this wish that does no more than express our ego and our refusal to depart.

We have got so used to the idea that we are indispensable. We are so convinced of our own importance! However, this is the most tenacious of enemies and we must get rid of it. It has the most formidable weapons: vanity, pretension, self-importance, and pride, in short, the worst possible facets of the human personality. Of course, the wish to continue has less to do with *serving Music and Art* than serving our own desires and making good our own shortcomings. These are the forces that develop our lack of generosity towards others: it is this need to feel like a *star* and to be unable to let go.

Quite often the spectacle becomes ridiculous and regrettable. We are not all Pablo Casals or Arthur Rubinstein, artists who improved with age just like a fine wine.

When it is not excellent, the wine turns to vinegar.

The image we have of certain *ageing* artists only goes to spoil the image we had of them when they were *young*. We ask ourselves, without finding an answer, why they are *still* there and why they insist. Their crises grow and they are no longer resolute. This desire to hang on is not just due to financial reasons, although they do exist. It is mainly this desire for fame, this primordial need to be reassured by the *bravos* of the public, given more to *the ghost or faded remains* of the artist in question rather than to their recent performances.

Similar to athletes, *knowing when to retire in time requires intelligence and a view of what is to come.* Leaving at the right moment is proof of wisdom, vision and generosity. In the words of Charles Dickens *"How cold the comfort in goodbye"* but *"One must also be able to listen to one's body",* in the words of a great Belgian doctor.

Signs of fatigue, exhaustion and spiritual depletion are all there. *Accidents* become ever more frequent: the technique, concentration, strength, and endurance fall away during the performance of what before was a *normal concert.*

It is useless, and sometimes cruel, to say that *the spirit is there*; to say that *the quintessence* of Art is there, in all its splendour. That might prove to be true in certain cases and in certain works: we spoke of Casals and Rubinstein and suffice to recall the last concerts played by Serkin with Beethoven's Sonatas Op. 110 and 111, or *The Emperor* of Claudio Arrau, at fairly advanced ages.

However, when the muscles no longer follow *it is useless to try and prove their lack of strength* by trying to play Bartok's Second Concerto, Liszt's Sonata or Prokofiev's Eighth Sonata. *The artist with any self-respect should have a clear idea of how ridiculous and grotesque he may look himself.*

It is not by *the mind or spirit* alone that you win the hundred metre race at the Olympic Games: the vital muscles and strength, *all the rest* that we need, make themselves cruelly felt.

2 - Windmills, or our "negative" Don Quixote

It seems that for an artist it is almost more difficult *to leave than to arrive.*

It is terribly hard to struggle against all these negative forces that during our years of training and throughout our career separate us from the works of music. Now, in the hour of our decline, these accursed forces attach themselves to our ego and become as in Faust, *the enemy of all time and forever.*

It is indeed Mephistopheles that tempts us to remain.

As before, the problem is that of getting rid of him. Everything must happen almost as if we were on the road to self-destruction. Clearly at this stage in the struggle, Mephistopheles is at the   peak of his persuasive capacities while we are struggling with our inner strife that weakens us. We are exhausted by these inner struggles: we have battled against them throughout our life with some degree of success and good fortune. Sometimes, we have been worthy in these struggles of comparison with Don Quixote tilting at windmills; yet sometimes we have been less worthy, and sometimes not worthy of all. But now the restrictions are more obvious than before: it is not the windmill that fights us, but there is no doubt that we feel we have managed to push these restrictions aside for a certain time, although without eliminating them or distancing them for a future that is already much shorter.

These restrictions are now ready to metamorphose into provocative goddesses for the young who follow us. *These goddesses expect us to pass them on* to the next generation. And so we must recycle ourselves, to prepare ourselves spiritually, to understand ourselves better,

251

without falling into sentimentality but adopting rational approaches.

In the words of Karl Marx *"In nature, nothing is lost, everything is transformed"*.

We must therefore hope that this transformation will aid substantially *the image that I have made of myself.*

3 - "Marcia Funebre sulla morte d'un Eroe"

The sadness experienced is infinite and profound. It is the end of a life.

We are no longer sure of having served Art, of having done everything.

We are no longer sure of having succeeded at anything. Everything seems to be a failure.

Negative forces express themselves in us more strongly than collapsing positive forces.

Recognition, rewards, speeches and medals can do little at such times. They even become hostile and perverse: they are worth no more than *a consolation prize* at some contest in the past. Looking at them you get the impression that *you are watching your own artistic death.*

However, we must respect this return to Silence, to the generating Aria of Bach's Goldberg Variations.

The return is to God.

This return is now ours.

We are not leaving the career, *but the career is leaving us.*

We are not leaving Liszt's Sonata, *Gaspard de la Nuit* or Opus 111. They are withdrawing their reverence for us, and this time *without booking the next meeting.*

This time it is not an *au revoir but a farewell.*

We swore, once, to serve them unconditionally. We are no longer able to do this. *"She [melancholy] dwells with beauty, beauty that must die"* was the superb conclusion of John Keats in his Ode on Melancholy. We must, therefore, hold to our oath and depart as silently as we arrived. We will keep them forever in our memory as we remember all our dead.

This presence will be so strong that this power will become incredible, because it is indeed God who speaks once again and calls us back once and for all to Him.

Words of premonition written by Jean d'Ormesson come to mind: *"There is something stronger than Death; it is the presence of those absent in the memory of the living."*

There is nothing more to add.

BOOK VI

Postludium: The ever-infinite renaissance...

But yet ....
the sun rises each day....
and day replaces night, just as in Ravel's *Daphnis et Chloé*.

Do not take my suggestions as negative. Quite the contrary, because I am an inveterate optimist and I do believe deeply in the best.

And I do believe in youth.

And it is precisely because of this that I want to provoke reactions. After all I still have hope, bearing in mind that there is no discord that cannot be resolved at some time, somewhere, even if in *another* work.
I am absolutely convinced of the transcendental power of Art as the supreme expression of the Spirit; not only of *our spirit, that of the artists, but that of God, the Creator.*
Above all I believe in renaissance because it signifies, first and foremost, a superior, constructive state of mind.

I do not believe in eternal darkness but in historical change. Suffice to observe the Infinite or the Cosmos, for example. What is the prevailing colour: the black of doubt or the clarity of the planets?

Birth itself is already the route towards Death, our final Destiny. But moving towards Death will also mean moving towards Understanding, Knowledge and Enlightenment. We are moving towards Consubstantiation and above all towards Renaissance. Perhaps into particles of the talent of others to come.

The major meaning of life is none other than understanding Morality, Religion, Philosophy and Art, the true proof of the immortality of the human soul.
In other words, this means nothing more, but really nothing more, than the possibility of choice being offered to the human being.
It is the enough for *one among them to choose*, the one with the talent, *so that the light shines for the others* who are less talented. The image of Life, *this fleeting moment between two Eternities*, goes to show this: the renewal of the human being, that being's spiritual regeneration and constant purification are an assurance of a future better than the one we knew. Seneca, tutor to Nero, had the following to say on this topic: *"The only way to avoid*

growing old is to die young".

This means *creating treasures for others* and not only *sharing what already exists.* That can only depend on us: our lack of regular creativity can only lead *to sharing the treasures produced by others.*

This would bring our social role as a human being down to a wretched level.

Just as we should *teach the art of fishing and farming to avoid hunger*, we should teach the art of creating new lighthouses able to produce the light for themselves, and to project it with greater strength and conviction than ours.

Our musical conformity, our petty bourgeoisie intellectual, our armchair habits and our lack of aesthetic, social and ethical courage, are the main cause of this mindlessness that strikes us all too often.

However, *I do not believe that the best* Music is behind us, although this does sometimes seem to be the case.

I do not believe this because out there somewhere there is always an individual called Bach, Mozart, Beethoven, Chopin, Liszt, Debussy, Ravel or Bartok, who picks up the gauntlet, looks it in the face and says NO to decadence.

History, the mother of all things, has taught us that any era that has caused a crisis has been underlain by obscurantism or renaissance. It is the concerned human being that has the possibility of choice. We can reflect in the Art of our day our distress in heart-rending artistic creations, but when all is said and done, a light appears somewhere, and it is the proof of the Love that God brings to us. It is not current day Music that can say the contrary.

Whenever Music wanders for a few seconds from the enlightened route it can only reflect anguish and moments from a life, but not a *whole* life.

I think that few periods in history have had such treasures as our own. Think only of the contemporary genii who have already been classified as classic. When you compare numbers there are *far more than in previous times.*

Like a divine gift we have received the Arietta of Op.111, Bartok's Third Concerto or Brahms' final messages, works from the end of a life in which we perceive the serenity of the artist able to accept his time *on* Earth *and in* Art as a privilege, as well as sharing words with God like the return of the prodigal son.

"Being an artist by the grace of God".

On the other hand, I do not think Art can be saved by a political system, whether of the right or left, as I have already said. We have already seen enough of what that produces all round: Music for the musicians and politics for... others less gifted.

I only believe in individuals, not in people, because talent, or genius, is not hereditary, far from it. It is, quite the opposite, a combination of qualities that joins *several beings into one* so that this one being can speak to the others with the authority of a prophet.

This is how we might view Moses, for example.

Consequently, it is not *a society* that can save anything, but *one* artist, or maybe *two or three*: a thinker who guides the others and makes them reflect. The whole is governed by *an* individual, by *a* brain, and not by a *group* or a *committee.*

We need a new Franz Liszt, for example, or a new Pope Julius II, a new Ludwig II of Bavaria, a new Lorenzo de' Medici, a new Dali and a new Karol Wojtyla, who, with their *follies* and vision, helped to build an infinitely better world.

What would the world be like *without the malady* of these exceptional beings?

Would we have known Wagner, Michelangelo or Leonardo? Would we be richer? Would we know Berlin without the wall?

I make no political or social references in recalling such men. What I do refer to is their vision of things: discover and protect Wagner, Chopin, Schumann, Berlioz, Borodin, Albéniz, Grieg... Set up theatres, festivals, centres, conservatories, museums... Support Michelangelo or Raphael... Support the Renaissance and create atmospheres that will promote work and development... Think of the glory of future generations...

This is what is known as forward thinking.

We must teach that we can make this twilight recede, the limits of the impossible, through intensive development and by shifting intellectual and emotional faculties, by making major demands, *by raising the bar and not by giving up, renouncing effort.*

Any brain that is not used is both a moral and social error. This would mean that we would agree today *to continue making slaves of people.* We must change attitudes from that of the *conquistador to that of the creator*, because the decline that we spoke of earlier *could be collective, not only personal.*

Our own personal decline is due to age, to relentless muscular and intellectual deterioration. Collective decline, on the other hand, is caused by spiritual sclerosis, in a misshapen mass, *in the refusal to think*, in the lack of ambition and collective intellectual thirst, *in the almost complacent acceptance of the self-destruction of the human being.*

So, we need a new type of artist.

It is clear and historical, and it is certainly in History that the cadence is felt, that sooner or later we must return to cultural and spiritual values.

We can no longer limit our appetites to mobile telephone games, facilities of every type, in relentless pursuit, *making ourselves giddy and to lose our awareness of all things.*

In the midst of all our technological development we should be able to find a spiritual compensation that will complete the rest. We cannot only depend on machines or on the beasts: once again we must decide for ourselves, assume our responsibility fully and prevent others from deciding for us due to our laziness and mass convenience, *"because alone, I can do nothing".*

Obviously, this position is the key to the concept. A different view of things gains no credit to our century.

We must begin again to thank Art and Music because, unfortunately, we used them to earn a living, as our work and not as our passion. We used them in an *absolutely incomplete* intellectual position.

Stendhal very wisely said that we should not only do our work for the love *of doing it*, but that we should also feel the passion of gratitude at *being able to do it*, and for the privilege of belonging to a race of major or minor creative people, able to make the world and others dream.

We have to relearn to be grateful for all the suffering that art forced on us *to make us artistic beings*. *We must* bless this suffering because it is through it that we have grown and achieved the transcendence impossible without it. We must relearn to express our gratitude for all the joy that art brought us, because it has shaped the mind and spirit in a way entirely different to a commercial way of thinking. We have to relearn how to thank life for allowing us to become a *musician*, because this brings us an ethical approach and grandeur of soul, and a nobility of mind impossible to obtain other than through aesthetic or religious channels.

We must also thank Heaven for having guided the others, the young and the less young, not just as an example to be followed, but *towards a succeeding model of someone greater than ourselves*. We must give thanks for having been able to enjoy, share and quiver with the great composers, the great artists, in moments of eternity and celestial contact with what is finest in the human soul. We must relearn to accept the duality of things, a major principle in numerous manifestations of art: that can only remind us that nothing is definitively played and that we are always in time to save our part… *but that the opposite is also possible.*

We could continue… but why?

And so, arriving at the end of the road, as in the last scale of Liszt's Sonata – and symbolically before the magnificent indecisive chords - *someone must take the final decision.*

I think it is for the artist - the one who has filled his mission as a disciple, as a missionary for God and of Music here on Earth - to do this and to take a look at the same time, still and *above all due to that*, at how the lights of art and life are lit for others and how, at the least expected moments, they extinguish for him.

Above all the artist must understand how these lights will continue to shine even when he is no longer there to see them.

A.D.V.

Photo at Liszt Hause in Weimar

Aquiles DELLE VIGNE, born in Argentine in 1946 to Italian parents, is recognized as a one of top piano professors in the world. Awarded Grand Prix in the "Albert Williams Competition", pupil of Claudio ARRAU, Eduardo del PUEYO and György CZIFFRA, DELLE VIGNE served as Jury or as President in the most important international piano competitions of the planet: five times in Sydney, Franz LISZT-Weimar, Monte Carlo, Rome, Paris, Bremen, Cincinnati, SCHUBERT Dortmund, Beijing, Casagrande, Pretoria, Osaka, Tokyo, Val Tidone, Bellini, Los Angeles...

He was Main Professor of the Piano Department of Codarts University in Rotterdam, at the Ecole Normale de Musique "Alfred CORTOT" de Paris, Visiting Professor at the Northern College of Music in Manchester – following Vlado PERLEMUTER -, at the Normal University of Taipei and taught 25 years at the Summer Academy Mozarteum Salzburg. Gave masterclasses in more than 40 countries, above all in Moscow and Saint-Petersburg Conservatories, Manhattan School of New York, Juilliard School, Toho University of Tokyo, Munich University. Recently, he founded his own Academy in Coimbra, Portugal (www.a2dv.pt), being followed by more than 30 pianists from several countries every year. DELLE VIGNE's class produced more than 160 international prizes in International Piano Competitions.

DELLE VIGNE performed and recorded several integrals: BEETHOVEN's 32 Piano Sonatas, LISZT's Etudes, MESSIAEN's Preludes, RAVEL's works for piano and violin with Alberto LYSY, Concerti by MENDELSSOHN for labels such as EMI His Master voice, B.A.S.F., Naxos, Empire Master Sound, Pavane. At present, he is recording the Années de Pèlerinage by Franz LISZT.
His first book, The Innermost Journey of a Pianist, was published in English, Italian and Spanish. His second one, The Interpretative Problem, was recently published in French and English.

DELLE VIGNE performed with some of the World's most important conductors, like Sir Yehudi MENUHIN, Leopold HAGER, André VANDERNOOT, Georges OCTORS, Emile SIMON, Edgar DONNEUX, Ferdinand TERBY, Juan Carlos ZORZI, ALBERTO LYSY, Eugene CASTILLO, Bogo LESKOVITCH, Jesus MEDINA, Edward TCHIVZEL, Henrique MORELENBAUM, Flavio SCOGNA, Claudio SANTORO..., with the National Orchestras of Belgium, Argentina, Mexico, Brasilia, R.A.I de Roma, Radio de Sofia, Camerata MENUHIN, Skopje, National Bogota, Chicago, Rio de Janeiro, Sao Paolo, Bern, in Europe, the three Americas, Asia, Australia. He performed MESSIAEN's Preludes for the Pope receiving formidable compliments from the composer.
"Only few pianists can go from a sparkling Mendelssohn to a thundering Liszt while passing an aristocratic, sophisticated and charming Ravel...", said Harold SCHOENBERG in the New York Times. La Reppublica of Roma called him "A prince of the piano". The PRS Rheinische Post "A Grand Seigneur of the pianists". Le SVZ of Salzburger Volkszeitung "From silence to a steel force".
DELLE VIGNE accomplished more than 35 tournées in Japan, 15 in Australia, in the three Americas, the whole Europe, Korea, Thailand, Hong Kong, Israel, Chine, Canada, Israel and Taiwan.

Aquiles DELLE VIGNE is based in Brussels, together with his wife Chantal Remy. Their children – now doctors and engineers - Laurence, Gabrielle and Guillaume also learned Music.

Printed in Great Britain
by Amazon